NATIVES MAKING NATION

T0294702

NATIVES MAKING NATION

Gender, Indigeneity, and the State

in the Andes

EDITED BY

Andrew Canessa

The University of Arizona Press

Tucson

The University of Arizona Press
© 2005 The Arizona Board of Regents
All rights reserved

www.uapress.arizona.edu

Library of Congress Cataloging-in-Publication Data
Natives making nation : gender, indigeneity, and the state in the
Andes / edited by Andrew Canessa.
p. cm.
Includes bibliographical references and index.
ISBN 978-0-8165-3013-7 (pbk. : alk. paper)
1. Indians of South America—Andes Region—Ethnic identity.
2. Indians of South America—Andes Region—Social life and
customs. 3. Indians of South America—Andes Region—Folklore.
I. Canessa, Andrew, 1965–
F2230.1.E84N38   2005
305.8'00980—dc22   2005011398

Manufactured in the United States of America on acid-free,
archival-quality paper.

16   15   14   13   12   11   7   6   5   4   3   2

CONTENTS

NATIVES MAKING NATION

1

Introduction

Making the Nation on the Margins

Andrew Canessa

In his oft-cited work on nationalism, Benedict Anderson writes that "in the modern world everyone can, should, will, 'have' a nationality, as he or she 'has' a gender" (1983:5). Possessing a national identity can be seen as being as natural as having a gender. Except that, of course, there is nothing "natural" about gender, as several decades of feminist and gender studies have shown. Similarly, there is nothing "natural" about having a national identity, as Anderson himself so clearly demonstrates. Gender and a national identity, and indeed race, may be naturalized but they are not "natural."

It is not simply that gender and national identity do not exist sui generis but that the fundamental conceptual distinction Anderson implies is seriously overdrawn. Insofar as everyone can have a nationality, this nationality is differentially assumed according to one's gender, race, and ethnicity: not all nationals are as national as others. Conversely, gender and ethnic/racial identities are constructed and lived through national ones.

This volume examines the ways in which identities—racial, generational, ethnic, regional, national, gender, and sexual—are mutually informing, even as they may be contradictory, among subaltern people of the Andes, where national sensibilities are not only strong but multiplying. Indigenous people are more likely now to claim an allegiance to a, say, Cumbe nation (Rappaport 1993) or an Aymara nation (Albó 1996) than ever before. Much has changed since the publication of Urban and Scherzer's influential volume, *Nation-States and Indians in Latin America* (1992); indians[1] are less likely to be confronted with crude assimilationist policies. It is nevertheless still the case that they face daily racism and discrimination, and struggle to assert an identity that is something more than a mere refraction of the dominant discourse. Despite the language of multiculturalism in many nations and even constitutional reform (van Cott 2000) any assertion of indian identity is likely to be resisted by at least some of the political and social elite.

If indigenous people struggle to assert and celebrate their identity, it is also the case that dominant national imaginings may include much that is indigenous. This inclusion of indian imagery in national ideology is, however, often at a far remove from the cultural practices of contemporary indians; it tends to be on the level of the folkloric rather than a lived culture. The relationship between indians and others is not simply one of local or even national concern, since by the beginning of the new millennium "The Indian" has become an international commodity, and indians are widely recognized around the globe for their "traditional" lifestyles and as guardians of the natural environment. Anthropologists may be irritated by this notion of the "hyperreal indian" (Ramos 1994) and its lack of correspondence with the lives of real people; but these images are used strategically by many activists and it becomes a practical issue for groups that deal with international tourism directly, as Elayne Zorn's essay in this volume shows.

The globalization and commodification of an image of indianness and its attraction to tourists as well as NGOs (which, in recent years, have been specifically targeting "indigenous communities"), impacts on metropolitan discourses: they co-opt indigenous cultures as exhibiting qualities that underline the uniqueness of the national culture. At the most trivial level, tourists can buy indigenous handicrafts as souvenirs in every Andean international airport as "typical" and "authentic" national souvenirs. The particularity of indigenous culture and language can be presented as marking the genuinely national even as it serves as the iconic marker of social and racial inferiority. In Bolivia today the ability to speak an indigenous language is highly valued among educated urban people as it is a useful passport to a job with an NGO; speaking an indigenous language as a rural and uneducated person serves as a marker of one's inferior social status. Chewing coca in rural areas is similarly a marker of inferior indianness, but when it is done in jazz bars in La Paz it is "cool."

Such images of indigeneity, colorful and exotic, bear little resemblance to the lives of real people; moreover, they can serve to dictate to indians the parameters of their own identity by defining what is "properly" indian or indigenous. They are, furthermore, often at sharp variance with political indigenous groups such as the EZLN in Mexico, the Movimiento Maya in Guatemala, CONAIE in Ecuador, and the various Katarista groups in Bolivia who directly challenge the nation-state and present alternative visions of the present and future. The strategic use of and mobilization around these concepts takes place in the context of the globalization of the concept of indigeneity itself (Hodgson 2002), which, in turn, informs activists' understandings and political maneuvering. Individuals embrace or contest the various images and languages of indianness and indigeneity in highly sophisticated ways (Warren and Jackson 2002). As Gow and Rappaport (2002) have noted, this may produce a strategic discursive multilingualism in activists as they speak the international language of indigenous rights to governments and nongovernmental organizations (NGOs) whilst addressing those they represent in a different, locally situated, language. It is therefore important to understand not only the words of political leaders directed to outside audiences but also how those without a political voice understand their identity within a national context, especially since most people do not organize politically. Many of the people represented in this book show a certain ambivalence to the nation-state, which can be seen as modern but soulless, civilized but harsh: indians themselves can view indian culture and practices as backward even as they offer meaning.

This volume looks at how metropolitan ideas of nation, those images and concepts employed by politicians, by the media, and through schooling, are produced, reproduced, and contested by those who, according to the dominant nationalist discourse, are on the geographical and social margins of the nation, namely, the people who populate the rural Andes and have long been regarded as ethnically and racially distinct from more culturally European urban nationals. These people marked as peripheral, these "natives," are shown to be actively engaged with the idea of the nation; they are making the nation in their own communities and in their own selves. This points to the irony contained in the title of this volume: dominant national discourses do not afford much space for native people to be actively involved in making the nation—it is simply not their place—yet indigenous people are significant in the ways they constitute and reproduce the nation. Of course, "native" and "nation" share a common root, and on one level it is hard to understand how native people could not be absolutely central to the idea of what constitutes the nation. Nevertheless, the dominant discourse has long been one that has pushed indigenous peoples to the conceptual fringes of the nation; indeed, indigeneity appears almost to be defined by its marginality from the dominant metropolitan culture.

Many of the other essays in the volume echo Taussig's thought that "rather than thinking of the border as the farthermost extension of an essential identity spreading out from a core, [we should] think instead of the border itself as that core . . . identity requires its satisfying solidity because of the effervescence of the continuously sexualized border, because of the turbulent forces, sexual and spiritual, that the border not so much contains as emits" (1993:151 in Stoler 1995:207). One could add that this is so because it is precisely on the border that the mutually implicating dyad of alterity and identity are created (Canessa 2000).

In the pages that follow I give an overview of some of the recent literature on race, gender, and the nation-state and argue for a holistic analysis of the three. This is followed by a look at nineteenth- and twentieth-century Andean history and the ways in which indians and indian issues have alternatively irrupted or been erased from the national consciousness of elites, and also how indians themselves and in their own fashion have engaged with the idea of the nation-state during this period. Finally, I consider some central themes of the book, such as the body and performativity, an integrated analysis of gender, identity, and the nation-state from the perspective of those at its supposed periphery, through which each of the contributors addresses the main concerns of the volume.

Subjects on the Margins

Indians certainly have long been deemed to have a problematic relationship to the nation-state, and it is often and widely assumed that they do not embrace or embody the nation as completely as people more obviously adept at metropolitan culture; but it is not simply in metropolitan regions that the nation-state is reproduced, as hegemonic ideas reach the very intimate lives of people, as Foucauldian analyses have shown (e.g., Jayawardena 1986; Mosse 1985; McClintock 1995; Stoler 1995). However, scholarship has rarely been devoted to examining how nationalist discourses are reproduced in the daily lives of people on the "periphery" of the nation. Even in studies, such as those of McClintock (1995) and Stoler (1995), that examine in depth the concern for subaltern racialized bodies, little space is devoted to how hegemonic ideas are reproduced by racialized subaltern people themselves; it is much more common to investigate how ideas of race and gender are internalized by the colonizers rather than the colonized.

The "margins," however, generate their own discourses about national identity, which may engage strongly with those emanating from the "center" but equally may provide very different understandings of who is indian or national. At the same time, urban elites may identify with indianness to mark their particularity as, say, Bolivians: the metropolitan and the marginal are constantly collapsing into each other. The essays in this volume take a fresh look at people who are notionally on the national periphery in terms of how they understand their own national identities.

A recent volume on women and the nation (Kaplan et al. 1999) treats women as "subjects on the margins" (p. 9). Kaplan's volume, which includes many examples from Latin America, analyzes these subjects as they are represented in various media, such as novels, films, and poetry, as well as public institutions. These "subjects on the margins" are given at best an attenuated voice: they speak through someone else's film, someone else's poetry. This is typical of much scholarship on nationalism that really "sees" subalterns only when they appear in the cultural media or political spaces of the dominant groups. Historians of the Andes who have shown how the nation is understood and contested by "subjects on the margins" are, however, an important exception (e.g., Abercrombie 1998; Nugent 1997; Rappaport 1998; Sanders 2003; Thomson 2003; and the work of THOA, e.g., Mamani Condori 1991). There are, however, few contemporary anthropological studies that examine nationalism or national identity from the "margins."

In a collection of anthropological essays on marginal people, *Consider the Lilies of the Field: Marginal People Who Live for the Moment*, the institutions of the state and, indeed, any enduring identity with the nation, are resisted and avoided by the people studied (Day et al. 1999). In a similar vein, whereas Anna Tsing's anthropological account of the Merana in the Philippines has much to say about how "marginal" people help constitute and, most important, react to the nation-state, for Tsing, the Merana "constitute the state locally by fleeing from it" (1993:26). Although this may sometimes be a response in the Andes, people are much more likely to engage with the nation-state than they are to flee from it. It is clear from these anthropological accounts that many people who are marginalized by the nation-state respond by rejecting it; but this is not the only option available to marginalized peoples.

The people who are the focus of this volume are certainly marginalized from the nation-state, both in terms of the exercise of state power as well as by national cultural ideology. To understand indigenous identity as being simply a function of marginalization, of the center pushing indians out and away from national power and discourses, as some anthropologists have done, is inadequate to understanding the complex interplay of indigeneity and the nation. Not only does it suppose a lack of engagement with national ideas on the part of indians themselves, but it reifies the very notion that nations are constituted in terms of metropolis and margins. Center and periphery, urban and rural, are, moreover, highly racialized concepts in the Andes as they are in other Latin American regions (Wade 1993). These concepts are also gendered, and a study of how Andean indians relate to the idea and reality of the nation needs to forefront gender and race in its analysis. This is a difficult task because gender, race, and nation, although distinct, flow in and out of each other at the level of meaning and practice.

The nation continues to be a central trope around which power is organized and exercised; and recent scholarship has shown how ideas of gender (e.g., Anthias and Yuval-Davis 1992) and race (e.g., Balibar 1991; Gilroy 1987, 2000) are not merely aspects of nationalism but fundamental to it. Postcolonial studies scholars have engaged closely with ideas of how the European imperial project had race and gender at its very core (McClintock 1995; Stoler 1995). What these and other studies show is that sexism and racism cannot be considered independently of nationalism because "race and gender are not distinct realms of experience, existing in splendid isolation from each other; nor can they be simply yoked together retrospectively like armatures of LEGO. Rather, they come into existence *in and through* relation to each other—if in contradictory and conflictual ways" (McClintock 1995:5).

Gender, race, and nation are therefore not concepts that can be added to each other in a simple way. Integration of these three major levels of social analysis has rarely been attempted, and it is only over the last two decades, since the works of Anderson (1983), Hobsbawm and Ranger (1983), Gellner (1983), and Smith (1986) began to seriously interrogate the "naturalness" of national sentiment, that scholars have examined the racial and gendered aspects of the nation.

One approach is to look at national ideas generated from certain sections of the population and see how these ideas are racialized and how they exclude certain groups of people. A good example is Gilroy's (1987) study, *There Ain't no Black in the Union Jack*. Similarly one can look, as Nira Yuval-Davis (1997) has done, at the gendered aspects of nationalism and the exclusion of women from the nation. Both of these works broke important ground and changed perceptions of nationalism, but, leaving aside the fact that neither study fully integrates race *and* gender in its analysis, such approaches make the implicit assumption that national identity is generated from the metropolitan centers. Furthermore, they assume that those who are notionally excluded identify weakly with the nation. There is no question that gender is central to the construction of nation as indeed is race in an imperial or (neo)colonial context.[2] If, however, the editors of a recent volume titled *Gendered Nations* can note that "questions of gender have been seriously neglected" in much of the recent work on nation (Blom et al., 2000:xv), it is even rarer to locate studies that combine race and gender in the study of the nation.

As this volume demonstrates, gender is often racialized and race gendered in the context of citizenship and the nation-state. In Latin America, Sarah Radcliffe and Sallie Westwood (1996) have looked at the various ways that gender is implicated in nationalist discourses; and Sarah Radcliffe (1990) and Mary Crain (1996) have explored the manner in which gender and ethnicity are reproduced and contested when women migrate to urban centers. These studies, however, are based on data produced in the metropolis and what is of concern is how the "marginal" are included or excluded when people move from the periphery to the center. Such dichotomizing obscures the many ways in which national culture is produced on the "periphery" by "marginal" peoples even if not through the production of novels, textbooks, or laws.

These approaches are insufficient to deal with the complexity of identities in the Andes of those "on the margins" and, indeed, in many other parts of the world. It is to these other national imaginings, and particularly their intersections with gender and indian identity, that this volume is principally addressed. Gender, indigeneity, and nation are not unlike the belts many rural Andeans wear, tightly woven with colors and threads interlocked and interlaced to produce a very attractive and functional item of clothing. To examine such a belt one thread at a time is really to miss the point of the belt and so the contributors to this volume, albeit from very different perspectives, take holistic views of how gender, indigeneity, and nation are constructed.

This volume concentrates on the central Andes, mainly Bolivia, with the one Peruvian case being from Lake Titicaca, which provides a border between the two countries. The advantage of such a tight focus is that it allows the contributors to draw from each other's material and permits the fine conceptual interlacing that is at the center of what this volume seeks to achieve. If we are to eschew the "Lego" approach to identity, then it is essential to examine identity from multiple but mutually informing perspectives; examples from disparate regions will necessarily give a more partial view. This novel approach to the study of gender, identity, and the nation enables each chapter to resonate with the others in complex and fruitful ways and the volume is organized in such a way as to facilitate these connections.

Race and Revolutions in the "Long" Nineteenth Century

It is widely accepted that modern nationalism was the child of the French Revolution, which introduced the ideas of a state organized around citizens with allegiance to a nation as opposed to one in which peasants showed allegiance to their lord and the lords to their king. This powerful transformation had at its root a reworking of the understandings of race. Until the Revolution, "race" was a concept that referred to aristocratic lineage. People with no political status simply had no "race" (Guillaumin 1995).[3] The Revolution expanded this concept to include the entire nation of French people—everyone now had "race"; everyone was French. This new racialized identity had, in fact, been developing in Europe for several centuries if not so clearly articulated as in the French Revolution.

Florencia Mallon (1995:8) and others have pointed out that the scenic backdrop for the inchoate European national consciousness was the "expanding" world and Europe's relationship with the Indies (West and East) in particular. This political baptism of the lower classes was, however, equivocal: excluded from full citizenship were women and nonwhites. Indeed, the contradictions of French liberalism were most obviously exposed in Haiti, where large numbers of slaves understood *liberté* to necessitate the abolition of slavery (cf. Ferrer 1999). Under the French Republics and through the French colonial period, there was always the possibility of colonial men being sufficiently acculturated to be considered fully French, thus furthering the myth of French republican *egalité*. In practice, however, the mass of French colonial subjects never became full French citizens as Fanon attested with such bitter eloquence (Fanon 1967). For, as Hannah Arendt (2004) also noted, French Republican rights as a citizen are reserved for those worthy of them, and this construction of worthiness was inherently racist (a point also made by Roediger [1991] about U.S. republicanism in the same period). French citizenship was in principle open to all, but in practice reserved for white, French-speaking males. Latin American republicanism, too, recognized the universal rights of man, but these rights were always contingent on the suitability of the citizenry (Anderson 1983; Stepan 1991).[4]

In the Andes, the idea of an inclusive nation-state based on universal franchise and rights is as old as the republics themselves. Anderson has pointed out that it was in these republics that modern national consciousness can first be identified (1983: ch. 4). The imagined national community of these "creole pioneers," as Anderson calls them, included neither blacks, indians, nor women as full and equal citizens.[5] It was not, however, only creoles who revolted against colonial rule in what has become known as the "age of revolutions." Haiti, most famously, resisted a republican model restricted to white, metropolitan Frenchmen; but it is not the only example within the Western Hemisphere of a subaltern revolt that challenged the racist assumptions of much revolutionary thought. As Sinclair Thomson (2003) illustrates, the Andes, too, had its emancipatory revolutions in the late eighteenth century: large-scale indian revolts in 1780–81, which offered an alternative vision of how the state should relate to the people it governs. The insurrections failed but have certainly not been forgotten; and the names of leaders Túpak Katari and Bartolina Sisa are regularly invoked in Bolivia today. More important, perhaps, "native American peoples nourished their own ideals of liberty and self-determination . . . [and] brought about effective and enduring practices of communal democracy and sovereignty that differed from Western liberal principles" (2003:276). As Thomson is at pains to point out, these insurrections were not just *indian* revolts and it is facile to characterize them as simply race wars: they were also struggles against autocratic power and for self-determination; they were conflicts about the structure of state authority and the position of subaltern peoples within it.

The indian revolutions ultimately failed and for much of the postcolonial period a national consciousness that included indian peasants was quite simply unimaginable for political and social elites; but this is not to say that the thousands of Andean communities did not, in fact, possess a national consciousness, nor that the memories of the emancipatory revolutions were simple erased. The "unimagined communities" (Thurner 1997:12) of indian peasants regularly engaged with the state and on various occasions argued for an inclusive republicanism (Larson 2004; Mallon 1995; Platt 1987; Thurner 1997).[6]

Tristan Platt's (1993) work on nineteenth-century indians in Potosí demonstrated how they created their own imagery of republicanism, particularly around the figure of Simón Bolívar. This republicanism was very different from that of metropolitan discourse and illustrates that one should not assume Andean peasants were beyond refiguring nationalist sentiments according to their own understandings. Platt demonstrated that there are more options than simply accepting the hegemonic idea of the nation-state or rejecting it.

Subaltern visions of the nation did not, however, coincide with those of the urban elite who considered themselves white and who continued to struggle with the "indian problem" and its "solution" through eugenics and immigration (Stepan 1991). Throughout the nineteenth century and beyond, the subaltern masses were alternately, and sometimes simultaneously, pitied and feared; but the postcolonial creole elites rarely saw the non-European majorities of their countries as anything other than a social or historical "problem" (Larson 2004:49) except, perhaps, when they proved useful in fighting postcolonial wars.

Historical and ethnographic accounts from the early part of the twentieth century are largely silent on the issue of subaltern national consciousness. It is not clear whether this is due to the cumulative effect of regionalism, dispossession, and disenfranchisement of indians, which intensified during the latter half of the nineteenth century, or a lack of scholarly attention. At any rate, by the early decades of the twentieth century, creole fear of indian insurrection combined with a hardening of biological racism led elites to "shut indians out of the creole notion of the nation-state" (Larson 2004:244). This imaginative expulsion, and the policies that accompanied it, served to obscure the long history of indian autonomy and indian struggles for inclusion within the nation-state; it also served to develop a racialized social geography with civilized urban creoles at the center and barbarous rural indians on the margins.

In her study of Andean nation-making between 1810 and 1910 Brooke Larson writes, "By 1910, creoles had reorganized their nation-states around rigid concepts of race, culture and geography, which aimed at controlling the ambiguous spaces of racial-ethnic crossing and mediation, while securing the boundaries of whiteness, urbanity and civilization" (2004:247). This racialized geography of the nation was to cast a long shadow across the century and into the current one as many of the essays in this volume clearly demonstrate.

Indigenismo, Mestizaje, and a New Nation in the Twentieth Century

If the early decades of the twentieth century marked the apogee of Andean nationalist racism and the exclusion of the indian, a very different process was unfolding in revolutionary Mexico (1910–1920), one that produced an idea of the nation that would eventually take hold in the Andes and much of the rest of Latin America too. Revolutionary Mexico rejected a republicanism rooted in a white, creole oligarchy for a broader-based nation that included all. This necessarily had a racial component for it replaced the right to rule based on European descent with one based on a new American culture defined by a mixed European and indigenous and African heritage: the white right to rule was being replaced by a different, but still racialized, model of *mestizaje*, one founded on the idea of racial mixing. This model is exemplified by the idea of the "cosmic race" (Vasconcelos 1961), which arose out of the Mexican Revolution, a new race of people neither European nor indian but Mexicans of mixed heritage, *mestizos*. There followed a major reevaluation of indigenous history and culture that spread over the course of the century to other countries with large indian and mixed populations such as Peru and Bolivia. José Uriel García (1973) suggested a similar model of progressive mestizaje for Peru in 1930; but in Bolivia, even as *indigenistas* such as Alcides Arguedas and other intellectuals saw a mestizo future, it was not necessarily one they wholeheartedly embraced (Larson 2004:242–43). In contrast to what occurred in Mexico, these ideas did not achieve political dominance in Bolivia and Peru until the latter half of the twentieth century

This new, mestizo, republicanism was championed by the rising middle classes but was characterized by a profound ambivalence toward indians. *Indigenismo*, the valorization of indian culture, was principally led by educated mestizos in the early decades of the twentieth century and concentrated heavily on the glorious past of indigenous culture, the Aztec and Inca civilizations. Rather in the way that the British recognized the value and even commonality of ancient indian and European civilizations (Sinha 1995:20), so too did Latin Americans learn to admire the ancient glories of the Aztecs and Incas. The decline of these civilizations needed, however, to be accounted for and, even though a large number of theories were put forward, there is a common theme of decline and degeneracy (Brading 1988; Sinha 1995:21; Thurner 1997:133–34).

Indigenismo was the cultural ideology of the rising provincial middle classes who sought to legitimize their new power by casting old creole elites as descendants of foreign oppressors, remnants of Spanish colonialism. Indigenismo, however, was rarely much concerned with contemporary indians beyond a paternalism that sought to civilize and modernize them; it was much more about creating a regional or national identity with the glories of indigenous civilizations securely in the past; and, indeed, most members of indigenista circles were mestizos and whites.[7] As Deborah Poole has shown for the indigenistas of Cuzco, they were more concerned with answering European artistic movements and developing a native bohemianism than with the conditions of labor of those indians who worked on their haciendas; of greater concern was the development of a romantic naturalism to regional identity. "The Indian, as a part of nature, was invoked as evidence of the generalized and environmentally circumscribed cultural intuition that separated all highland peoples from their coastal compatriots" (Poole 1997:187). Whites could absorb autochthony through the landscape, what García called "syncretic tellurism" (ibid.); and there are echoes of this when whites and mestizos today strategically adopt an autochthonous identity through adopting particular indian practices.

Meanwhile, contemporary indians were often seen as anachronisms or degenerate and miserable epigones, having little in common with their illustrious ancestors. The national project required indians to become assimilated into a new and modern nation, to become, in fact, mestizos. As Brading has noted, "The ultimate and paradoxical aim of official indigenismo in Mexico was . . . to liberate the country from the dead-weight of its native past, or, to put the case more clearly, finally to destroy the native culture which had emerged during the colonial period" (1988:88; see also Anderson 1983:13).

It was not until the 1930s that indians once again were given a role in the imagination—but not in concrete terms—of some elites in the 1930s: scholars have sited the rise of a broad consensual national consciousness in the fall of the Leguía presidency and the rise of the middle classes in Peru (Nugent 1997) and the 1932–35 Chaco War in Bolivia (e.g., Arze Aguirre 1987). David Nugent's work in northern Peru at the beginning of the twentieth century illustrates the important point that the sense of nation does not always emanate out from the center. In provincial Chachapoyas it was the rising middle classes who saw modern ideas of the nation as encompassing equality, individual rights, progress, and so on (1997:308) and who pushed for change. It is worth noting that the indian minority surrounding Chachapoyas did not appear to have a voice or opinion about the nation even as this group became an object of concern by the new political classes.

In Bolivia the Chaco War had a profound effect on how the nation was to develop. This disastrous war, which resulted in the deaths of tens of thousands of undertrained indian troops, at the same time created a common experience among men, many of whom later pushed for the creation of a modern nation-state based on equal citizenship for all. The generation of the Chaco was responsible for the Revolution of 1952. The Revolution and its aftermath saw the dismantling of the feudalistic hacienda system under a major land reform, the introduction of mass education, and the abolition of the category of "indian" in law, to be replaced by "*campesino*," peasant. It was in this postrevolutionary period that citizenship was meaningfully acquired by the mass of indians but this was accompanied by powerful assimilationist policies that sought to turn "indians" into "Bolivians," leaving little space for any expression of indian or indigenous identity: modernity was mestizo.

Contemporary indian culture was consequently regarded as regressive and anachronistic, and it was the expectation of successive governments that through political liberty and education, retarding indian culture would inevitably be erased. This was, indeed, one of the primary aims of universal education for several decades in Bolivia. As one commentator put it, mass rural education was about "Bolivianization" much more than it was ever about pedagogy (Choque et al., 1992).

The progressive side of these new political ideologies was a concern for the oppressive conditions under which indians lived and even the intimate details of their lives. This should not surprise us. As George Mosse (1985) has shown for several European countries, once nationalism is seen to be about creating a new kind of person, then physical hygiene, personal practices, and moral qualities become increasingly important. In the Andes, as in much of Europe, the nation came to be conceived as a political community of citizens: the ideas of nation and citizenry were intimately linked and intertwined (Eley 2000:33) and this sense of citizenship is profoundly gendered. Here, as in many other instances, citizenship and military service are closely linked: it was the sacrifice of indian soldiers in the Chaco War that persuaded many of their middle-ranking officers that they deserved full inclusion in the nation-state, and today indian men dominate the ranks of the Bolivian army (Gill 1997). It is through the masculinizing spaces of military service that many men lay claim to their citizenship (Canessa, this volume).

Whereas the army could break or mold indian men, the household sphere presented a challenge as a space that did not produce proper citizens (Larson, this volume). In particular, it was women's roles as mothers of new citizens that caused the greatest concern. Focusing eugenicist concerns on subaltern women was a widespread phenomenon in Latin

America (Stepan 1991), though the concern for the education of women was central to the development of national sentiment in many countries around the world (Jayawardena 1986). Better housewives and better mothers are central to the modern nation-building project.

Indian women in the past as well as now are often seen as inhabiting, at best, the folkloric margins of the nation, if not as retarding agents preventing national progress. There are, moreover, echoes of the public policy concerns of the thirties and forties today: schoolteachers will berate children for their footwear, peasant dress, food, and housing and equate these with moral failings that undermine national progress (Canessa, Van Vleet, this volume). The "Mothers" Clubs that visit every indian community also serve to inculcate a particular ethic of hygiene and ethic of care as well as a specific ideal of femininity: hard-working, strong, and highly competent farmers with several children are seen by the state as simply "mothers," and not very good mothers at that. These women appear very far from the long-suffering, self-sacrificing, and infinitely patient "mothers" that so dominate understandings of the "good mother" in metropolitan society.

It is not only in their social roles and lack of appropriate domesticity that indian women in particular are considered cause for concern: ideas of national belonging and national identity are focused on the physical bodies of indians in myriad ways. Their closeness to the earth, from the adobe homes in which they live to the earthenware pots that they use to produce their food, mark indians as primitive and dirty and less civilized (Orlove 1998). Their speech and clothing also mark indians as not belonging in the nation-state. Full citizenship therefore remains elusive for the more indian, the less urban, and for women (Stephenson 1999; Luykx 1999). Moreover, the issues of whiteness and hygiene are especially focused on the bodies of indian women (Stephenson 1999; Weismantel 2001; Seligmann 2000), who, more clearly than men, are marked as being particularly indian and "other" (Canessa, this volume; de la Cadena 1995). As many of the contributors to this volume show, indian women and indian women's bodies are problematic in terms of the national imagination, not only as markers of difference but for being the perceived sites for the reproduction of indian homes and families. Whereas indian men are much more likely to be seen to contribute to the nation through their wage labor or military service, indian women are seen as being outside the nation-state and contaminating intruders when they do enter public domains as market traders (Seligmann 2000). As Weismantel (2001) has shown, the bodies of urban indian women, *cholitas*, excite as much sexual frisson as fear as their dress and behavior so jar with metropolitan norms.

It is worth remembering that for many of the people discussed in this volume national citizenship has been only recently, and still not fully, conferred. The road from hacienda serfs to peasants to citizens is one that many indians have traveled in their lifetimes and there continues to be a tension between the model of national citizenship imagined by urban elites and those on the periphery. A particular example is the comment made to me by a shopkeeper in the town of Sorata in Bolivia: "These indian peasants do not know how to live; they have not yet learned citizenship." He was referring to peasants from the hinterland migrating to Sorata (as his parents had done) who, according to him, dragged down standards in local schools and generally acted as a brake on the town's progress. Of course, the peasants he is talking about may not entirely agree: as many of these examples given in this volume show, there is a dynamism to the way people imagine, reimagine, contest, and reshape the idea of the nation-state and their membership of it in the contemporary Andes.

It is not simply that indians and indian women do not conform to the national ideal but, rather, that the national ideal of progress is constructed in contradistinction to the rural, indian, and feminine. Indian women, even as they epitomize backwardness and pollution, are at the very heart of the national imagination (cf. Abercrombie 1992). It is through the interplay of racial discrimination and gender hierarchy that the national ideal is constructed and, moreover, that racialized class inequality is reproduced and reinforced. This implication of race and gender in the dynamics of political control has a long tradition in Latin America as Verena Martínez-Alier (1974) has shown for nineteenth-century Cuba; McCaa (1984) and Stern (1997) have shown for colonial Mexico; and Twinam (1999) has shown for Latin America more generally.

In any racialized system of power, gender and sexuality are of primary concern. It is through controlling elite female sexuality that racial stratification can be maintained and through racial mixing that it can be undermined. This is particularly so when, as in much of Latin America, it is widely believed that people and populations can be "whitened" (Graham 1990; Skidmore 1974; Stepan 1991; Wade 1993; Wright 1990). Whitening is not simply the strategy by which wealthy mestizos marry poorer white women so that their offspring look more European, but whitening is also about adopting the outward behavior and mores of the dominant classes; above all, as has been widely noted, "money whitens." The ideology of mestizaje, therefore, offers the possibility of personal and racial improvement. This may appear to be more progressive than a system of rigid racial stratification but, in fact, depends on a broad acceptance of a racial hierarchy and is much more difficult to resist and mobilize against. So long as these ideas are widely accepted and the boundaries are multiple and fluid, personal advancement through whitening will be a frustrating process. One example is the experience of rural schoolteachers who see education as a means to personal and racial advancement but are constantly reminded of their rural roots and indian background (Luykx 1999; Canessa 2004).

Indian women are therefore not only "more indian" to use de la Cadena's phrase (1995), but indian men, by association, are also more feminine, for, as gender is produced and reproduced at different levels of the hierarchy, gender and race are overlaid on each other. When creole Bolivians invoke an indian deity, either out of solidarity or as a marker of national identity, it is almost always the earth goddess, the Pachamama (cf. Rivera Cusicanqui 1996:42). The Pachamama was invoked in public protests against water privatization in Cochabamba in 2000, but not the male Andean deities most associated with water, the *achachilas*. It is probably no coincidence that in Bigenho's chapter the mestizo-creole singers of indian music are all women, which raises the question that if indian women are more indian, are white women less white?

Collapsing the Center and Fraying the Fringe

People "on the fringes" of the nation-state may resist or embrace the metropolitan national imagination, and the chapters in this volume show that they will often do both in complex ways. It is not, therefore, necessarily the case that the nation being made on the margins must be one recognizable as a national culture based on universally shared values. This volume shows that making the nation is an individual as well as a collective act and that people construct a national imagination through a variety of activities, such as eating, having sex, dealing with tourists, learning at school, making music, and so on. The meanings generated on the margins occur in a context of a powerfully hegemonic national idea but there are many spaces to contextualize and transform this idea in small and large ways. We must be careful not to exaggerate the level of agency individuals or communities have, but we must be equally careful not to assume that people either passively consume or simply reject nationalist ideology.

This volume suggests that subaltern Andeans respond to the nation and the state in myriad ways: sometimes the nation is rejected; sometimes it is embraced; frequently the nation is refigured, reinterpreted, and reconstituted in local contexts and in often surprising ways. These studies expose a paradox in the relation between indians and the nation, which is that the nation can be claimed as a source of power and distinct identity whilst simultaneously serving to oppress by making some types of national imaginings unattainable. So, as shown in many of our examples (e.g., Bigenho, Canessa, Van Vleet), people can lay claim to an indian identity in some contexts whilst rejecting it in others. One important aspect of this is that the identity claims that can be made are sometimes compromised by the need to make them within a discourse of citizenship.

People in the Andes do not generally make an outright rejection of the hegemonic nation, nor do they fully embrace it. In the words of Layoun, "the peoples of the nation often negotiate . . . nationalism and its boundaries in far more various and inventive ways than they are given credit or apparent narrative license for" (2001:9). Given the short historical depth of the idea of mass national identity in the Andes, the internal borders of race, class, and gender around which this identity is constructed are open to multiple interpretations. Zorn's essay illustrates how national boundaries and identities are both reinforced and undermined by transnational links. Here the people of Taquile build on their "typical" weaving art to simultaneously assert their "traditional" culture and become "modern." The Peruvian national imaginary, which constructs their marginality, is traversed as marginality and is used to create transnational networks. The borders between tradition and modernity, center and periphery, national and international are perforated and twisted at every turn. Zorn touches on these themes most directly in her discussion of tourism and transnationalism: as the world economy becomes increasingly globalized, one's marginality can be transformed into a means of communicating with the world. Through mass and global communications, Europeans and North Americans may have a better idea of how indians live in the Andes and the Amazon than they do of the social elites of these regions. As Zorn's work in this volume shows, marginality can be transformed into a transnational commodity as mass travel has created markets for "exotics." The people of Taquile illustrate well how the center and margin, national and international, "true" Peruvianness and indianness are telescopically related: they loom large or small depending on which lens you look through and all are ultimately collapsible.

In a comparable vein, Marcia Stephenson shows that the dichotomy between center and periphery, civilization and barbarism is collapsed in the *chuqila* dance. Here, adolescent girls are the main protagonists, and through the course of the dance the standard national geography is subverted, whereby the mountain peaks and undomesticated landscape are seen as the source of morality and civilization: out of the landscape productive connections between people are made and moral communities created. In this way the chuqila dance inverts the dominant national imagery wherein urban space is seen as civilized and the mountains and indian communities in them seen as barbarous.

If Zorn and Stephenson look at the tropes of center and periphery in terms of a racialized geography, many of the other contributors to this volume look at center and periphery in much more intimate spaces. In these examples, just as with those mentioned above, center and periphery are constantly twisting into each other rather like a Möbius strip. In Bigenho's study of singers, creole women celebrate "indianness," but this particular version of indianness is also quintessentially Bolivian and therefore universal on that level. At the same time, the indians they recall from their nostalgic youthful days on country estates are not three-dimensional people but appear to form a natural part of the landscape. Indeed this is precisely how indians were largely represented in early twentieth-century art in Bolivia, as part of a dramatic landscape. So the creole women are celebrating indianness and bringing it into the heart of national identity, but this has nothing to do with indians qua people who are resolutely on the descriptive margins of their imagination and memory.

In Andrew Canessa's contribution to the volume, center and periphery, and the racialized structure these articulate, are reproduced analogically in the most intimate spaces of a "remote" indian community. Here the gendered images of nation are recast at the level of gender relations in the personal lives of men and women; what might appear as abstract gendered imagery of the nation reappears in the concrete lives of individuals. These are the very "hearths and minds" that, as Larson shows, the state considered so problematically distant from the nation-building project. Indeed, it still does as it tries to inculcate a particular domesticity on indian women. As we twist through the Möbius strip, the domestic lives of indians concern makers of public policy and consequences of public policy structure the domestic lives of indians, but not, of course, in ways either would easily imagine.

Van Vleet's essay demonstrates how the dyad of center and periphery are constantly appearing and disappearing. The story of Reina's shoes illustrates how ideas of what is white and metropolitan and what is rural and indian can shape the desires and frustrations of an eleven-year-old girl. But the story of Reina and Marisa reverses the polarity of a standard national imagining that contrasts active (white) men and passive (indian) women. These girls may not be consciously aware of the implications of their acts in defining ethnicity and nationality, but the desire and ability to choose one's clothes and shoes occur in a political and national context. These adolescents, in crossing and recrossing boundaries, of incorporating particular notions of center and periphery within themselves, are constantly challenging key notions of gender and indigeneity and, as a consequence, how the nation is imagined.

All the writers here discuss how identity is created and contested through physical processes, and one way of reading these activities is to see identity as performative in the sense used by Judith Butler. In the Andes, essentialized differences between people are produced through cultural processes. That is, the racialized differences between indians and non-indians are understood to be rooted not in immutable characteristics but, rather, in social and cultural practices, which nevertheless produce differences that inhere in the body: difference is essentialized and even seen as biological, but these differences are produced through practice and are therefore mutable (cf. Weismantel 2001:191–92). As Stoler asserts, "A notion of essence does not necessarily rest on immovable parts but on the strategic inclusion of different attributes, of a changing constellation of features and a changing weighting of them" (Stoler 1997:200 in Wade 2002:64).[8]

Larson illustrates how "indian bodies, hearths, and minds" became central to the nation-building project in the 1930s. Indians, and particularly female indians, became a concern of public policy as various political elites sought to draw indians into a modern nation-state. All subsequent chapters reflect some of the implications of such policies. Larson and Bigenho's chapters together illustrate the opposing and frequently contradictory tendency of seeing indians as being on the periphery and requiring assimilation and *simultaneously* as being at the heart of national culture and identity. Subsequent chapters provide a counterpoint by taking the perspective of indians themselves—as opposed to social and political elites—and investigate in a number of ways how indian men and women, youths and elders, negotiate, resist, absorb, and transform a sense of national identity. The chapter by Elayne Zorn takes this process a stage further and looks at how international tourism has a role of transforming indian culture from being considered absolutely marginal in terms of national imagery into something that is deemed iconic of national culture. The book thus progresses from elites' perceptions to indians' perceptions to a more globalized concept of indigeneity and nation.

The body and kinesthesis are also central themes around which the volume is organized. It is in the body that genders, races, and national subjectivity are often believed to inhere. It is, for example, fairly common in nationalistic discourse to see the female contribution as being one of a mother producing citizens and soldiers. Here a woman's national and gender identities are clearly overlapping, the one informing the other. Mrinalini Sinha's (1995) work on colonizer and colonized in British Bengal is an interesting attempt to explore how Bengali men partially absorbed and reacted to British ideas about their race and masculinity. Sinha's analysis is restricted to the Bengali social and educational elite; but in illustrating how the effeminacy of the educated Bengali male was understood as an interplay between race and bodily practices, she demonstrates how gender, race, and national identity (in this case Englishness and a Bengali indian identity) may be conceptually separable but nevertheless intersect at the level of the body. As Judith Butler has shown for gender (1990) and Peter Wade for race (2002), difference may be simultaneously performative and essentialized: what the body *does* and what the subject is understood to *be* are often inseparable. As Mary Weismantel points out, "the body, in Andean thinking, is an object built up over time. As it ingests, digests, and expels substances from the world around it, it provides its owner an identity drawn from worldly substances" (2001:191–92). To share food is to produce a shared identity that is rooted in metabolic processes. It is not, however, only ingestion and digestion that produce a physical change: other quotidian physical processes such as dressing, dancing, and weaving are not merely outward manifestations of a racialized identity but work to *produce* that identity.

The body is therefore the most immediate mode through which identities—gender identities, indian identities, and national identities—are produced. The contributors illustrate how identity is performative and is produced through clothing (Van Vleet), sexuality (Canessa), music (Bigenho), dance (Stephenson), and weaving (Zorn). It is at the level of the body that the three elements of gender, indian, and national identity come together, and because identity is rooted in the body and bodily practices, it is often also essentialized in terms of gender and race. We move away from standard studies of indigeneity and nationalism, which focus on political movements and parties, toward a level of analysis rooted in daily practice. Each chapter looks at bodies and performance in different but overlapping ways: bodies as a focus of government policy (Larson) and bodies as international icons (Zorn); bodies that dance (Van Vleet, Stephenson) and sing (Bigenho); bodies that weave and work (Zorn, Larson); and bodies that through violence and sexual practices illustrate and encode identity and difference (Canessa). These acts are understood not simply on the level of cultural practices, because they produce meanings that are essentialized in terms of "being." Bigenho's singers expect her to feel Bolivian through singing; Stephenson's dancers embody the boundaries of the community and the nation; Canessa gives the example of one man who believed himself to become truly Bolivian through sexual activity; in Van Vleet's chapter what girls wear and dance has a transformative, but certainly temporary, effect on their ethnic identity; and on Taquile, as Zorn shows, the act of weaving is economic as well as serving to constitute gender identity and ethnic difference. One's own identity and, as a consequence, the way one imagines the nation then become corporeal acts.

This has consequences for national feeling and identity because the nation does not only exist on the level of imagination, representation, and cultural production, but is also experienced kinesthetically through gendered and raced bodies. By the same token, the nation can be experienced and reproduced and, therefore, have meaning, on the level of the individual as much as it can as a collective representation.

To sing, to eat, to weave . . . these are simple, quotidian acts. Yet in the performance of these acts, as bodies move in particular spaces and contexts, they do so within certain understandings of gender, race, and nation. The physical acts may affirm, undermine, challenge, or reshape these understandings, but as the essays in this volume show, they are never innocent of them.

Note on Terminology

To draw an overly clear distinction between white and mestizo and urban on the one hand and indian and rural on the other is deeply problematic: the relationships between whites, indians, and mestizos have been long, often violent, and frequently intimate. The distinctions between these groups are more likely to be characterized by ambiguity than clarity. No single term could possibly encapsulate the multiplicity of meanings and references that ethnically diverse subaltern Andeans evoke. Although the terms "indigenous" and "indian" are becoming increasingly common in the context of political mobilization, the vast majority of people identified as such continue to eschew any identification of that kind; nor do they generally describe themselves as "Quechuas" or "Aymaras," terms usually used to refer to the languages people speak, rather than the people themselves, although these national/ethnic terms are increasingly common in urban and peri-urban regions.

The term "indian" itself is highly derogatory in Spanish, as the chapters by Van Vleet and Canessa illustrate, and its use is controversial. Some scholars prefer to use the term "Andeans," but it is both imprecise and runs the risk of essentializing and homogenizing groups of very different people (Starn 1994). When speaking about particular groups the authors use the terms people use for themselves, which generally refer to places of origin; but when speaking of the large numbers of multifarious peoples who are deemed to be culturally and politically marginal to the nation, it sometimes seems preferable to avoid euphemisms and use a term that has historical continuity and points directly at the subaltern position of the people we are writing about. Over the past centuries, although the position of the "indian" as well as the way that identity has been understood has changed (Harris 1995), it has always denoted a difference in status and power and, moreover, it has been non-indians who have decided who is and is not an "indian." The term "indian" is *not* neutral: it points precisely to the unequal power relation that we seek to interrogate.

The word "indigenous" is drawn from natural history, where it means "belonging naturally to the region." In some contexts the term can imply a certain "naturalness" to indigeneity and an association with particular landscapes and environments, which suggests that people can be considered as simply part of the flora and fauna of a region. Unlike "indian," however, its wide use is much more recent. It consequently has the advantage of being less loaded; although its apparent neutrality obscures the neocolonial processes out of which it arises. In this volume the term is generally used to refer to contemporary political mobilization, to native languages, and as a more neutral term to refer to the ethnically distinct subaltern people of the Andes.

The word "indian" in the Americas does not refer to national origin; that is, the people referred to by the term in this book are not from India. We therefore follow the usage of writing this word in lower case in the same way as other such terms, for example, mestizo, mulatto, creole (Abercrombie 1998:xviii; Wade 1997:121). In every instance of their use in this volume, the terms "indian" and "indigenous" are understood to be socially and culturally constructed, to have contested meanings, and to refer to a multifarious group of people who share a subaltern position vis à vis the state. Both terms are inherently ambiguous and problematic: we avoid the clumsiness of constantly using "scare quotes" to indicate this as indeed one of the principal thrusts of the book is to challenge a key assumption of the designation, namely marginality from the nation.

Acknowledgments

I am very grateful to Michelle Bigenho, Susan Paulson, Lucinda Platt, Melanie Wright, and Elayne Zorn for their useful and insightful comments on earlier drafts of this introduction, as well as to the two anonymous reviewers from the University of Arizona Press. They have made significant contributions to the content and style of the piece. I am, of course, responsible for any remaining errors or infelicities.

Notes

1. For a discussion of the term "indian," see the Note on Terminology at the end of this chapter.

2. In the Latin American context see, for example, Wright (1990), Skidmore (1974), Wade (2000), Placido (2001).

3. In a rather similar way, Aristotle did not recognize that slaves had a sex: Aristotle, who was immensely concerned about the sex of free men and women, recognized no sex among slaves. "A woman," as Vicky Spellman puts it, "is a female who is free; a 'man' is a male who is a citizen; a slave is a person whose sexual identity does not matter." For Aristotle, in other words, slaves are without sex because their gender "does not matter politically" (in Laqueur 1990:54).

4. As in France, exceptionalism plays an important role. Emiliano Zapata rose from his indian origins to be a revolutionary leader and national hero of Mexico; Pelé is a great black footballer and symbol of Brazil who for a while was

the partner of blonde television star Xuxa. People can point to these and other exceptions to demonstrate the inclusive nature of nationalism, but most people of color are heavily discriminated against and, because of economic and political marginalization, have limited chances to enjoy the benefits of full citizenship.

5. In Latin America, "creole" refers to those of "pure" Iberian heritage born in the Americas. More generally, it refers to those people who are unambiguously white and is in contrast to those who are considered to be of "mixed race" such as mestizos. In certain contexts, as an adjective, it can refer to cultural forms that are American but not indigenous, such as creole cuisine.

6. Historical scholarship has demonstrated how subalterns may embrace nation-building ideas even as they transform them according to their own agendas and worldviews. For example, Ferrer has shown for Cuba in the nineteenth century how black and mulatto insurgents took the liberal rhetoric of their white comrades in the anticolonial struggle at face value and pursued an egalitarian and emancipatory agenda within the independence movement. In the process these soldiers and intellectuals offered alternative visions of what it was to be Cuban and a citizen. In a similar vein, Vaughan (1997) has shown how the Yaqui of Mexico struggled against state control by asserting a different model of nationhood to the one prosecuted by the Mexican government through the expansion of the education system.

7. There were, however, some exceptions, most notably the Peruvian photographer Martín Chambi.

8. As Wade has noted (2002:61–64), even at the height of "biological racism" in the West there was a continuing tension between a belief that race was a "fixed" quality and the uneasy acceptance that environment played a role in transforming that fixed essence.

Bibliography

Abercrombie, Thomas. 1992. "To Be Indian, to Be Bolivian." In *Nation-States and Indians in Latin America*, ed. Greg Urban and Joel Sherzer. Austin: University of Texas Press, 95–130.

———. 1998. *Pathways of Memory and Power*. Madison: Wisconsin University Press.

Albó, Xavier. 1996. "Making the Leap from Local Mobilization to National Politics" (Bolivia: Report on Indigenous Movements). *NACLA Report on the Americas*. March.

Anderson, Benedict. 1983. *Imagined Communities*. London: Verso.

Anthias, Floya, and Nira Yuval-Davis. 1992. *Racialized Boundaries: Race, Nation, Gender, Colour and Class and the Anti-Racist Struggle*. London: Routledge.

Appelbaum, Nancy, Ann Macpherson, and Karin Rosemblatt, eds. 2003. *Race and Nation in Modern Latin America*. Chapel Hill: University of North Carolina Press.

Arendt, Hannah. 2004. *The Origins of Totalitarianism*. New York: Schocken Books.

Arze Aguirre, René Danilo. 1987. *Guerras y conflictos sociales: El caso rural boliviano durante la campaña del Chaco*. La Paz: CERES

Balibar, Etienne. 1991. "Racism and Nationalism." In *Race, Nation and Class: Ambiguous Identities*, ed. Etienne Balibar and Immanuel Wallerstein, 37–67. London: Verso.

Barth, Frederick. 1969. *Ethnic Groups and Boundaries*. London: Allen & Unwin.

Bigenho, Michelle. 2002. *Sounding Indigenous: Authenticity in Bolivian Musical Performance*. New York: Palgrave.

Blom, Ida, Karen Hageman, and Catherine Hall, eds. 2000. *Gendered Nations: Nationalisms and Gender Order in the Long Nineteenth Century*. Oxford: Berg.

Butler, Judith. 1990. *Gender Trouble: Feminism and the Subversion of Identity*. New York: Routledge.

Brading, David. 1988. "Manuel Gamio and Official Indigenismo." *Bulletin of Latin American Research* 7, no. 1:75–90.

de la Cadena, Marisol. 1995. "'Women are more Indian': Ethnicity and Gender in a Community Near Cuzco." In *Ethnicity, Markets, and Migration in the Andes*, ed. Brooke Larson and Olivia Harris. Durham, N.C.: Duke University Press.

———. 2000. *Indigenous Mestizos*. Durham, N.C.: Duke University Press.

Canessa, Andrew. 1998. "Procreation, the Person and Ethnic Difference in Highland Bolivia." *Ethnos* 63, no. 2:227–47.

———. 2000. "Fear and Loathing on the Kharisiri Trail: Alterity and Identity in the Andes." *Journal of the Royal Anthropological Institute (incorporating Man)* 6, no. 4:705–720.

———. 2004. "Reproducing Racism: Schooling and Race in Highland Bolivia." *Race, Ethnicity and Education* 7, no. 2:185–204.

Choque Canqui, Roberto, et al. 1992. *Educación indígena: ¿Ciudadanía o colonización?* La Paz: Aruwiyiri.

Colloredo-Mansfeld, Rudi. 1999. *The Native Leisure Class: Consumption and Cultural Creativity in the Andes*. Chicago: Chicago University Press.

Crain, Mary. 1996. "Negotiating Identities in Quito's Cultural Borderlands: Native Women's Performances for the Ecuadorian Tourist Trade." In *Cross-Cultural Consumption*, ed. D. Howes. London: Routledge, 125–37.

Day, Sophie, Evthymios Papataxiarchis, and Michael Stewart, eds. 1999. *Lilies of the Field: Marginal People Who Live for the Moment*. Boulder: Westview.

Dore, Elizabeth, and Maxine Molyneux. 2000. *Hidden Histories of Gender and the State in Latin America*. Durham, N.C.: Duke University Press.

Eley, Geoffrey. 2000. "Culture, Nation, and Gender." In *Gendered Nations: Nationalisms and Gender Order in the Long Nineteenth Century*, ed. Ida Blom et al. Berg: Oxford.

Fanon, Franz. 1967. *Black Skin, White Masks*. London: Pluto.

Ferrer, Ada. 1999. *Insurgent Cuba: Race, Nation, and Revolution, 1868–1898*. Chapel Hill: University of North Carolina Press.

García, José Uriel. 1973 [1930]. *El nuevo indio*. Lima: Colección Autores Peruanos.

Gellner, Ernest. 1983. *Nations and Nationalisms*. Oxford: Blackwell.

Gill, Lesley. 1997. "Creating Citizens, Making Men: The Military and Masculinity in Bolivia." *Cultural Anthropology* 12, no. 4:527–50.

Gilroy, Paul. 1987. *There Ain't No Black in the Union Jack: The Cultural Politics of Race and Nation*. London: Hutchinson.

———. 2000. *Between Camps: Race, Identity and Nationalism at the End of the Colour Line*. London: Allan Lane.

Gow, David, and Joanne Rappaport. 2002. "The Indigenous Public Voice: The Multiple Idioms of Modernity in Native Cauca." In *Indigenous Movements, Self-Representation, and the State in Latin America*, ed. Kay Warren and Jean Jackson. Austin: University of Texas Press.

Graham, Richard, ed. 1990. *The Idea of Race in Latin America, 1870–1940*. Austin: University of Texas Press.

Guillaumin, Colette. 1995. *Racism, Sexism, Power and Ideology*. London: Routledge.

Harris, Olivia. 1995. "Ethnic Identity and Market Relations: Indians and Mestizos in the Andes." In *Ethnicity, Markets, and Migration in the Andes*, ed. Brooke Larson and Olivia Harris. Durham, N.C.: Duke University Press.

Hobsbawm, Eric. 1990. *Nations and Nationalism since 1780*. Cambridge: Cambridge University Press.

Hobsbawm, Eric, and Terence Ranger, eds. 1983. *The Invention of Tradition*. Cambridge: Cambridge University Press.

Hodgson, Dorothy. 2002. "Comparative Perspectives on the Indigenous Rights Movements in Africa and the Americas." *American Anthropologist* 104, no. 4:1037–49.

Jayawardena, Kumari. 1986. *Feminism and Nationalism in the Third World*. London: Palgrave.

Kaplan, Caren, Norma Alarcón, and Minoo Moallem, eds. 1999. *Between Woman and the Nation: Nationalisms, Transnational Feminisms, and the State*. Durham, N.C.: Duke University Press.

Laqueur, Thomas. 1990. *Making Sex: Body and Gender from the Greeks to Freud*. Cambridge: Harvard University Press.

Larson, Brooke. 2004. *Trials of Nation Making: Liberalism, Race, and Ethnicity in the Andes, 1810–1910*. Cambridge: Cambridge University Press.

Layoun, Mary. 2001. *Wedded to the Land? Gender, Boundaries, and Nationalism in Crisis*. Durham, N.C.: Duke University Press.

Luykx, Aurolyn. 1999. *The Citizen Factory: Schooling and Cultural Production in Bolivia*. Albany: State University of New York Press.

Mallon, Florencia. 1995. *Peasant and Nation: the Making of Postcolonial Mexico and Peru*. Berkeley: University of California Press.

Mamani Condori, Carlos. 1991. *Taraqu: 1866–1935: Masacre, Guerra y "Renovacion" en la Biografia de Eduardo L. Nina Qhispi*. La Paz: Taller de Historia Oral Andina.

Martínez-Alier, Verena. 1974. *Marriage, Class, and Color in 19th Century Cuba*. Ann Arbor: University of Michigan Press.

McCaa, Robert. 1984. "Calidad, Clase, and Marriage in Colonial Mexico: The Case of Parral, 1788–1790." *Hispanic American Historical Review* 64, no. 3:477–501.

McClintock, Catherine. 1995. *Imperial Leather*. London: Routledge.

———. 1996. "No Longer in a Future Heaven: Nationalism, Gender and Race." In *Becoming National*, ed. G. Eley. Oxford: Oxford University Press.

Mosse, George. 1985. *Nationalism and Sexuality: Middle-Class Morality and Sexual Norms in Modern Europe*. Madison: University of Wisconsin Press.

Nelson, Diane. 1999. *A Finger in the Wound: Body Politics in Quincentennial Guatemala*. Berkeley: University of California Press.

Nugent, David. 1997. *Modernity at the Edge of Empire: State, Individual, and Nation in the Northern Peruvian Andes, 1885–1935*. Stanford, Calif.: Stanford University Press.

Orlove, Benjamin. 1998. "Down to Earth: Race and Substance in the Andes." *Bulletin of Latin American Research* 17, no. 2:207–22.

Placido, Barbara. 2002. "'It's All to Do with Words': An Analysis of Spirit Possession in the Venezuelan Cult of María Lionza." *Journal of the Royal Anthropological Institute* 7, no. 2:207–24.

Platt, Tristan. 1987. "The Andean Experience of Bolivian Liberalism: Roots of Rebellion in Nineteenth-Century Chayanta." In *Resistance, Rebellion, and Consciousness in the Andean Peasant World, 18th to 20th Centuries*, ed. Steve Stern. Madison: Wisconsin University Press, 280–326.

———. 1993. "Simón Bolívar, the Sun of Justice and the Amerindian Virgin: Andean Conceptions of the Patria in Nineteenth-Century Potosí." *Journal of Latin American Studies* 25, no. 1:159–85.

Poole, Deborah. 1997. *Vision, Race and Modernity: A Visual Economy of the Andean Image World*. Princeton, N.J.: Princeton University Press.

Radcliffe, Sarah. 1990. "Ethnicity, Patriarchy, and Incorporation into the Nation: Female Migrants as Domestic Servants in Peru." *Society and Space*, 8: 379–93.

―――. 1996. "Imaginative Geographies, Post-Colonialism and National Identities: Contemporary Discourses of the Nation in Ecuador." *Ecumene* 3, no. 1:23–42.

Radcliffe, Sarah, and Sallie Westwood. 1996. *Remaking the Nation: Place, Identity and Politics in Latin America*. London: Routledge.

Ramos, Alcida. 1994. "The Hyperreal Indian." *Critique of Anthropology* 14, no. 2:153–71.

Rappaport, Joanne. 1993. *The Cumbe Reborn*. Berkeley: University of California Press.

―――. 1998. *The Politics of Memory: Native Historical Interpretation in the Colombian Andes*. Durham, N.C.: Duke University Press.

Rivera Cusicanqui, Silvia. 1996. "Prólogo." In *Ser mujer indígena, chola o birlocha en la Bolivia postcolonial de los años 90*, ed. Silvia Rivera Cusicanqui, 1–84. La Paz: Ministerio de Desarrollo Humano.

Roediger, David. 1991. *The Wages of Whiteness: Race and the Making of the American Working Class*. London: Verso.

Sanders, James. 2003. "Belonging to the Great Granadan Family: Partisan Struggle and the Construction of Indigenous Identity and Politics in Southwestern Colombia, 1849–1890." In *Race and Nation in Modern Latin America*, Nancy Appelbaum et al. Chapel Hill: University of North Carolina Press, 56–86.

Seligmann, Linda. 2000. "Market Places, Social Spaces in Cuzco, Peru." *Urban Anthropology* 29, vol. 1:1–68.

Sinha, M., D. J. Guy, and A. Woollacott, eds. 1998. "Feminism and Internationalism." Special issue of *Gender and History* 10, no. 3.

Sinha, Mrinalini. 1995. *Colonial Masculinity: The "Manly Englishman" and the "Effeminate Bengali" in the Late Nineteenth Century*. Manchester: Manchester University Press.

Skidmore, Thomas. 1974. *Towards Black into White: Race and Nationality in Brazilian Thought*. Oxford: Oxford University Press.

Smith, Anthony. 1986. *The Ethnic Origin of Nations*. Cambridge: Cambridge University Press.

―――. 1995. *Nations and Nationalisms in a Global Era*. Cambridge: Cambridge University Press.

Starn, Orin. 1994. "Rethinking the Politics of Anthropology: The Case of the Andes." *Current Anthropology* 35 no. 1:45–75.

Stepan, Nancy. 1991. *The Hour of Eugenics: Race, Gender and Nation in Latin America*. Ithaca, N.Y.: Cornell University Press.

Stephenson, Marcia. 1999. *Gender and Modernity in Andean Bolivia*. Austin: University of Texas Press.

Stern, Steve, ed. 1987. *Resistance, Rebellion, and Consciousness in the Andean Peasant World, 18th to 20th Centuries*. Madison: Wisconsin University Press.

————. 1997. *The Secret History of Gender: Women, Men, and Power in Late Colonial Mexico.* Chapel Hill: University of North Carolina Press.

Stoler, Ann Laura. 1995. *Race and the Education of Desire.* Durham, N.C.: Duke University Press.

————. 1997. "On Political and Psychological Essentialisms." *Ethos* 25, no. 1:101–6.

Taussig, Michael. 1993. *Mimesis and Alterity.* London: Routledge.

Thomson, Sinclair. 2003. *We Alone Will Rule: Native Andean Politics in the Age of Insurgency.* Madison: University of Wisconsin Press.

Thurner, Mark. 1997. *From Two Republics to One Divided: Contradictions of Postcolonial Nationmaking in Andean Peru.* Durham, N.C.: Duke University Press.

Tsing, Anna. 1993. *In the Realm of the Diamond Queen.* Princeton, N.J.: Princeton University Press.

Twinam, Ann. 1999. *Public Lives, Private Secrets: Gender, Honor, Sexuality and Illegitimacy in Colonial Spanish America.* Stanford, Calif.: Stanford University Press.

Urban, Greg, and Joel Scherzer, eds. 1992. *Nation-States and Indians in Latin America.* Austin: University of Texas Press.

Van Cott, Donna Lee. 2000. *The Friendly Liquidation of the Past: The Politics of Diversity in Latin America.* Pittsburgh: Pittsburgh University Press.

Vasconcelos, José. 1961. *La raza cósmica: misión de la raza iberoamericana.* Madrid: Aguilar.

Vaughan, Mary. 1997. *Cultural Politics in Revolution: Teachers, Peasants, and Schools in Mexico, 1930–1940.* Tucson: University of Arizona Press.

Wade, Peter. 1993. *Blackness and Race Mixture: The Dynamic of Racial Identity in Colombia.* Baltimore: Johns Hopkins University Press.

————. 1997. *Race and Ethnicity in Latin America.* London: Pluto.

————. 2000. *Music, "Race," and Nation: "Música Tropical" in Colombia.* Chicago: University of Chicago Press.

————. 2002. *Race, Nature and Culture: An Anthropological Perspective.* London: Pluto

Warren, Kay, and Jean Jackson, eds. 2002. *Indigenous Movements, Self-Representation and the State in Latin America.* Austin: University of Texas Press.

Weismantel, Mary. 2001. *Cholas and Pishtacos: Stories of Race and Sex in the Andes.* Chicago: University of Chicago Press.

Wright, Winthrop. 1990. *Café con Leche: Race, Class and National Image in Venezuela.* Austin: University of Texas Press.

Yuval-Davis, Nira. 1997. *Gender and Nation.* London: Sage.

2

Capturing Indian Bodies, Hearths, and Minds

The Gendered Politics of Rural School Reform in Bolivia, 1920s–1940s

Brooke Larson

For a good while now, feminist scholars have illuminated the complicated gendered processes that accompanied modern state-building and development policies in twentieth-century Latin America. Just as modernizing a European nation's devised social policies to cope with an emerging mass society pressing new political claims and bringing social ills into close proximity of urban educated elites, so too did Latin America's liberal and populist states develop educational, immigration, and eugenic plans to manage their explosive demographic, social, and political problems associated with all the opportunities and ills of modernity. In the era of World War I, government reformers drew from biomedical and social ideas articulated in a transnational professional milieu and adapted them to suit their definition of national need or racial heritage. Latin America's varied postcolonial contexts therefore shaped and mediated the political and social significance, and outcome, of those reform efforts in the interwar era. According to Nancy Stepan, Brazil's reformism proved to be the vanguard of tropical medicine policies and sanitation sciences, whereas Argentina cast its fate with the eugenic process of whitening through aggressive immigration policies and military violence against its interior indian population (1991). The Mexican Revolution, by contrast, made its development policies progressive compared with those of Argentina and Brazil. The revolutionary rupture of its oligarchic liberal state permanently altered the ideological landscape and transformed the national state, making it more beholden to the country's laboring classes and anxious to bring them into the ambit of the populist state. This it largely accomplished through federal agencies of education, agrarian reform, and health under Cárdenas during the 1930s (Stepan 1991; Vaughan 1997).

In the Andes, modernizing and reformist elites confronted a more difficult task. On the one hand, they lacked the institutional or ideological resources that neighboring nations enjoyed—Chile's relatively stable political system, Brazil's biomedical establishment, Argentina's immigration option, or Mexico's unifying revolutionary state apparatus—in order to mobilize their own societies for purposes of social control and economic development in an increasingly competitive global economy. On the other, Bolivia's creole reformers (that is, Spanish-speaking Bolivians of European descent who considered themselves to be progressive nationalists) were deeply preoccupied with the "dead weight" that their own racially heterogeneous, poor, and illiterate populations had placed on their modernizing and culturally homogenizing projects. As they gazed upon their interior landscapes of mountains, provincial potentates, and indians mired in feudal servitude or else erupting in episodic upheaval, creole elites often turned pessimistic about their nation's racial unfitness or diseased body politic (Arguedas 1909). Anxiety about the future progress of Andean society might then provoke deeper unease about modernity itself. Was Mexico's postrevolutionary paradigm of mestizaje (that is, racial-cultural fusion) to serve as the Andean template of integration, or did race mixture hasten nineteenth-century "degenerative processes" of racial and republican decline? How might the Andean nation-state uplift and integrate its indigenous populations while preempting a Mexican-styled social revolution? Might Andean scientists and health workers manage to engineer sanitary cities and healthy bodies, purged of disease, alcoholism, and other vices, without the kind of public health campaigns that Brazil boasted? No less urgent, if attempts to attract white European immigration to the Andes were proving to be a colossal failure, how might public education be made to civilize, moralize, and uplift the Andean nations? These questions vexed and divided creole elites (see de la Cadena 2000). Furthermore, as Nancy Stepan notes, tropes of economic and cultural progress could easily be reversed as "degeneration [became] the major metaphor of the day, with vice, crime, immigration, women's work, and the urban environment variously blamed as its cause" (1991:24). At any historical moment or place, social policy making might be motivated by a fragile calculus of optimism and pessimism, hope and fear—and never more so than in the Andes, where weak states and fractured elites competed with each other over regional/racial projects (as in the polarizing Lima/Cuzco struggle in Peru), or where international conflicts or internal rural uprisings suddenly altered internal political balances (as in Bolivia after the 1899 indigenous uprisings or the Chaco War in the early 1930s).

But sooner or later, modernizing states began to expand the notion of "public interest" to encompass realms once thought of as "private." As the old patriarchal and seigneurial order crumbled, peasants flooded into the cities, and urban laboring groups mounted all sorts of democratizing challenges, Latin America states and social reformers sought new modes of "population management," which could burrow into the intimate interior of the family. Nationalist ideologies quickly fastened on family, as they did on race, to promote cultural reforms designed to reproduce healthy, efficient, patriotic citizen-workers or peasants. Brazil and Mexico offer striking historical examples of strong corporatist states taking aggressive measures to "rationalize domesticity" in the service of broader political, economic, and eugenic projects. As Mary Kay Vaughan writes, "Public appropriation of reproductive activities such as education, hygiene and health care demanded new interactions between households and the public sphere: [and] the appointed household actor was the woman, the mother" (Vaughan 2000:196). State policies therefore fastened onto gender as both a precept and a tool in their attempts to subordinate popular households to the interests of national development, social order, and patriarchal power (see also Besse 1996; Dore 1997; Dore and Molyneux 2000; Klubock 1998; Mayer 2002; Rosemblatt 2000; Stephenson 1999; Weinstein 1996).

There is no doubt that the new gendered policies had tangible, often beneficial, effects. Public health programs of disease control, the introduction of rural schools, and the regulation of work did improve living standards for certain social sectors and did empower women and children in new ways. But feminist scholarship has shown that the states' efforts to rationalize the household and, in Eileen Findlay's words, "impose decency" on the gendered body politic were hardly driven by emancipatory aims (Findlay 1999). On the contrary, progressive social reforms hoped to reconfigure gender inequality during Latin America's turbulent passage to industrial capitalism and corporatist state building.

This paper explores the Bolivian state's halting efforts to burrow into the intimate spaces of the rural Aymara world in order to remake indians into productive peasants over the course of the 1920s, 1930s, and 1940s. Although the Bolivian state was riddled by partisan and ideological conflicts, and singularly impoverished and ineffectual in comparison to Mexico or Brazil, it managed to mount an extraordinary project of rural education, which ultimately came to target *el hogar campesino* (variously connoting peasant hearth, household, family) as the terminal point of the state's evolving "cultural revolution" in the countryside (the term "cultural revolution," although most often associated with Maoist reform is, here, borrowed from Philip Corrigan and Derek Sayer's [1985] idea of the slow, contested process by which the modernizing state imposed a normative [hegemonic] order). Rural school reform was aimed at the cultural production of Bolivia's modern campesino class, but it was not simply about "incorporating indians into the national culture." It was equally driven by the need to fix racial, class, and gender hierarchies in ways that subordinated the indian peasantry to the state, especially as rural insurgents pounded on the gates of Bolivian cities in the 1930s and 1940s. Paying close attention to shifting social fields, I examine how the changing calculus of elite needs, aspirations, and fears shaped rural school reform, which became a crucial site for rearticulating gender and race categories in the process of educating campesinos. I am especially interested in how social reformers came to focus rural development policy on the Aymara family and body—where "cultures and habits" stubbornly resided.

Colonial politics of Bolivian rural schooling, of course, lay close to the surface. As historians have vividly shown in the studies on European projects of colonization in Africa, the Bolivian state's efforts at domestic and bodily reform were highly specific colonial projects springing out of the tensions of westernizing an ethnically plural postcolonial society and designed, at least in part, to "remake memory, tradition, and identity" (Comaroff and Comaroff, citing Bourdieu, 1992:70). La Paz, Bolivia's young rough-and-tumble capital, was redefining its national function as Bolivia's major internal metropolis. Its progressive policy makers, agents, and intellectuals set themselves the task of discovering, knowing, uplifting, and managing the rural Aymara world of the *altiplano*, the highland plateau. Ultimately, the city's civilizers wanted the erasure of those indigenous communal memories, traditions, and identities, which lay at the core of local Aymara communities, political culture, and mobilizations. Arguing over the racial destiny of the Bolivian nation, creole elites managed to forge a common mandate to bring the Aymara (and the Quechua) population into the ambit of the modernizing Bolivian state. Although by the 1940s some policy makers were increasingly subordinating race doctrines to the fashionable post–World War II discourses of gender and class, this semantic shift barely disguised their most ambitious colonial project to date—the making of a disciplined, gendered peasantry at the margins of modernity.

Race, Habits, and Habitats

Around the year 1920, La Paz's creole elites embarked on a remarkable campaign to remake the Aymara indian population into the nation's essential rural labor force. Wrestling with theories of *raza y medio* (race and environment), the capital's civilizing vanguard rediscovered the "purity" and "authenticity" of Bolivia's pristine Aymara population, isolated in its mountainous habitat and splendidly adapted to the harsh climate of the altiplano. Beyond the romantic imagery of the pristine indian and gentle critiques of feudal landlordism, the discovery of the utilitarian and telluric Aymara race had tangible implications. Creole writers fastened on the Aymara population, once the scourge of caste warfare across the altiplano, as the nation's future rural labor force. The poet, politician, and pedagogue Franz Tamayo, declared in his newspaper column in 1910 that Bolivia's indians supplied "ninety percent of the nation's energy," because the indian was born for only one destiny: "to produce, to produce incessantly in whatever form, be it agricultural or mining labor, rustic manufacturing or manual service in the urban economy" (Tamayo 1910:64). It was dawning on the liberal vanguard that Bolivia needed to harness the 500,000 indians who inhabited the altiplano, and who made up almost 25 percent of the nation's entire population. Indeed, La Paz had already become the colonial metropolis of Bolivia's campaign to break up remaining ayllu lands, advance the edge of rails and *latifundismo*, and extend the reach of the federal bureaucracy and army into the outlying provinces (Mamani Condori 1991; Rivera Cusicanqui 1986). But by 1920, it was clear that the country's principal eugenic project, that of white European immigration, was failing badly. Not only was Bolivia failing to inject white blood into its national veins, as Brazil and Argentina were doing, but it could not even promote modern agriculture under its semi-feudal hacienda regime (see Guillén Pinto 1919). Yet agricultural development on the altiplano was crucial if Bolivia was to supply its growing cities with domestic staples and diversify its mineral-skewed economy. The solution? To turn the Aymara peasant into a productive yeoman and artisan. The peasant was to become the rural counterpart, producing for the domestic market, of Bolivia's strategic mine worker, producing wealth for the export market. No Bolivian writer in the 1920s articulated this goal in quite such stark economic terms; this sort of developmental language would take hold and spread in the late 1930s and 1940s. But Bolivia's vanguard reformers in the 1910s and 1920s did appreciate the uses of environmental determinism to naturalize the Aymara indian as the nation's primordial laborer. They fashioned discourses of raza y medio to accomplish three basic objectives: (1) to identify the "natural aptitudes" of the indian (hardworking, stoic agro-pastoralists; miners of great strength and endurance; and stoic, disciplined soldiers); (2) to fix the indian in his "natural habitat" (the isolated high-country of the altiplano, where the air was as pure as the indian's blood); and (3) to map his destiny in the nation as the rural laboring force.

These new anthropological truths buttressed the pedagogic turn away from "traditional schools," which had promoted the older, imported European curriculum based on "mere reading and writing," "memorization," "verbalism," "scholasticism," and other forms of "intellectualism." The Liberal Party's earlier commitment to universal education (based on the teaching of Spanish literacy plus a little scriptural study) came under harsh scrutiny after 1914, just about the time that La Paz's vanguard rediscovered the authentic indian and heralded the new (anti-cosmopolitan) spirit of cultural nationalism. Bolivian pedagogues decided around 1920 that they needed to do things their own way, calibrated carefully to Bolivia's environment, history, and race(s). That turn inward toward a "national pedagogy" produced a crucial prescription that was to govern popular education for the next twenty years. It was the idea that indians needed a separate system of rural education, geared to their "racial aptitudes" and "natural habitat." In short, indians needed special work-training schools (escuelas de trabajo), located in isolated rural settlements far away from the corruption of the city, and staffed by indian teachers trained in special rural teacher training schools (or, rural normal schools).

In 1919, the Ministry of Instruction issued a comprehensive school reform plan, calling for the reorganization of Bolivia's pioneering escuelas normales rurales (Umala, Puna, and Sacaba), teacher training colleges. Government inspections had deemed them to have failed in their mission to create indian teachers because, among many other shortcomings, they were located in towns and producing "mestizo preceptors" who had refused to teach in rural indigenous primary schools and, worse, had ended up migrating to the cities and meddling in political life (Ministerio de Instrucción Pública 1919:251–56). The new pedagogy would merge rural teacher-training (the rural "normal" school) with the new agricultural work-school so that the two institutions could calibrate their curricula to manual labor training and teaching. The new normal pedagogy would teach three subjects: practical knowledge in agriculture; new methods of soil preparation; and methods to improve small industries (textiles, ceramics, brick making, hat making, carpentry, and ironwork). Apprenticing in these agro-pastoral and artisan crafts, indians would learn through "active methods" of education, conducted in the Spanish language. Thus conceived, the process of hispanization (*castellanización*) would be linked to hands-on knowledge rather than to literacy. In 1919, Minister Daniel Sánchez Bustamante explained that "all school lessons would have one material objective, manual labor, and one moral objective, to instill the value of socially useful labor" (ibid., 163). But the new pedagogy was also driven by an equally powerful concern about stabilizing the racial and spatial location of Aymara people, as they tried to gain access to literacy, knowledge, and mobility. In a revealing 1918 report to the congress, the ministry stated unequivocally that the new work-school was designed to guard against indians turning into *cholos* (hispanizing indians) "so they would not abandon their own domain, by converting themselves into extortionist *corregidores* or into electoral mobs; [with their newly acquired knowledge], they will know how to exploit the land and . . . they will understand that the modest citizen should function only within the limits of his own sphere" (Ministerio de Instrucción Pública 1918:57–58). These contradictory motives expressed a larger postcolonial dilemma: the ruling elite's need to promote economic progress (especially the formation of a disciplined rural labor force on the altiplano), while securing the internal borders of race, gender, and class (Stoler 1996). This dilemma would not soon go away, and Bolivia's progressive reformers constantly felt themselves pulled between the promises of modernity and the imperatives of social order, between economic hope and racial fear.

"The education of the indian in his medium" thus became the leitmotif of rural school reform in 1920. But it posed another, perhaps deeper, dilemma for La Paz's colonizing pedagogues: namely, how to simultaneously preserve and alter indians in their "natural habitat." This classic dilemma of the (post)colonial civilizer (see Chatterjee 1993; Sider 1987)—to construct and transform racial difference—comes to light in an illuminating 1918 field report, written by two teachers possessed of sharp ethnographic intuition. Mariaca and Peñaranda were director and teacher, respectively, in the rural, teacher-training normal school located in the tiny town of Umala, on the coast of Lake Titicaca. Already their school was plagued by problems, and it would soon be denounced as a failure by official inspectors. But these teachers used their bitter field experience to critique indigenista orthodoxies about race and environment. (*Indigenismo* refers to the political, literary, and ethnographic production of educated creole elites, who arrogated to themselves the authority to study, diagnose, represent, assimilate, reform, or celebrate the indian race(s) that inhabited their nation.) Specifically, they criticized indigenista reformers for having failed to draw a conceptual distinction between the indian's *physical* and *social* environments. It was true, they argued, that highland indians needed to be rooted in their "natural" rural domain and instructed in work-schools, so they could take their appointed place in the nation as rural laborers and artisans. But if the rural normal school had to mold indigenous laborers in harmony with their habitat, it had an equally powerful mandate to wrench them from their social milieu, one that was "saturated by prejudices and backward customs, the locus of alcoholism and demoralization" (Mariaca and Peñaranda 1918:11).

Specifically, rural schooling needed to fight against the overpowering tendency of moral regression, once the indian child left the enlightened sphere of learning and slipped back into the stupefying routines, debauchery, and other vices of village life. For these teachers, poised on the cutting edge of rural school reform yet demoralized by their own field experiences, the new pedagogy had to shift the focus of attention from the physical to the social and moral environment of the population in order to diagnose, and then eradicate, the indian pupil's "bad habits and customs." Implicitly, the child and the family were set in place as the object, mechanism, and rationale for state intervention, and their bodily habits of hygiene, consumption, clothing, diet, housing, and sexuality would soon be targeted for resocialization.

But how exactly were rural teachers to manage the moralization of their indian pupils? Unhindered by practical matters, these teachers envisioned a new kind of communitarian, agro-pastoral, normal school for indians. It would become a beacon radiating productivity and enlightenment into the dark rural hinterlands. This so-called school colony (*la colonia escolar*) was to revolve around the idea of the indian boarding school (*el internado*), where teachers would be able to inculcate values and monitor routines of everyday life in classrooms, workshops, and fields. The boarding school complex would be housed in vast pavilions, surrounded by cultivated fields and pastures. Not only would "satellite" primary schools channel the most adept indian pupils to the agro-normal, but the "solar" normal school would become the axis of expanding agro-industrial colonies—attracting parents (*los padres de familia*) and other "healthy and hardworking elements" into their cultural orbit.

This brave new world, reminiscent of the totalizing utopian community of work, piety, and civilization under the colonial Jesuit system of *reducción* was certainly bold. Yet it also borrowed curricular elements (specifically, hygiene, homemaking, and industrial labor) from contemporary North American boarding school models that had been functioning on the western "indian" frontier of the United States since the late nineteenth century (Szasz 1974). Bolivian educational reformers were also attracted to the North American ideal of segregated "Negro" industrial schooling, as exemplified by Hampton and Tuskegee institutes (see Guillén Pinto 1919, for example). In any event, these Bolivian teacher/reformers obviously struck a chord, for in 1919 Alfredo Guillén Pinto, another young, up-and-coming educational reformer, published a major study extolling the idea of special education (based on rural vocational training) for the indian races (ibid.). The minister of public instruction was also convinced that Bolivian rural school reform needed to refocus attention on the socialization of indigenous youth in newly established *internados*, and in 1919, he called on the congress to establish insulated boarding schools so as to promote middle-class values—temperance, thrift, cleanliness, and hard work—and "instill an awareness [in indians] of what it means to live like a civilized race, capable of continual improvement" (Ministerio de Instrucción Pública 1919:263).

The reformed rural normal schools became rural colonies of productivity, discipline, and acculturation and were thus able to reconcile the contradictory goals of reproducing and transforming the Aymara race without causing any fundamental social disturbance. They set out to lay the conceptual groundwork for the state's intervention into peasant cultural practices in the 1930s and 1940s—although creole projects of rural school reform in those years were chasing varied, often divergent, political objectives. Both left- and right-wing political regimes in those decades learned to turn the rural indian school movement to larger political and ideological purposes in specific historical moments. In the 1930s, the indian boarding school complex, institutionalized as the indian school nucleus (*el núcleo escolar indigenal*), became a crucial, albeit contested, site for projecting populist, socialist, and syndicalist political projects onto the Bolivian peasantry in the aftermath of the Chaco War (Choque 1996; Pérez 1992). By contrast, as we shall see below, the post-1940 rightist governments used rural indian school reform to accelerate the cultural assimilation of indians in a fast-track project of economic development, social control, and cultural mestizaje.

The tentative expansion of the state into the rural communities during the 1920s was accompanied by an explosion of interest in the interior world of the indian. Following in the footsteps of Bautista Saavedra's classic 1904 ethnography of the ayllu, a new generation of professionals probed even deeper into the ayllu, extracting truths about the nature of Aymara or Quechua family life. José Salmón Ballivian's "El indio íntimo: Contribución al estudio biológico social del indio" (1926) plunged the reader into the minutiae of everyday rituals of work, consumption, sexual relations, communal ceremony, and political life. We learn, for example, that Aymara couples were nearly "asexual" due to the stupefying effects of coca (a finding that surely provoked the anxiety of reformers eager to promote peasant procreation, rural repopulation, and regional economic recovery). Another pathbreaking study came in the form of a celebrated thesis delivered to Bolivia's first Teachers' Congress held in 1930. Published in 1932, María Frontaura Argona's *Towards the Indian Future* (*Hacia el futuro indio*) electrified Bolivia's emerging leftist and populist vanguard by calling for rural education, civilization, and agrarian reform to forge the indian races into a skilled, propertied peasantry, emancipated from centuries of servitude but living in harmony with Bolivia's other races and social classes. That a young, unknown woman teacher would crystallize the vanguard position of the new teachers' union was certainly notable. But Frontaura also tried to refocus the emerging public debate over gender and national identity on the imperatives of her indigenista cause. In a chapter titled "A Psychological Glossary of the Indian Woman," Frontaura offered a fascinating diagnostic examination of gender, race, and region, by mapping gender across the older geo-environmental-ethnic dichotomy, made famous by Alcides Arguedas (1909), between the "soft" valley culture of the Quechua and the "harsh" highland culture of the Aymara races. Injecting gender into that familiar geo-racial polarity, Frontaura drew an innate distinction between the sweet, sensitive, compliant, civilizable, religious Quechua woman, molded by the gentle valley climate and easier economic prospects, and the hardened Aymara woman who was made, if not of bronze, then of "steel" (36–38). Frontaura's essential Aymara woman was unique: "Never has nature molded a woman equal to the Aymara. . . . Every muscle fiber is insensitive to pain and exhaustion, as if she were made of compact metal." "Nowhere in the world is there another woman like her." "She is constituted purely of nerve." "Her will power is stronger than that of any other race on earth. When she sets her mind and robust character to accomplish something, she will do it at any cost or sacrifice. Her strength to resist defies all reason" (40–41). What were the determinants of such a singular character? A combination of nature and nurture: gender and race were molded by years of pain, maternal neglect, stoicism, mysticism, and deprivation inherent in the material and cultural milieu of Aymara society.

These early ethnographic incursions into the Aymara family framed a crucial moral issue that would continue to haunt the ethnographic imagination of Bolivian reformers and educators for the next two decades. Both authors alluded to the innate fragility, instability, deprivation, and ultimate dysfunction of the Aymara family. Salmón Ballivián's brief biography of an indian ritual authority (*alfaréz*) was really a meditation on the ways that the ayllu's civil-religious rituals brought financial ruin, fragmentation, and dispersion to the indian family. Such illogical customs and accumulated debt, he argued, ultimately forced Aymara men to cast off from family and ayllu in search of livelihood, trade, and wage work in distant mines, cities, and haciendas. Meanwhile, their women and children stayed back on the land, eking out a precarious existence in wretched isolation (123–28). María Frontaura, in turn, worried about the destabilizing practices of domestic life, such as Aymara mothers abandoning their young children to go off into the *puna* (high altitude lands) to pasture their animals or to pursue long-distance trading activities in the cities. Worse yet, Aymara daughters were socialized in ways that encouraged their mobility and absence from the home. For against proper female roles, young preadolescent daughters were sent off into the mountains to pasture sheep, and they sometimes accompanied their fathers on long llama-train treks to mines, markets, or into the fields (42). Although they grew strong and agile from these journeys, Frontaura's Aymara girls continued to suffer isolation, physical abuse, and deprivation in the confines of their own home. Thus, they came to embody a curious contradiction of resistance and resignation, strength and docility—the combustible elements that made up the Aymara "woman of steel." However these writers diagnosed the instability of the indian family, they concurred that Aymara home life boded ill for the future regeneration of the race and the hope of forging an organic "Bolivian family."

But who exactly was paying attention? Certainly there was a flurry of creole interest in the indian problem after the 1927 indigenous uprising of Chayanta. Although the epicenter of indigenous unrest was located in

Quechua-speaking communities and on haciendas in the southern high-lands, far from La Paz, its repercussions were felt across the northern alti-plano. Threats of rebellion in the north plunged the Bolivian congress into intensive debates over the "psychological, economic, and moral causes" of unrest among the nation's indian population. And many politicians worried publicly about the growing network of "communist agitators" that were supposedly infiltrating indigenous communities and stirring up trouble (Congreso Nacional de Bolivia 1928:50–80, 134–41, 209–11). Such political talk put pressure on the government to crack down on popular and insurgent forces in both city and countryside during the late 1920s and early 1930s (Klein 1969: chaps. 4 and 5; Rivera Cusican-qui 1986: chap. 2; Mamani Condori 1991: chap. 3). The brewing 1927 crisis also spurred reformers to inject a new sense of urgency into the perennial issues of indian land, labor, and education (see, for example, various newspaper articles and editorials in *El País* and *La Defensa* [September and October, 1927]). The deeper structural issues of communal land rights were pushed aside, however, while the government turned to "safer" cultural reforms, such as promoting indigenous school reform. Rhetoric about indian education was hammered into institutional policy in 1930 and 1931, with the creation of a semi-autonomous Bureau of Indian Education, created to organize and oversee rural primary schools and indian teacher training (Ministerio de Instrucción Pública 1931).

But it was the Chaco War (1933–1935) more than any other event that suddenly transformed the indian family from an esoteric subject of anthropologists into a highly publicized national concern. First, because the nation suddenly needed to restore the "indian [man] to the active life of the nation" (in the headlines of one news article) in order to mobilize him for the defense of the *patria*, fatherland, against the "barbarian Guar-aní nation" of Paraguay, and second, because the war itself unleashed all sorts of popular sectors that began to lay claim to citizenship and welfare rights in return for their hardships and sacrifices for the Bolivian na-tion. The postwar state, driven now by a new "military socialist" order, had to attend to multiple, mobilizing groups of ex-combatants, orphaned children, and widows, whose welfare was suddenly deemed the respon-sibility of the postwar Bolivian state. In particular, women invaded the public sphere to demand new social reforms. Bolivian feminist scholar-ship and, more recently, Marcia Stephenson argue that both elite and popular organizations of women catalyzed social reforms that "contested the public-private divide," brought urban working-class women into the purview of the populist state, and cast mothers as the new guardians of national peace and reconciliation (Stephenson 1999:24–26; THOA 1994; Medinaceli 1989; Lehm and Rivera Cusicanqui 1988). Most visible to the urban elites were La Paz's urban market and laboring women, many of them unionized and anarchist *cholas*, who frequently took to the streets to demand labor legislation, municipal licenses to sell their goods on the streets, and other forms of citizenship rights (Gill 1994; Stephenson, chaps.1 and 4). In response, the government created a host of new ministries of public health, welfare, and labor to cope with, and contain, this explosion of new social groups clamoring for recognition and reform (Rivera Cusicanqui 1996).

In this political climate, indigenous school reform made important advances (Choque 1996). Under a semi-autonomous state organization, the General Direction of Indian Education, sixteen *núcleos escolares* flourished as the tangible outcroppings of the earlier *imagined* school-colonies, once promoted by the Ministry of Instruction and several progressive teachers around 1920. These new community-based "nuclear" schools tried to put into practice, in varied regional contexts, the notion of the integrated and insular indian boarding work-school complex, designed "to radiate" knowledge and enlightenment to satellite primary schools and their surrounding peasant villages. And as envisaged by the earlier indigenistas, each of these communitarian schools aimed to train and civilize their male and female pupils, as well as the padres de familia who participated in the life and work of the boarding schools. In short, these rural schools were faithful to many of the same separatist principles and methods of teaching that were promoted by the first generation of pedagogic reformers around 1920. In general, the sixteen rural nuclear schools were to mold Aymara and Quechua indians into virtuous indian laborers and consumers, stabilized in their own "natural habitat" but wrenched from their "backward" cultural lifeways and reinstalled in these enlightened enclaves.

Yet the wrenching experiences of the Chaco War and the growing radicalization of popular political forces in the mines, cities, and countryside began to alter and polarize the pedagogical objectives of indian school reform. The núcleos escolares gradually became enclaves of leftist, syndicalist, and nativist ideologies and social actions, or so they were perceived in many political quarters. In 1936 the rural school of Vacas was born in the lap of the local syndicalist movement of peasants; Caquiaviri anchored itself in the volatile Aymara town, famous for its history of uprisings; and the famous indian school experiment in the altiplano town of Warisata became a nucleus of nativism and resistance against feudal-like landowners on its borders. It is true that all of Bolivia's initial núcleos escolares had to negotiate different relations to local indigenous communities, surrounding regional elites, leftist and syndicalist organizations, and the federal bureaucracy. But as a whole, the Indian School movement of the 1930s represented a potent multiethnic alliance among shifting factions of radical political parties, middle-class teachers and intellectuals, a growing movement of peasant syndicalism, and radicalized indigenous peasant leaders (see esp. Perez 1961; Salazar 1997).

At the local level, these school/communities (made famous by Warisata's self-designated title of "school-ayllu" [*la escuela-ayllu*]) were experimental microcosms of interethnic democracies in practice. Communitarian schools promoted the direct participation of indigenous families in the cooperative labor and local governance of the rural school. In various ways, the new rural nuclear schools tried to introduce elements of agro-labor, hygiene, and physical education into their curricula, but those schools were increasingly shaped and mediated by leftist and nativist slogans calling for the "emancipation of the indian," "the raising of class awareness," "the restoration of the ayllu," "the destruction of the old feudal order," and/or the "the advancement of citizen rights." All these official communitarian schools promoted, to a greater or lesser degree, the direct participation of indigenous families in the cooperative labor and local governance of the rural school, and thus they brought the peasant family into the very center of building, debating, and often co-governing the local school. And in the case of Warisata, the boarding school actually became the locus of a reconfigured community. As the 1930s progressed, however, polarizing political forces began to turn these experiments in rural school reform into local battlegrounds over the right of Bolivia's indigenous people to education and, more fundamentally, to land, citizenship, and social justice in the postwar society.

The year 1940 marked an abrupt end of postwar populism and reform and ushered in a new era of imperialism, repression, and what Josep Barnadas (1976) has called "the feudal reaction." A new conservative group of reformers seized control of indian education, redirecting its social purpose and methods toward the linked imperatives of economic modernization, social stability, and counterinsurgency. Once more, only this time with teeth, the state fastened on gender and family, and specifically the peasant household (el hogar campesino) as a strategic point of cultural and political incursion.

Gender, Household, and Family Values

"If Warisata's [old] slogan was 'the community for the school and in the school,' now we can say 'the school [is] at the service of the community and in the peasant home.'" In his speech to the Bolivian congress in 1947, the minister of education used this slogan to synthesize the government's critical pedagogic shift toward issues of gender, family, and the body. The minister explained:

> The "Work School," eulogized by Warisata, retains its validity, but now it is directed toward the *improvement of the rural family*. If the dynamism which once flourished in Warisata were now to be redeployed for the benefit of the peasant household, Bolivia's rural living standards would soar to unimaginable heights; each material conquest would be irreversible and useful. . . . [Thus] the contribution of rural school reform ought to be clear and well-defined: to teach the campesino to take better advantage of his own labor and to concern himself with his standard of living. With proper tools and techniques and with aspirations similar to those of more evolved rural sectors, the man of the countryside will have more possibilities for self-improvement. . . . Furthermore, increased agricultural production will contribute to cheapening [the cost of] living in Bolivian cities which, paradoxically, must feed themselves today with imported products.
>
> The rural school must also concern itself with the health of the campesino, to ensure that our male campesino is imbued with the principles of a healthy life, and that he practices the fundamental [routines] of personal cleanliness, good diet, good housing, and systematic prophylaxis. To achieve such elementary success in the interior of the indian household is the immediate imperative of the rural school" (Congreso Nacional de Bolivia 1947:131–33; emphasis added).

The ministry's message to the congress was stark: Bolivia's rural development pivoted on the intimate socialization of campesino. The "new" rural work-school was to remake the peasant family—mainly through the resocialization of the male campesino—and harness it to Bolivia's project of agricultural development. Capitalist development of the countryside, feeding the cities, the reproduction of the rural labor force, and the self-sufficiency of the Bolivian economy all depended on forging, and monitoring, the nuclear farm family under the direct influence of federal bureaucrats, schoolteachers, agronomists, and health and social workers.

To accomplish those goals, state agencies would have to destroy, or reverse, the dangerous indigenista school reforms of the 1930s. In fact, the whole ideological thrust of agrarian modernization after 1940 was to repudiate the indigenistas' aims and methods of indian school reform during the earlier populist era, and Warisata became the favorite target of attack. The smear campaign began in 1940, marking the government's abrupt ideological shift toward work and hygiene, family farming, and capitalist rural development. Under the conservative regime of Colonel Enrique Peñaranda, the Ministry of Education (via the newly formed Consejo Nacional de Educación) launched a massive attack on Bolivia's original sixteen núcleos escolares for having sowed the seeds of indigenous unrest, destabilized rural communities, neglected the health and welfare of rural families, and deviated from the "biological need" of the nation to create a segmented labor market of healthy productive peasants (Consejo Nacional de Educación 1940). According to the "tribunal of judges" commissioned to evaluate ten years of indigenista school reform, Warisata and the other núcleos escolares had failed to transform indigenous populations into modern agro-pastoralists, letting them practice their "primitive" agricultural methods in communal work projects. More deviously, the communitarian schools had violated the national interest by training indians in artisan skills, awakening new economic aspirations and vocations, thus tempting them to abandon their natural sphere and migrate to the cities. The judges proclaimed "the ultimate goal of the school is the making of great agriculturalists because indians are magnificently adapted to the harsh climate and thus irreplaceable" (ibid., 140). But on the issue of land reform, the new pedagogues equivocated. For example, Vicente Donoso Torres, the architect of pro-development (*desarrollista*) rural school polices, took a classically evolutionist stance. Agrarian reform, a la Mexico, was needed in Bolivia, but he warned against attacking Bolivia's "feudal regime of landholding" until the time that indians were "prepared" to enter into new forms of property relations. Better to pass laws improving relations between landlords and laborers, regulating minimal salaries, prohibiting religious fiestas (where the indian revelers consume great quantities of alcohol and coca), and organizing peasant production cooperatives with access to an Agricultural Bank for advances in seeds, tools, machinery, and capital to jump-start agro-pastoral industries (Donoso Torres 1946:180–81). Bolivia's cultural, political, and economic progress would have to be carefully channeled through school reform, before the peasantry was "readied" to take its place as property owners!

Clearly, the peasantry's preparation for entry into the modernizing nation as propertied citizens was contingent upon the deep resocialization of the peasant family. To mold the campesino man into Bolivia's modern (albeit still landless) farmer was one aim; to mold the campesina woman into Bolivia's hygienic housewife and mother was its essential complement. It was the educational philosopher Vicente Donoso, who had the clarifying word on the gender issue, as well. Writing generally on "the education of the Bolivian woman," Donoso joined a chorus of social reformers, writers, and labor organizers eager to nationalize motherhood as the womb, nurturer, and healer of the war-torn Bolivian nation (see Gotkowitz 2000; Stephenson 1999, chap. 1). Donoso engendered a transracial discourse on the "aptitudes" and "indispensability" of the woman in building the "Bolivian family" (both real and metaphorical). And he listed the complementarity of gendered traits. Women possess sweetness, patience, thrift, love, and reconciliation; men boasted valor, impulsiveness, profligacy, combativeness, and intransigence. Such "complementarities," of course, composed the organic basis of the nuclear family—regardless of geo-racial particularities. Naturalizing womanhood in bourgeois European terms, in vivid contrast to the stoic, strong, combative Aymara woman sketched in Frontaura's 1932 ethnography, also rationalized the rigid sexual division of labor, sentencing all women (regardless of race, ethnic, or class categories) to "their fundamental responsibility . . . , the organization of the family, basis of the community, the patria, and humanity. On this premise, the education of the woman should prepare her, above all, for the happiness of the home" (Donoso Torres 1946:168). As far as cultivating conjugal bliss in the campesino family, however, Donoso and his colleagues had one primary prescription: hygiene. "The new schoolhouses need supplies of drugs and soap because the educational question, as regarding peasants, must first deal with the extirpation of lice and filth" (Consejo Nacional de Educación 1940:5). Indeed, the lack of hygienic reform had been one of the great sins of the earlier communitarian schools, according to the grand inquisitors of 1940 (ibid., 107). In later years, rural school curricula would move beyond issues of health and hygiene to set up highly ritualized regimes of child rearing, food, fashion, sleeping arrangements, architecture and spatial layouts, and modes of sociability in the interior of the peasant school and family (see Stephenson 1999, chaps. 3 and 4).

In the view of social reformers, the new rural work/hygiene regime of the 1940s responded to Bolivia's urgent development needs, especially the need to stabilize the farming family as the nucleus of agro-production/reproduction on the altiplano. But as I have already hinted, it also responded to shifting social anxieties under the converging pressures of rural labor unrest and leftist mobilizations across Bolivia. In fact, I would argue that the overriding issue among reformers in the early 1940s was not the promotion of economic development, but the maintenance of social peace and harmony in the turbulent countryside. Vicente Donoso, himself, feared that Bolivia was on a collision course in the race between development and social revolution: "It is urgent to realize this peaceful evolution before it turns into a social revolution of the masses. It would be fatal for the nation, especially if it followed the path towards world communism, with its simplistic program to cure poverty by dissolving private property, without taking into account human and environmental difference" (Donoso Torres 1946:181). In that Donoso and other creole reformers could not conceive of indigenous men and women as proactive political subjects capable of mobilizing their own people in pursuit of land, labor laws, schools, and citizenship rights, they heaped most blame on leftist parties, rural teachers, and the expelled directors of the communitarian schools. The 1940 council of educators, for example, warned that "under the pretext of educating the indian in his own ayllu, the [radical indigenistas] have crusaded unjustly and unpatriotically against whites and mestizos, turning countryside against city, and using racist doctrines to wage a dangerous war against national unity" (Consejo Nacional de Educación 1940:105). By the mid-1940s, conservatives thought Bolivia was caught in a spiral of violence and anarchy amid the brief Villarroel regime, the Indian Congress of 1945, the spreading rural sit-down strikes (*huelgas de brazos caídos*), the Ayopaya peasant uprising of 1947, and the brewing miners' strike in Catavi. One writer warned that "professional political agitators, propagandists with new ideas, and semi-literate lawyers and notaries (the infamous *tinterillos*) were whipping up the rural indian masses and plunging Bolivia into a state of internal warfare not seen since the end of the Chaco War" (Jáuregui Rosquellas 1947:530–31).

What could save Bolivia from the impending social cataclysm? Nothing less than the rapid biocultural conversion of indians into mestizos! Vicente Donoso put it best: "What we need to do is incorporate the elements of universal civilization into the life of the indian, to benefit him in his own medium . . . because the *end product of the Bolivian indian has to be mestizaje*" (Donoso Torres 1946:179, emphasis in the original). Furthermore, mestizaje need not wait for biological race mixing to take effect. The state could regulate de-indianization by banishing "ethnic clothing" (*lluchu*, ponchos, short *bayeta* pants, *ojotas*, and *ckepi*), which always stigmatized men as "indians" no matter that they knew how to read and write, or spoke Spanish. This critical redefinition of Bolivia's racial destiny as mestizo did not deviate radically from earlier indigenista national imaginings, but oligarchic reformers now harnessed it to their other overarching goals—rapid capitalist development of agriculture and rural counterinsurgency. In 1940, the Consejo Nacional de Educación was already formulating Bolivia's racial project: henceforth "mestizaje would become the ethnic goal of Bolivia, instead of the formation of racial groups with their own languages, devoid of nationalist spirit, and separated [from the rest of the nation] by hateful rivalries and incomprehension" (Consejo Nacional de Educación 1940:137). The gendered nature of rural social policies (hygiene, development, and schooling) would create out of Bolivia's unruly and heterogeneous populations not only a disciplined and docile peasant class, but a racially purified homogeneity on which a unifying Bolivian "nationhood" ultimately might be erected. All they needed was a strong, well-endowed partner to launch these fundamental reforms.

Enter the United States, with its hemispheric interest in promoting social order, capitalist development, and friendly governments. Bolivia, of course, was strategic to the United States because it lay at the geopolitical core of South America, and also because its oil and tin were desperately needed in the war effort. Of course, Washington envisioned a much broader imperial project springing out of urgent geopolitics of the Second World War. It needed to secure the hemisphere against the twin threats of fascism and totalitarianism, and in the early 1940s FDR turned his Good Neighbor Policy precisely to those ends. Under the newly formed Institute of Inter-American Affairs, the U.S. government sought new ways to insert itself into the interior of Latin American societies by promoting education, development, and health programs. An official 1955 report explained the original rationale behind the first bilateral aid program in Bolivia, established in the mid-1940s:

> The urgency of the times brought an awareness that the economic condition of individual countries is important to the stability of the hemisphere, and the United State consequently offered to go in as a partner . . . in projects for raising the standard of living. The resulting cooperative programs being grassroots affairs, with immediate

advantages to people and to communities, were successful in their own technical right, and have survived and greatly influenced political thinking. (SCIDE 1955:8)

It was this last objective, to sway political thinking, that immediately concerned the U.S. embassy in La Paz. In 1945, at the height of political turbulence and unrest, the embassy dispatched weekly reports on the dangers of indigenous discontent and insurgency, the spread of labor strikes, and the growing communist menace (United States Record Administration, 1945). It urged Washington to increase its institutional and ideological presence in Bolivia, by deploying the new Inter-American Cooperative Education Service (SCIDE) to spread American values and goodwill. Under its first director, the U.S. rural educator Ernest Maes, SCIDE put most emphasis on rural indian education and health care. By all accounts, U.S. development aid was beginning to assume political significance as an arm of counterinsurgency.

More significantly, SCIDE's crusade to bring western aid, culture, and ideology to rural Bolivia took its technicians directly into the domestic sphere of the rural campesino household. SCIDE's 1948 *Teacher's Manual* mapped the technician's pathway into el hogar campesino: the first objective, it explained, was "to form in the campesino good living habits with respect to diet, dress, house, personal health, and civic, social and religious practices." The next three objectives had to do with agropastoral education, followed finally by the goal of socializing peasants to become good family and community members, as well as socially useful citizens. In short, SCIDE organized the rural curriculum around two primary subjects—agricultural education and sanitary education (Ministerio de Educación 1948; Nelson, 1949:21). Its priorities matched those of the Consejo Nacional de Educación. But SCIDE's program specifically promoted the use of peasant women as conduits for the realization of economic and cultural progress. For if Bolivia was to spread "good living habits," it needed to fix the peasant woman in her own specific "natural habitat"—the nuclear family. Although Bolivian reformers themselves had recognized el hogar campesino as a crucial locus of cultural colonization, they had generally targeted the male campesino as the contact point. Just as most creole men could not conceive of indigenous people as active political subjects, so too they rendered the campesina as a subordinate, almost invisible, subject within the peasant patriarchal household.

Now, however, SCIDE's technicians publicly authorized rural women as agents of eugenic improvement and cultural change. Yet their blueprints for domestic and gender reform also revealed a profoundly ambivalent stance toward patriarchal power. On the one hand, SCIDE professionals reported that "the most inaccessible group in the average community is the adult women," and that indian girls rarely attended school because of their traditional jobs in the home and tending sheep (SCIDE 1955:41). SCIDE had encouraged campesina girls to step forward and enter primary schools, and in 1955 reported that "a really signal achievement for the normal school [of Warisata] is that the Amautas [communal authorities] have taken an interest in the home life instruction and more of them are sending their daughters to school." Another experimental SCIDE school in the old núcleo escolar of Kalaque reported that female attendance had grown from 9 to 14 percent in its nineteen rural schools during the late 1940s and early 1950s (ibid.: 41, 42). On the other hand, SCIDE's social education programs reinforced or, borrowing from Vaughan (2000), "modernized," the institution of patriarchy, by trying to domesticate the wild and feisty Aymara woman into an ideal middle-class housewife. And we all know where delusions of domesticity can lead! The 1948 *Rural Teacher's Manual* is a hilarious guide to "domestic economy" worthy of Doctor Spock and Martha Stewart, 1940s-style. It maps out in copious detail the practical knowledge that rural Andean teachers should convey to their female students—everything from infant care, food preparation, home remedies, and vitamin supplements to techniques of ironing, setting the proper table, pretty color coordinations, and choosing sewing patterns flattering to the slim figure (Ministerio de Educación 1948)! Funny, absurd, and seemingly trivial, these blueprints of cultural reform nevertheless reveal the extent to which the Bolivian state, now in alliance with U.S. aid workers, was trying to infiltrate the indigenous family, reorganize gender, assimilate indians into a homogenous national culture, and forge a rural working class.

In the post–World War II climate of optimism, the United States obviously had set itself a utopian task, encouraged as it was by the paternal sentiments and social anxieties of Bolivian statesmen and intellectuals. Ten years later, SCIDE noted its considerable achievements in rural education, hygiene, and development in the six *núcleos escolares campesinos* under its control. But overall Bolivia's first bilateral aid project had made barely a dent in rural indian illiteracy (estimated at around 85 percent in 1955); it had failed to spread "technical education" to most of the nation's 700 rural schools; and, more fundamentally, it had even failed to forestall social revolution (SCIDE 1955:14–15). Rural unrest began escalating in the late 1940s, and it culminated in a series of coordinated political actions among dissident factions of the peasantry, miners, and middle class in 1952. Yet SCIDE weathered those storms. Slowly, patiently it laid the ideological foundation of a new cycle of rural school reform, to be carried out by a new political vanguard in the aftermath of the 1952 Revolution. It fell to the postrevolutionary populist state to carry forth SCIDE's project of rural school reform in the mid-1950s on the road to modern mestizaje, patriarchy, and the formation of a modern rural labor force.

Conclusions

Borrowing conceptual elements from Foucault and Bourdieu, anthropologists Jean Comaroff and John Comaroff have studied how, in the colonization of South Africa, the imposition of new bodily routines and moral regimes represented the most intimate and penetrating forms of imperial power and social control that accompanied the expansion of capitalism and British colonial rule. Studying the work of missionaries among the Tshidi people, the Comaroffs show how the agents of empire tried to transform native memories, traditions, and identities into individuated and bounded selves, upon whose bodies were to be inscribed new categories, values, and identities that added up, ideally, to docile colonial subjects (Comaroff and Comaroff 1992, esp. chaps. 3 and 10). Such imperial projects of deculturation that the Comaroffs describe for South Africa in the late nineteenth century were remarkable neither for their scale nor for their innovation, however. Changing notions of person and body have been were integral to the creation of Christian disciples and colonial subjects in the Amerindian highlands of Latin America since the mid-sixteenth century. Indeed, the Andean region provided one of the original theaters of European imperial biopower, as the Spanish state and missionaries began to hammer out policies of cultural and bodily reform (Silverblatt 2004). In the 1570s and 1580s, Viceroy Francisco Toledo engineered successive "civilizing" campaigns to eradicate polygamy and other "barbarous" customs, nucleate indigenous settlements, restructure ethnic hierarchies, impose legal and moral norms, extract tribute and labor from every "strategic hamlet" in the viceroyalty, and convert the heathen and extirpate the idolaters. Missions and schools were established to spearhead that cultural revolution. That Toledo's project largely failed in many of its overarching goals is testimony to the vast historic distance obtaining between imperial utopias and local forms of autonomy and adaptive resistance throughout the Andean highlands over three centuries of Spanish rule.

In the early twentieth century, Latin America's aspiring nation-states took up the unfinished project of molding indian minds and bodies into a homogeneous mass of docile national, class, and gendered subjects. Blunt material conditions (export-driven capitalism, liberal ideologies and land reform policies, growing agrarian violence surrounding the practice of land divestiture and peasant resistance, massive rural-to-urban migration, a sprawling urban underclass and its attendant social ills) demanded new modes of population management and cultural reform. Among other reforms, the education of the masses suddenly loomed large. In the Bolivian Andes, where bio-cultural "whitening" vis-à-vis European immigration was proving to be unviable, political elites seized on the idea of indian education as both a powerful symbol and potential tool of indigenous incorporation into the modern Bolivian nation. By 1910, educators and intellectuals were embracing the nationalist ideal (popular in Argentina, Chile, and other Latin American nations) of "national pedagogy," designed to shape national subjects in harmony with Bolivia's environmental, racial, and social specificities.

Unpacked and examined critically, this notion of "national pedagogy" is fraught with contradictions. While the idea of national pedagogy embraced Enlightenment principles of universal schooling and citizenship, it also invoked race and environmental theories to define the bio-cultural character of the indian race(s) and, on that basis, to limit indigenous access to schooling and knowledge (even were they able to attend a functioning rural school in the first place). Concretely, indigenista racial theorists advocated a segregated system tailored to the "innate character" of the indian. Translated into policy, separate "work" schools were to prepare indians for their selected and limited entry into the national economy and polity as rural wage laborers on the otherwise uncolonizable altiplano. Vocational training had another significance: it pushed literacy to the edge of the curriculum in the rural indian school, since to read and write was deemed a useless, if not dangerous, source of knowledge among a feisty, often litigious peasantry.

We have here, then, a tangible locus of what Andrew Canessa has called "the [state's] opposing and frequently contradictory tendency of seeing indians as being on the periphery and requiring assimilation and *simultaneously* as being at the heart of national [economy], culture, and identity" (see the introduction). Throughout the early twentieth century, Bolivian reformers and indigenistas were caught on the horns of the post-colonial dilemma—the need to construct and mediate racial difference (to contain agrarian unrest, preserve creole caste privileges, and control the geopolitical and racial mobility of indian peasants) and the need to eradicate it in the service of a homogenizing national culture. It is a common irony among modernizing Latin American nations that, to the degree that states did manage to tame their interior "indian" frontiers, they tended to uplift those vanishing cultures and lost civilizations to iconic status and include them in their emerging repertory of civil celebrations. Such was the fate, of course, of Argentina's gauchos, Peru's Incas, and to a far lesser degree, Bolivia's ancient Aymara outpost of Tiwanaku. In Bolivia, thanks to the robust presence (and perceived threat) of indigenous peoples, political elites only belatedly and ambivalently embraced indigeneity as the mark of authentic Bolivianness (although see the interesting case of creole women appropriating Aymara music as "authentic Bolivia" in chapter 2 of this volume). Indeed, Bolivia's most common strand of indigenismo took a conservative, reactive stance against the putative ills of modernity (indian migration into the cities, vice and criminality, spread of popular literacy, suffrage, and other forms of "political mischief"). Much like Cuzco's romantic indigenistas of the 1920s, Bolivian elites wanted to deploy racial discourse and school policy to reproduce and upgrade the "unique aptitudes" of the Aymara labor force on the altiplano. In the 1920s, gender supplied a complementary prop to naturalize racial and subracial categories.

But, as we have seen in this chapter, there was nothing natural or fixed about elite notions or calibrations of gender, race, class, and nation. In different historical moments, the social meanings and uses of those categories rearticulated and changed with the times, especially under the impact of revolution (as in Mexico during the 1910s) or war (as in Bolivia in the 1930s). In both cases, the imperatives of reconstructing state power and bringing indians into the fold forced a radical reconfiguration of race, gender, and national identities. In the case of Bolivia, we perceive an unfolding national narrative in which gender began to trump race as the main modality by which political elites began to redefine the boundaries of difference and sameness. Such discursive and normative shifts were deeply grounded in the dangerous disjunctures that accompanied the Chaco War and its aftermath. During the war, issues of gender, physicality, and psychology became subjects of national debate, as the Bolivian state contemplated the need to mobilize, discipline, and dispatch tens of thousands of indian male bodies to the front lines in the Chaco War. In the immediate post-Chaco era, national unity and popular redemption called for radical experiments in communitarian schools and multiethnic coalitions. Bolivia's devastating military defeat also called for a massive effort to integrate the indian masses into the nation, if it were ever to be able to integrate the masses and defend its borders. In the meantime, the state confronted a new set of self-defined subjects (veterans, widows, mothers, and orphans), who militantly demanded public recognition and reparations for their own horrific sacrifices in the Chaco War. Gender and generation, as well as patriotic sacrifice and honor, now began to permeate both official and popular notions of national belonging.

But the ideological uses of gender, race, and nation took on new dimensions in the 1940s. The specter of indigenous mobilization, mining strikes, and the spread of "worldwide communism" in the mid-1940s jolted Bolivian conservative reformers and their new U.S. allies. Transracial notions of gender now became tools for promoting de-indianization, mestizaje, and cultural integration. In particular, nationalizing womanhood as the womb, nurturer, healer, and heroine of the war-torn nation became a critical trope in the 1940s. At the same time, Bolivia engendered rural school curricula in order to hasten the cult of domesticity and its particular order of values and dispositions. Now the indian woman was to be anchored in her own "natural habitat"—the peasant hearth and home. In many ways, the new curricular emphasis on bodily reform and family values sprang from the nation's urgent developmental needs to cultivate new habits of hygiene, work, and consumption. But, as I have tried to show, the impulse toward what the Comaroffs call "homemade hegemony" also came out of the intense struggle over power in this radically polarized, hierarchical society. Ironically, the Bolivian reformers' search for a Mexican-styled paradigm of mestizaje and rural development was aimed at building a hegemonic social order that would skip over, and preempt, a radical social uprising on the scale of Mexico's 1910 revolution. The state's failed effort to deploy indian education to integrate the peasant masses and preempt revolution represents, in my view, an exquisite episode in historical irony. But it is not the outcome, so much as the process, that interests us here. For it shows how, in the struggle to define indian education, a nation's cultural engineers wrestled with recursive notions of gender, race, and class to keep its rural indigenous people at the margins of the nation and modernity.

Acknowledgments

An earlier version of this chapter was published in *Proclaiming Revolution: Bolivia in Comparative Perspective*, edited by Merilee Grindle and Pilar Domingo (London and Cambridge, Mass.: University of London and Harvard University, 2003), 183–209. It is reprinted here with permission from the publishers.

Bibliography

Arguedas, Alcides. 1932 [1909]. *Pueblo enfermo*. 3d ed. La Paz: Puerta del Sol.

Barnadas, Josep. 1976. *Apuntes para una Historia Aymara*. La Paz: CIPCA.

Besse, Susan. 1996. *Restructuring Patriarchy: The Modernization of Gender Inequality in Brazil, 1914–1940*. Chapel Hill: University of North Carolina Press.

Bourdieu, Pierre. 1977. *Outline of a Theory of Practice*. Cambridge: Cambridge University Press.

de la Cadena, Marisol. 2000. *Indigenous Mestizos: The Politics of Race and Culture in Cuzco, Peru, 1919–1991*. Durham, N.C.: Duke University Press.

Chatterjee, Partha. 1993. *The Nation and Its Fragments: Colonial and Postcolonial Histories*. Princeton, N.J.: Princeton University Press.

Choque, Roberto. 1996. "La educación indigenal boliviana: El proceso educativo indígena-rural." In *Estudios bolivianos* 2:12–182.

Comaroff, John, and Jean Comaroff. 1992. *Ethnography and the Historical Imagination*. Boulder, Colo.: Westview.

Congreso Nacional de Bolivia. 1927. *Redactor, Congreso ordinario, 1927*. Vol. 5. La Paz: Renacimiento.

———. 1928. *Redactor de la Honorable Cámara de Diputados*. La Paz: Brazil.

———. 1947. *Redactor, Congreso extraordinario, 1947*. Vol. 1. La Paz: n.p.

Consejo Nacional de Educación, Bolivia. 1940. *El estado de la educación indigenal en el país*. La Paz: n.p.

Corrigan, Philip, and Derek Sayer. 1985. *The Great Arch: English State Formation as Cultural Revolution*. Oxford: Blackwell.

Donoso Torres, Vicente. 1946. *Filosofía de la educación boliviana*. Buenos Aires: Ed. Atlantida.

Dore, Elizabeth. 1997. "The Holy Family: Imagined Households in Latin American History." In *Gender Politics in Latin America: Debates in Theory and Practice*, ed. Elizabeth Dore, 101–17. New York: Monthly Review Press.

Dore, Elizabeth, and Maxine Molyneux, eds. 2000. *Hidden Histories of Gender and the State in Latin America*. Durham, N.C.: Duke University Press.

Findlay, Eileen J. Suárez. 1999. *Imposing Decency: The Politics of Sexuality and Race in Puerto Rico, 1870–1920*. Durham, N.C.: Duke University Press.

Frontaura Argona, María. 1932. *Hacia el futuro indio*. La Paz: Intendencia de Guerra.

Gill, Leslie. 1994. *Precarious Dependencies: Gender, Class, and Domestic Service in Bolivia*. New York: Columbia University Press.

Gotkowitz, Laura. 2000. "Commemorating the Heroínas: Gender and Civic Ritual in Early Twentieth Century Bolivia." In *Hidden Histories of Gender and the*

State in Latin America, ed. Elizabeth Dore and Maxine Molyneux, 215–37. Durham, N.C.: Duke University Press.

Guillén Pinto, Alfredo. 1919. *La educación del indio: Contribución a la pedagogía nacional*. La Paz: González y Medina.

Jáuregui Rosquellas, Alfredo. 1947. "Reflecciones sobre la cuestión indigenal: Sublevaciones y levantamientos." In *Boletín de la Sociedad Geográfica Sucre* 62:522–32.

Klein, Herbert S. 1969. *Parties and Political Change in Bolivia, 1880–1952*. Cambridge: Cambridge University Press.

Klubock, Thomas. 1998. *Contested Communities: Class, Gender, and Politics in Chile's El Teniente Copper Mine, 1904–1951*. Durham, N.C.: Duke University Press.

Lehm, Zulema, and Silvia Rivera Cusicanqui, 1988. *Los artesanos libertarios y la ética de trabajo*. La Paz: Gramma.

Mamani Condori, Carlos. 1991. *Taraqu: Masacre, Guerra, y "renovación" en la biografía de Eduardo L. Nina Qhispi, 1866–1935*. La Paz: Aruwiyiri.

Mariaca, Juvenal, and Arturo Peñaranda. 1918. *Proyecto de organización de una escuela normal agrícola de indígenas en el altiplano*. La Paz: Boliviana.

Mayer, Enrique. 2002. *The Articulated Peasant: Household Economies in the Andes*. Boulder, Colo.: Westview.

Medinaceli, Ximena. 1989. *Alterando la rutina: Mujeres en las ciudades de Bolivia, 1920–1930*. La Paz: CIDEM.

Ministerio de Educación (Departamento de educación rural and Programa cooperativo de educación), Bolivia. 1948. *Guía de instrucción para maestros rurales*. La Paz, n.p.

Ministerio de Instrucción Pública, Bolivia. 1933. *Memoria, 1931*. La Paz: Eléctrica.

Ministerio de Instrucción Pública y Agricultura, Bolivia. 1918. *Memoria y anexo*. La Paz: Moderna.

———. 1919. *Memoria y anexo*. La Paz: Moderna.

Nelson, Raymond. 1949. *Education in Bolivia*. Washington: U.S. Government Printing Office.

Pérez, Elizardo. 1992 [1961]. *Warisata: La escuela-ayllu*. 2d ed. La Paz: Hisbol/Ceres.

Rivera Cusicanqui, Silvia. 1986. *"Oprimidos pero no vencidos": Luchas del campesinado aymara y qechwa, 1900–1980*. La Paz: Hisbol.

Rivera Cusicanqui, Silvia, ed. 1996. *Ser mujer indígena, chola o birlocha en la Bolivia postcolonial de los años 90*. La Paz: Plural.

Rosemblatt, Karin Alejandra. 2000. *Gendered Compromises: Political Cultures and the State in Chile, 1920–1950*. Chapel Hill: University of North Carolina Press.

Saavedra, Bautista. 1987 [1901]. 2d ed. *El ayllu: Estudios sociológicos*. La Paz: Juventud.

Salazar Mostajo, Carlos. 1997. 3d ed. *Warisata Mía*. La Paz: Juventud.

Salmón Ballivián, José. 1926. "El indio íntimo: Contribución al estudio biológico social del indio." In *Ideario aimara*, 105–63. La Paz: Salesiana.

Servicio Cooperativo Interamericano de Educación [SCIDE]. 1955. *Rural Education in Bolivia*. La Paz: Institute of Inter-American Affairs.

Sider, Gerald. 1987. "When Parrots Learn to Talk, and Why They Can't: Domination, Deception, and Self-Deception in Indian-White Relations." In *Comparative Studies in Society and History* 29:3–23.

Silverblatt, Irene. 2004. *Modern Inquisitions: Peru and the Colonial Origins of the Civilized World.* Durham, N.C.: Duke University Press.

Stepan, Nancy. 1991. *The "Hour of Eugenics": Race, Gender, and Nation in Latin America.* Ithaca, N.Y.: Cornell University Press.

Stephenson, Marcia. 1999. *Gender and Modernity in Andean Bolivia.* Austin: University of Texas Press.

Stoler, Ann Laura. 1996. *Race and the Education of Desire: Foucault's History of Sexuality and the Colonial Order of Things.* Durham, N.C.: Duke University Press.

Szasz, Margaret. 1974. *Education and the American Indian: The Road to Self-Determination, 1928–1973.* Albuquerque: University of New Mexico Press.

Tamayo, Franz. 1988 [1910]. *Creación de una pedagogía nacional.* La Paz: Juventud.

Taller Andino de Historia Oral [THOA]. 1994. "Indigenous Women and Community Resistance: History and Memory." In *Women and Social Change in Latin America,* ed. Elizabeth Jelín, 151–83. London: Zed Books.

United States Record Administration. 1945. Record Group 39, 824, 401/3–145; Adam to Secretary of State, March 1.

Vaughan, Mary Kay. 1997. *Cultural Politics of Revolution: Teachers, Peasants, and Schools in Mexico, 1930–1940.* Tucson: University of Arizona Press.

———. 2000. "Modernizing Patriarchy: State Policies, Rural Households, and Women in Mexico, 1930–1940." In *Hidden Histories of Gender and the State in Latin America,* ed. Elizabeth Dore and Maxine Molyneux, 194–214. Durham, N.C.: Duke University Press.

Weinstein, Barbara. 1996. "Remaking the Worker at Home and at Play." In *For Social Peace in Brazil: Industrialists and the Remaking of the Working Class in Sao Paulo, 1920–1964,* 219–49. Chapel Hill: University of North Carolina Press.

3

Making Music Safe for the Nation

Folklore Pioneers in Bolivian Indigenism

Michelle Bigenho

In the 1990s, the past became a profitable refuge of Latin American music projects. *Buena Vista Social Club* brought Cuban octogenarians to international stages, and Carlos Vives's album *Clásicos de la Provincia* connected music of "grandfathers" with provincial roots of national Colombian music. In these projects, the past and the provinces were skillfully blended in music of a national ilk. A Bolivian ensemble called *Música de Maestros* (Music of the Masters) has been involved in a similar, although less commercially successful, national music project that draws on the powerful metaphors of both past epochs and provincial geographies. In this Bolivian national music project, the metaphorical work of imagined time—the national past—and imagined space—the diversity of the provinces—is entwined with representations of indigenous cultures. In 1995, Música de Maestros embarked on a more specific project of recalling a moment of the Bolivian national past. In a recording titled *ReCanTanDo* (*Singing Again*, 1998), the ensemble accompanied mestizo-creole women who in the 1940s and 1950s were considered "pioneers" of Bolivian song. In this case "Bolivian song" refers to indigenous genres from the countryside, music that had been previously rejected in urban areas, and that had to be made palatable to the tastes of national elites. What does it mean to be a mestizo-creole pioneer of indigenous Bolivian song? What is the significance of mestizo-creole women singing indigenous genres that come to stand for the Bolivian nation? Implicit to both of these interrogatives is the issue of mestizo-creole representations of an indian world, the symbolic work of these representations as Bolivian national projects, and the powerfully gendered aspects of these symbolic realms. To address these questions, I draw from interviews conducted in 2000 and 2001 with Irma Vásquez, Chela Rea Nogales, María Luisa Camacho, Norah Camacho, Elsa Tejada, and Esperanza Tejada, and build on extensive ethnographic work, since 1993, with Bolivian folklore workers. The women I interviewed have public performance personas in Bolivia, and all of them wished to be named in this work. However, for their privacy, I have attempted to maintain anonymity in relation to their specific statements.

In the 1940s and 1950s these mestizo-creole women were permitted to sing for the nation, but within set parameters that have been used to control women in the spheres of music performance and nations. Many authors have written about masculine hegemony in the spheres of both national projects (Gill 1997; Radcliffe and Westwood 1996; Taylor 1994) and music performance (Grossberg 1991; McClary 1991; Rose 1994; Waksman 1999), and many of these authors critically examine the traditionally accepted location of the feminine within both of these spheres, carefully detailing the multiple subversions of this dominance. In national projects, women are presented as mothers of citizens, and female sexuality is confined to the private space of the heterosexual couple that produces citizens for the nation (see Parker et al. 1992:7; Radcliffe and Westwood 1996:141–51; Stephenson 1999; Taylor 1994). In the performative context, women are often staged as tragic victims of their own public display of sexuality; men can use sexuality on stage and live to tell about it, but women symbolically die if they attempt the same performative feats (see McClary 1991:148–66). When these mestizo-creole women took on the roles of folklore pioneers, they worked well within these closely circumscribed gendered boundaries of performative and national spaces, even though they considered their own actions radical in their time. Ultimately they transformed sounds that were previously disliked by their own social classes into Bolivian national music, making expressions of marginalized indian music the root of a mestizo-creole patriotic core (see Canessa, introduction to this volume).

The analysis I present of these women's stories emphasizes an often overlooked dyad of colonial/postcolonial studies: the mestizo-creole woman and the indian man. Gendered analysis of race and nation in Latin America has to some extent been marked by a foregrounding of the meeting between the white man as ultimate colonizer and the indian woman as ultimate colonized subject.[1] A gendered analysis of cultural resistance and/or its cooptation may come to emphasize the special role played in national projects by the doubly marked indian woman. For example, in an article on the role of Andean women in the Andean rebellions of 1910 to 1950, the authors state: "The Andean woman is the privileged repository of cultural resistance. In her weaving activities as well as in her specialized ritualistic role, the woman actively produces symbols and interpretations that form an important part of the collective identity of the Andean communities" (Taller de Historia Oral Andina and Rivera Cusicanqui 1990:179). While the gist of this cited article focuses on the much-needed project of locating indigenous women within the history of Andean rebellions, the assignation of "privileged repository" is perhaps the point I find most troubling, as stated here, but also as implicitly assumed in both nationalist projects and in some gender-focused studies. I will not present mestizo-creole women as repositories of national traditions, but rather as participants in a symbolic exchange that occurs with indian men, entails the appropriation of indigenous expressions, and transforms indian expressions into national ones. This interpretation brings into focus the phantoms of the gendered analysis of nation, and sheds light on the nuanced ways that gender and race play out in the pageant of nationalism.

In the 1940s Bolivia had just emerged from the defeat of the Chaco War (1932–1935) and the creole elites were facing increasingly well-organized peasant indigenous groups who would not remain quiet about the critical agrarian issues of Bolivia's countryside. With the backdrop of a changing indigenous countryside, these mestizo-creole women participated in the cultural politics of indigenism that preceded and continued through the 1952 Revolution. Mestizo-creole women's performances of indian music resonated with several contemporary Latin American projects of indigenism—where national or regional elites turned to the indian cultures around them to shore up national or regional identities. During the 1940s several indigenista projects were under design. In Cuzco, Peru, local elites were "inventing" the pre-Columbian tradition of Inti Raymi, the Inca Festival of the Sun (de la Cadena 2000:157–62; see Hobsbawm and Ranger 1983). In Ecuador, indigenistas built a national ideal on the symbolic values of pre-Columbian civilizations and the Instituto Indigenista Ecuatoriano aimed to improve the indian through integration policies (Radcliffe and Westwood 1996:69). Coming out of the Chaco War as the vanquished power, the Bolivian state also sought to create a sense of national unity through indigenist policies. But, rather than a project aimed at incorporating indians into the nation-state, the folklore careers of these women highlight a cultural politics directed at Bolivian mestizo-creoles. Indigenista politics cannot be reduced to mere smoke and mirrors of national or regional elites. The stories I reference will show how mestizo-creole folklore workers came to identify with the indianness they performed on stage. These performances still excluded flesh-and-blood indians; but the feelings expressed by my interviewees reflected much more than a mere manipulation of indigeneity. I will suggest that this Bolivian indigenismo, in the realm of music, requires reflection on at least three bodies: (1) mestizo-creole women's bodies that literally become instruments of song, and symbolically become mothers of the nation by drawing on ideologies of essentialized indigeneity; (2) the indian body that these women perform on stage; borrowing from Michael Taussig (1993), I will call this the mimetic indian body; and (3) the Bolivian nationalist body politic that is served by these two previously mentioned bodies. Within the context of Bolivian indigenism, and working through state-run programs, these folklore singers played crucial roles in making indian music safe for mestizo-creole nationalism.

When May Women Sing?

As these singers reflected on their careers, they emphasized the radical artistic moves they made in an earlier time, but their stories also reflected the very traditional feminine positions they continued to occupy. While their artistic work in the 1940s and 1950s marked a significant change in the soundscapes of Bolivia, these pioneers of Bolivian song did not venture far from home and from traditional expected roles within their families. All of these women talked about learning music within the contexts of their families, and most of them emphasized the roles their fathers played as key figures in their musical training. One singer came from a family of musically inclined women, but they all played within traditional home and school spheres: "My mother was a pianist. My mother liked to play the piano. She wasn't a pianist of . . . she was a pianist of her home, of her house." Her aunt studied mandolin at a high school run by nuns, "so in my blood I carry something of an artist." Another singer told me her father played in an *estudiantina*, a style of ensemble consisting primarily of plucked string instruments in which most of the parts are doubled or tripled. One woman located her artistic "lines" through both maternal and paternal ancestry: "I have my ancestors. . . . My grandmother played guitar and mandolin, my maternal grandmother; my father played guitar and the brother of my mother as well. They made me sing when I was a little girl." Two singers said their love of folklore came from their father, who was born in a rural village, played violin and piano, became a music teacher in the school of Quillacollo, and played in the Cochabamba Symphony. He liked all kinds of music, "but folklore was what he liked best," they insisted. While he taught music to all of his children, only their brothers played musical instruments, and he did not teach his daughters to read music. One of these women began studying music at the conservatory, but she said her school schedule left her no time to continue this pursuit, which would have included learning how to read music. In general, these women learned to sing within family contexts, often to the exclusion of learning other instruments, and often without the more formal training for reading written music.

I asked the women about how they felt as young single women singing in the bohemian contexts of La Paz. Within my reference to "bohemian" was my assumed interpretation of late-night, male-dominated performance contexts where people consume a significant amount of alcohol. In each case, the women quickly distanced themselves from an association with these scenes or spoke of being carefully chaperoned within these spaces that might compromise a young woman's honor. In response to this question, several women used the narrative strategy of an imagined brotherhood between the musicians and themselves. One singer commented, "The bohemian life is . . . well, then it was so spiritual, so pure. We were all brothers and sisters. We shared, we felt the same desire to triumph, to improve something, . . . to share the happiness of being together." Another singer claimed, "I was always respected. We all acted like brothers and sisters, even when we traveled." Another woman responded to this question in terms of both the limited ways women were allowed to move and the demands of work obligations outside of music: "Women can't get around as easily as men. [Men] stay up all night. But we had our artistic life anyway." She described how they went to work in a folklore nightclub (*peña*) between 11:00 p.m. and 3:00 a.m., how they would arrive in a taxi from home and immediately take a taxi home after playing their pieces. "We didn't stick around after the show. We didn't want to, but they wouldn't have let us either." She further explained: "Why [did I leave immediately]? Because I worked. I am a pharmaceutical biochemist. So I had to go to work. . . . Besides, we were *señoritas* and it wasn't right."

Another narrative strategy was to emphasize the prestige of one's performance contexts. In describing her singing career as an "exclusive artist" of Radio Illimani (the government broadcasting station with which every one of the singers I interviewed had at one time been contracted to sing), one singer said she was not permitted to sing in restaurants or hotels. "That was something you did not do." "Why?" I asked. "Because it was prohibited. It wasn't good. Yes! We had to always sing in theaters. I sang in the Monje Campero, in the Tesla film house." From these comments a picture emerges of carefully watched young women who were allowed to perform in specified respectable contexts.

All of these women began singing as young single women. Some later married. Today most of them are single, divorced, or widowed. Most of them commented on the antagonistic relationship between a singing career and a married life. One woman gave up her singing for work and family: "I had a job in a commercial house. I couldn't divide myself in two. So I had to dedicate myself to work or art. And then I got married and I had to stop singing for several years. . . . For reasons of my family, I could not prolong my artistic situation. . . . I had to work." Another woman described singing as the activity that filled her soul and spirit, but when she married it was not possible to continue singing. "I had children, a family . . . I also worked; I was a kindergarten teacher." One singer described the resistance of her husband to her singing. She spoke of her husband's opposition to not only her career, but to her very act of singing: "I would start singing in the shower, anywhere, maybe while I was dusting the house, and he would say 'Please! Be quiet!' He didn't like it when I sang." In general, these women mentioned marriage as a point of interruption in their singing careers, and even those who never married reiterated the impossibility of maintaining both a married life and a singing career. Two of the women gleefully talked about continuing their singing careers as single women, something they saw as impossible in the lives of their married sisters.

For these folklore pioneers, the act of singing itself was couched within comfortable gendered patterns. Carefully chaperoned single women might sing under fatherly or brotherly protection. When married, they found it problematic, impossible, or simply out of the question to continue their singing activities. The bodies of single mestizo-creole women were temporarily permitted, even encouraged, into the activity of song, as long as their performances did not disrupt the expectations of marriage and child bearing. These singers were not radically breaking with gendered expectations of mestizo-creole life; they told a story of women who acted well within the patterns of Marianismo, with all the accompanying expectations of motherhood and protection of feminine honor. Marianismo, a "disciplinary technology" that constitutes the white woman as subject (Nelson 1999:216), is prevalent in many Latin American contexts and presents the ideal of femininity as the chaste, self-sacrificing mothering figure, often patterned after the Virgin Mary of the Catholic Church (see Gutmann 1996:21; Radcliffe and Westwood 1996:141; Stevens 1973). As my interviewees remembered their youth, they painted a picture of performing under carefully chaperoned conditions, and clearly described sacrificing their "art" for the demands of married family life. While they did not necessarily break with expected white feminine roles, they consistently told a story of radical social change, and they portrayed themselves as spearheading these changes within an artistic realm.

Romancing the Rebellious Indian

In retelling the story of their artistic careers, these women explicitly talked about the shift they made in the kinds of songs they performed. They began their careers by singing what they called "foreign" genres: *tangos, boleros,* and *valses* (Peruvian and Argentine waltzes); but in the 1940s they shifted to what they called "national," "Bolivian," "native," and "autochthonous" genres. The shift was not easy, they said, and in some cases they felt themselves pitched against the opinions of family members. One singer couched this challenge in terms of "having to raise the consciousness of Bolivians." On a performance stage, mestizo-creole women's bodies began to represent mimetically the indian body–a body scorned by mestizo-creoles. They call themselves "pioneers," and others refer to them with this moniker. The term *pioneer* ties a sonorous incantation to region, and in this case to rural, peasant, or indian regions of Bolivian territory. In mimetically bringing the indian body to a performative stage, these women came to identify personally with an idea of indigeneity, a romanticized image that fixed natives to bucolic landscapes. The term *pioneer* carries the weight of discovery and of firstness. In this case "discovery" was about knowing something in a different way, about transforming something marginal and previously despised by urban mestizo-creoles into something central and cherished as a point of national identification.

Discovery of indianness emerged through memories of bucolic rural vacations. While most of these women have lived their lives in cities (La Paz and Cochabamba), they remember fondly a contact with the rural provinces around these urban contexts. They discussed visits to family lands that were described as stunning landscapes: "Our father's estate was on the shores of Lake Titicaca with a view of the Illimani."[2] Like other indigenista projects (see Poole 1997), the remembered highland landscape served as inspiration for these singers' artistic creations. A visit to the farm in the provinces meant a break from school, a break from the city, a vacation in the country. Of course, the position of those who worked in the Bolivian countryside under extremely exploitative labor relations stood in glaring juxtaposition to these vacation stories.[3] In the 1940s the Bolivian countryside around La Paz and Cochabamba was characterized by large landed estates (*haciendas*) on which peasants, without access to their own land, were forced to work as peons. Dissatisfaction with these land/labor arrangements, skewed in favor of the few, was coming to a head in Bolivia's post–Chaco War period.

From 1932 to 1935 people from all over the Bolivian territory met in the trenches of the unsuccessful Chaco War with Paraguay. In the war's aftermath people who may not have even considered themselves as "Bolivian" before the war began to make claims upon the nation for which they or their brothers, fathers, or husbands fought (Albó 1987:381; Arze Aguirre 1987; Montenegro 1943:235–39; Ranaboldo and SEMTA 1987; Rivera Cusicanqui 1986:45–48; Stephenson 1999:25). One of the singers I interviewed related the end of the war to a kind of openness to hearing a new Bolivian music: "With the question of the Chaco, I believe that the whole world was asleep. Because of the impact, the pain of having lost part of our territory, of Bolivia having lost many sons, . . . In the war they died and the whole world was with a sleeping heart and soul, dead from the pain of it. You go to Germany or to somewhere where there has been a war, everyone walks crestfallen with pain. No one even remembers music. . . . Then little by little the people began to wake up and they didn't have any entertainment."

While my interviewees spoke of beautiful, inspiring rural landscapes, they also expressed an awareness of the exploitative social relations of the time. When they referred to the people who lived in what were their own inspirational landscapes, they used the terms *campesinos* and *indios* interchangeably. A possessive adjective was often placed in front of the term: "our indians" or "our campesinos." "You know, the ones who were on the family estate." "The pongos, those who don't exist anymore since the Agrarian Reform" (1953). This comment was made by a singer who spoke extensively and favorably of President Gualberto Villarroel. Villarroel's presidency was marked by the First Indigenous Congress of 1945, the first context in which the labor system of pongos was abolished. During this congress, campesinos from all areas marched to the city of La Paz and Francisco Chipana Ramos or "Rumi Sonqo" presided over the multitudinous gathering. Rumi Sonqo was photographed next to President Villarroel and began to speak of himself as the president of indians while Villarroel was the president of whites (Rivera Cusicanqui 1986:64).[4] The Indigenous Congress proposed reforms in agricultural labor relations, but stopped short of proposing reforms to land tenure. This approach was consistent with a prominent political discourse about "modernizing" labor relations in the countryside and then "civilizing" the indians through education (Malloy 1989:165), even as these educational projects proved contradictory to the other postcolonial projects of policing racial and class boundaries (Larson, this volume).

The Indigenous Congress was a radical event, and in many ways its symbolic effect and the resulting fear and anger of the landed elite contributed to the upheavals that cost President Villarroel his office and his life. While these singers did not talk about the First Indigenous Congress, one singer mentioned Villarroel's presidency several times, emphasizing how Villarroel promoted Bolivian popular music through Radio Illimani, and how she worked under contract with this broadcasting station. As she spoke of Villarroel, she recited the phrase often connected with his name, "I am not an enemy of the rich, but I am more of a friend to the poor." While these women seemed quite aware of the social inequalities of their context and seemed to express support for the more inclusive politics of Villarroel, they were also members of the very social class that was running in fear of the subsequent indigenous rebellions. Indian sounds formed part of that landscape of conflict. Jacques Attali has suggested that the transformation of noise into music is indeed a site of political struggle, and a place where future symbolic modes of production can be heard in incipient forms (1985). As Silvia Rivera Cusicanqui has suggested, the eerie sound of the *pututu*, an indigenous instrument often crafted from a cattle horn, was enough to send some hacienda owners fleeing for their lives (1986:58). According to Rivera Cusicanqui, the 1947 rebellions marked the moment from which the National Revolutionary Movement (Movimiento Nacional Revolucionario, MNR) began crafting homogenized "campesinos" out of culturally diverse indians (1986:63). Another step in this process was taking control of indian sounds, and I would suggest that part of this nationalist project had to be aimed at mestizo-creoles and families of the landed elite. Frightful sounding indian music had to be tamed, and the singing bodies of mestizo-creole women became the instruments through which dangerous indian sounds became Bolivian national music.

The singers did not talk of the dangers of this music, but in some cases they did mention the perceived melancholic sound of indian music as a reason for its initial rejection by more affluent sectors of society. One woman discussed the "sadness" of indian songs that were played only in isolated villages for local fiestas. "We dared to play this music." Part of making indian music safe for Bolivia included discovering and championing genres from the different regions of the country, from the highlands as well as from the warm lowlands of eastern Bolivia. Naming the regions of La Paz, Chuquisaca, Oruro, Potosi, and Santa Cruz, one singer said, "It was a time for discovering our music. . . . We were the first to disseminate Bolivian folklore [in the 1940s], even though in this period you did not hear much folkloric music because it was a little bit sad and the public did not like it much because of the characteristics of the music and the lyrics that were somewhat tear-jerking at first. Later, people developed an awareness and this music became accepted. Our music made it to the Bolivian public at full volume and it was accepted with pleasure. So at that time *taquiraris* and *carnavalitos* [genres from the eastern lowlands], other more cheerful rhythms, were accepted by all social sectors, by the cultured and by the common people." This singer championed the genres of the lowlands, emphasizing their "cheerfulness" as a reason for their broad acceptance. Social differences had to be bridged through music and these differences were often imagined in terms of different geographic environments that were thought to determine the essential cheer or gloom of a people's music. One singer barely contained her enthusiasm for those genres from the warm lowlands: "Taquiraris and carnavalitos make you vibrate. . . . [In the lowlands the people] carry in their blood the cheerfulness of the eastern part of Bolivia. It is not like here [in La Paz] where one is scorched by the cold."

One singer attributed eventual acceptance of indian music to the policies of Villarroel, making particular reference to the programs this president sponsored at Radio Illimani. "From then on [1945], Bolivian music became accepted, the national music in all the Republic. Because before that, there was shame in Bolivian homes. . . . People said that only indians or cholos (urbanized indians) sang that, but it had not penetrated the field of the aristocracy. . . . Now you see, from then on national music, Bolivian music, has been accepted." One singer mentioned a slow process of acceptance of Bolivian music, with a quicker acceptance of music that was, "How can one say [it]? Something more serious, like those classic *cuecas* of Eduardo Cava, Simeón Roncal, Teófilo Vargas, and [Humberto]

Iporre Salinas." Here she suggested the quick acceptance of genres that could be viewed as "Bolivian"—rather than the Argentine tango, for example—but that had ties to the elites in the cities of Sucre, Cochabamba, and Potosí (cuecas) and to the compositions that emerged in the 1930s within the "golden age" of mestizo-creole music composition.[5]

The cueca, a song-dance genre of mestizo-creole association, shares with the tango its gendered forms of romantic conquest. But unlike this "foreign" dance, in the cueca, dancers never touch their partners, but rather dance around each other, waving a tempting handkerchief in one hand, always at the point of touching their partners, but never quite doing so. Even before urban elites began listening and dancing to Bolivian cuecas, they danced to the music of the Argentine-modeled "typical orchestra" (*orquesta típica* or simply *la típica*). The typical orchestra—with an instrumentation of piano, bass, *bandoneón* (related to the accordion), violin, and drum set—performed the preferred genres of tangos, *paso dobles*, boleros, and valses (Rolando Encinas, personal communication 2004). Even though Bolivians have compositions in these genres, not one of these musical forms is considered quintessentially "Bolivian." As reflected in the nostalgia of elderly Bolivians today, the tango certainly had its moment of popularity in the city of La Paz, but as a genre that would play a key role within Argentine social processes of national identification (Savigliano 1995; Taylor 1998; Vila 1991), the tango would never do as sonorous raw material for Bolivian nationalism. While cuecas were becoming recognized as "Bolivian," the claim to fame in the case of my interviewees rested with their performative associations with nativeness and indianness. As one of the singers insisted: "We only play native music now, once in a while a cueca."

As a consolidation of the political processes put into motion after the Chaco War, the cultural politics of the 1952 Revolution moved marginalized indian expressions to the center of a nationalist project, but it did so in ambiguous ways. The revolutionary project brought universal suffrage, universal education, the abolition of the hacienda system (Agrarian Reform of 1953), the nationalization of mines, and the unionization of peasants. The liberal model of citizenship embodied in these politics explicitly sought to create, from the different ethnicities and classes of the Bolivian territory, an "imagined community" (Anderson 1991) of mestizos—seeking to make of them uniform and productive Bolivians, even as it implicitly reinforced existing social hierarchies (see Rivera Cusicanqui 1993:62–89). Within relatively recently formed political parties, the marginalized flesh and blood "indians" came under the new label of "peasants" (Albó 1987:381), and the symbolic world of indianness was corralled into the heart of the national body politic. Two of the singers—who began their singing careers later than the other women who were interviewed, and on the very eve of the 1952 Revolution—spoke in terms that sat squarely within the politics of the MNR. "Before, folklore was not viewed positively because it was the music of cholos, the music of campesinos, and the people of the towns said, 'no, no, I prefer to dance vals, tango, any music except folklore.' They despised [folklore] because it was music of the common people (pueblo)."

While these singers continued to occupy traditional women's roles, they viewed their own folkloric singing as a radical leap in their own social circles. They were not revolutionaries, and in fact they belonged to a social class that stood to lose in a revolutionary project. With the Revolution of 1952 and the Agrarian Reform of 1953, these women were put in the paradoxical position of championing the musical traditions that belonged to the very peasants to whom their families actually lost land. One singer described her reactions to the Revolution and the Agrarian Reform: "For us it was painful because they took away our land, but nevertheless, musically, spiritually, we continued singing that music. It was the music of our country, the music we loved. And we continued to sing with even more enthusiasm."

In their art, folklore singers were inspired by urban bourgeois romanticizations of Bolivia's rural indians. Much like Elayne Zorn's discussion of the way the marginal place of Taquile became the iconic representation of Peruvian nationness (this volume), the stories told by my interviewees—although featuring very different contexts of state, social class, and historical moment—highlight a similar project that mines the imagined social and geographic margins to produce the symbolic wealth of national culture. The singers I interviewed were very aware of the social chasms across which they were leaping, even though they framed these differences in terms of socioeconomic gaps and rural-urban divides, rather than in terms of ideologies of racial or cultural differences. National music had to bring together under one flag the "aristocracy" and the "lowest classes," the "people of towns" and the "campesinos."

The Work of Mimesis

In copying indigenous things, these women imitated the sounds of indigenous instruments, used indigenous languages in their performances, and dressed in indian clothes. These mestizo-creole women were fascinated by musical sounds produced by indian men. The playing of highland Andean indigenous instruments has been considered a predominantly masculine activity in which women often participate with the instrument of their own voices (Bigenho 2002:139–68; Meisch 2002:189; Turino 1993:41, 49). My interviewees waxed poetic, not about the singing of indian women, but about the sounds of the environment and of instruments played by troupes of indian men. The women I interviewed claimed to imitate with their voices the sounds produced when indian men played native instruments. One of the singers remembered her own attraction to the music from the area of her family's farm in Santiago de Huata: "The way they played their instruments caught my attention. I would follow a troupe of *sikuris* (pan pipes) to see exactly how they were playing . . . with our voices, we imitate the way they always play, the way they play in fifths."

How were these mestizo-creole women drawn into the world of potentially dangerous indian sounds? The singers talked about visually inspiring rural landscapes that moved them to compose a national music. They also detailed their experiences in rural soundscapes, blending in their stories, ambient sounds, and indigenous wind instruments: "I had been born in a little village called Italaque and this village is surrounded by rivers of crystal clear waters. And I loved to listen to the trill of the birds, the noise, the sound of the river. . . . Imagine it! . . . In the time when I was born, in the plaza of my village there were forty [troupes] of sikuris."[6] This singer moved to the city of La Paz at the age of two and returned to Italaque on vacations during the school year. She associated Bolivian music with sad sounds wafting through a rural landscape. She remembers having gone to the hills to sing and to listen to the echo of her own voice. The way she talked about natural sounds in connection with her own inspiration to compose does not differ greatly from the way indigenous men have described their musical inspirations in ambient sounds (e.g., see Bigenho 2002:209–13), although these men may connect their experiences with spirits of the water or the *sirena* (see Sánchez Canedo 1988). While this woman definitively attributed to the sikuri players the role of "creators of Andean music," she described her own process of taking inspiration from the sounds and landscape she so intimately described. When she made this statement about the sikuris, she was showing me a scrapbook of an exhibition on Italaque held in La Paz's House of Culture. With each photo of this cherished landscape she herself had written a few lines of poetry. Mestizo-creole women imitated the musical sounds produced by indian men and narrativized this experience through a sentimentality about the sound of rural landscapes and a strong identification with wind instruments, particularly the sikuris. Mestizo-creole female voices imitated male-produced, potentially dangerous, indian sounds.

While the women imitated musical sounds as produced by indian men, they usually dressed in women's costumes. When one singer was showing me a scrapbook, she pointed to a picture of a young woman dressed in a full gathered skirt (*pollera*), high-heeled boots, a shawl (*manta*), and a bowler hat—the "typical dress" of the *chola paceña*. "This is my work costume," she said. While this singer is from La Paz, two other singers from Cochabamba told me of many different costumes: "We went dressed like indians, as campesinos. The cholo is already creole. On the other hand, the campesino is pure." While they told me about utilizing many different Bolivian costumes, they insisted that their preference was always to wear the "representative" costume of Cochabamba. All the women spoke with great pride about their chola and indian costumes, but the meanings of this pride are distinct from those felt by the young woman who, in 2001, returned to her village armed with polleras to participate in the annual Carnival celebrations (Van Vleet, this volume). For her, the chola clothes demonstrated wealth and an ability to succeed and be a consumer in a more cosmopolitan context. For the folklore singers of the 1940s this form of dress represented the indigeneity they were bringing into the service of a mestizo-creole nationalist culture.

Yet another group of singers spoke of dressing "as indias," emphasizing the feminine costume they always used when they were younger. They giggled as they spoke of performing today with ponchos, "always in the colors of the flag," to conceal their heavier silhouettes that have come with age. At the concert for the launching of the compact disc *Singing Again*, the invited soloists wore ponchos, a masculine garment in the countryside of Bolivia. In their youth they donned costumes that evoked their perception of indian women. When they returned to the stage as mature women, they assumed a masculine attire.

Another woman enthusiastically told me about creating her own fashion for the stage through a creative use of the *aguayo* (colorful woven cloths that are used to carry bundles tied on one's back): "I always liked to capture people's attention. So I made myself little jackets of aguayo and everyone just stared at me because this seemed ridiculous. And now you see everyone doing this." She had many different costumes from different areas of Bolivia, but the item of clothing about which she spoke with most affection was an item worn by men: a poncho from the area of Charazani. This garment was given to a male relative of hers who visited the area in a government capacity during the presidency of Villarroel. She told me that the mother of this relative gave her the poncho as a gift. I pictured the formal event in which a symbolic item was passed between an indian man and a mestizo-creole man of the government, and the way this piece of clothing was sidetracked into the symbolic work of those mestizo-creole women who were making indian sights and sounds safe for the nation. The act of putting on costumes should not be underestimated in its power. While most of the women spoke lightheartedly about the ways they prepared themselves for visual presentation on a performance stage, they reached a level of identification with that otherness that was quite striking. The comment that most drove home the power of mimesis in this process was made by this same singer: "The day that I die, they are going to bury me in typical dress, with my poncho and my black hat on top of my coffin."

Folklore singers relied on a multisensorial portrayal of indigeneity. Along with the sounds of indigenous instruments, and sartorial suggestions of indianness, the languages of Aymara and Quechua were other markers of indian that these singers consciously adopted in their performances, and the women remember vividly the critiques they received for making such choices. As one woman said: "They told us, 'Why do you sing that stuff in Aymara? You are not indiacitas.'" One singer told me she speaks Aymara very well because she spent her vacations in the countryside, on the family properties, and in that context she interacted with "the Aymara children, with those who tended the estates, the properties." The singers from Cochabamba claimed a slightly different experience with the indigenous language of Quechua. Their stories about Quechua painted a picture of a language that crossed classes in Cochabamba: "We like [Quechua]. We speak Quechua. . . . Here in La Paz, the children don't want to speak it. They are ashamed. They are Aymarists. In Cochabamba everybody speaks Quechua, doctors, wherever you go. So my father would say at the lunch table, 'Now it is prohibited to speak Spanish, just Quechua. I will teach you.' In the whole world there is not a word for love larger than the one in Quechua. It is the word 'chunkituy.' Like 'te quiero,' 'je t'aime,' and 'I love you.'" The translations of English, French, Spanish, and Quechua are purposely lumped together to indicate an equality, and in some cases even a superiority in the expressive capacities of the Quechua language. One of the singers, in the context of a discussion about her fluency in the Aymara language, and her role as a teacher of this language, stated with pride, "I felt very indigenous!" I could underscore the irony of such statements as made by middle-class mestizo-creole women, but the sincerity with which they spoke leads me to ask how and why such a level of identification with indianness was reached. Indigenista projects are often correctly labeled and critiqued as projects about indians sans flesh-and-blood indians. But an analysis should not overlook the weight of folklore singers' statements about "feeling indigenous" or wanting to be buried in indian clothing. They signal the incredible degree to which indigeneity has become the lens through which many mestizo-creoles feel themselves to be Bolivian.

When I reflect on my own participation with the ensemble Música de Maestros, I remember publicity interviews in which I am often asked, "How does it feel as a *North American* to perform *Bolivian* music?" I suspect they long to hear me answer enthusiastically, "Oh! I feel completely Bolivian!" I am somewhat reluctant to disappoint them with the truth: that I do not feel at all Bolivian. Because I thoroughly enjoy the musical endeavor in which I have become immersed, I usually deflect the question, saying something sincere, such as what an honor it is to play with this ensemble, or how much pleasure I get out of performing particular genres and compositions. Of course there are differences between the gringa anthropologist who starts playing Bolivian national music and the Bolivian mestizo-creole artist who sings indigenous genres of her country. When the performer comes out of the process saying she feels very indigenous, the powerful symbolic work of the mimetic and nationalist bodies is revealed.

Taussig discusses mimetic processes with a particular attention to copying and embodiment within colonial and postcolonial contexts (1993). He describes first contact as that initial encounter of conquest in which the conquered attempt to know the conquerors by imitating them, by embodying them. Taussig uses the term "second" or "reverse contact" to refer to the moment when Western colonial powers confront the images of themselves as fashioned by their own colonized others (1993:xv, 249). He points to the visceralness and tactility of the embodied copy of colonizing figures—whether they are Cuna curing dolls made in the image of Europeans or the Hauka possession rites in which the Nigerian participants are possessed by personages of the French colonial administration (see also Stoller 1997). In these cases, the colonized, through a process of sympathetic magic and embodiment of the other, are tapping into the perceived powers of their colonizers. People of the Andes have been no exception in this realm of imitation, embodiment, and transformation of otherness. Many musical instruments that are associated today with Andean indigeneity are the product of Spanish conquest and colonization (see Stobart 2001; Turino 1984), and the production of chola clothing falls within these same historical processes of mimesis and mestizaje, a mixing of elements perceived to come from both indian and Spanish traditions(see Barragán 1992). When mestizo-creole women embody in musical sound, linguistic expression, and forms of dress what they perceive as indianness, they are moving from Taussig's second contact to a third, fourth, or fifth contact in the endless chain of mimesis. The magic of mimesis has taken one more turn, this time in the service of a national project.

Conclusion: Mothers of National Music

The singing bodies of mestizo-creole women imitated the dress, musical sound, and linguistic utterances of a perceived indian world. How did these bodies, engaged in the process of singing and mimesis, serve the nationalist body of Bolivia? Marcia Stephenson has suggested that the upper-class woman gained status as the imagined mother of the Bolivian nation, and the horrors of the Chaco War led to upper-class pacifist organizations and the emergence of a "social motherhood."[7] Another social motherhood may have been at work here: mestizo-creole women sang and mimetically became indian so these dangerous sounds could be tamed and put to the service of a nationalist narrative. The early stage careers of the women interviewed cover a period of 1940 to 1957, from just after the Chaco War to just after the 1952 Revolution. It was a period of intensified indigenist politics. Josefa Salmón, in her study of Bolivian indigenismo, discussed the renewed relevance in the 1940s of Franz Tamayo's book, *Creación de una pedagogía nacional*, which was first published in 1910; in this text, Tamayo suggested that the indian was the source of an authentic nationalism, the fountain of nationalist energies (Salmón 1997:77). At the same time, Tamayo also located the Bolivian source of thought and intelligence among mestizos. Mestizo-creole women, who in the 1940s began singing indian genres, transformed into a comfortable realm of Bolivian music what had previously been heard as noises that fueled the fears of landed elite.

I suggest that the symbolic mothering of Bolivian national music occurred through an otherwise taboo relation between white women and indian men. Diane Nelson discusses discourses of whitening and mestizaje in Guatemala, outlining how the policing of white women's sexuality goes hand in hand with acceptance of extramarital relations between white men and indian women (1999:219; see also Canessa, chap. 5; Weismantel 2001). When mestizo-creole women began singing music played by indian men, they became part of this otherwise prohibited dyad of white woman and indian man. White men and indian women may produce mestizo citizens, but white women and indian men engendered national music. The taboo relation was tolerated as long as the women remained single, and as long as they were carefully chaperoned in their activities. Through this symbolically taboo relation, previously marginalized and dangerous music became a safe main attraction for a pageant of Bolivian nationalism.

Acknowledgments

I greatly appreciate the time that Chela Rea Nogales, María Luisa Camacho, Norah Camacho, Irma Vásquez, María Luisa Tejada, Elsa Tejada, and Esperanza Tejada took to share their stories with me, and they did so with a great enthusiasm for the music they perform. I thank the director of Música de Maestros, Rolando Encinas, who has continued to allow me to perform intermittently with this ensemble and who facilitated contact with the women who are central to this chapter. In revising this work, I have benefited from the helpful comments and suggestions of Andrew Canessa, Julie Hemment, Beth Notar, Joshua Roth, Barbara Yngvesson, and anonymous reviewers at the University of Arizona Press. I alone am responsible for any shortcoming in the analysis of these pages. To Hampshire College I am grateful for the funding of part of this research through their summer faculty development grants in 1999, 2000, 2001, and 2002.

Notes

1. Lesley Gill's work on Aymara military recruits in Bolivia is an obvious exception to this trend (1997). In the context of story sambas in Brazil's Carnival, Alma Guillermoprieto also mentions the absence of the white woman and the black man (1990).

2. The Illimani is a snowcapped peak visible from the city of La Paz.

3. The singers' memories of vacation landscapes also might be contrasted with the memory of landscape among the Cumbales of Colombia. As documented by Joanne Rappaport (1994), the Cumbal landscape is remembered in relation to land struggles and in relation to the local social organizations and systems of authority.

4. For a reading of this period from the perspective of another prominent

campesino leader, see the biography of Antonio Alvarez Mamani (Ranaboldo and SEMTA 1987).

5. These compositions became an important part of the repertoire of Música de Maestros (see Bigenho 2002).

6. In my fieldwork I have never come across this many musical troupes in a single fiesta; memory and nostalgia may have led her to exaggerate the number of troupes present at this fiesta. In the late 1990s, the number of troupes that played pan pipes in Italaque numbered thirteen (Rolando Encinas, personal communication 2004).

7. In reference to this discussion, Stephenson (1999:25) details the formation of the *Legión Femenina de Educación Popular America* (Feminine Legion of Popular Education America).

Bibliography

Albó, Xavier. 1987. "From MNRistas to Kataristas to Katari." In *Resistance, Rebellion, and Consciousness in the Andean Peasant World: 18th to 20th Centuries*, ed. Steve J. Stern, 379–419. Madison: University of Wisconsin Press, 379–419.

Anderson, Benedict. 1991. *Imagined Communities: Reflections on the Origin and Spread of Nationalism*. Rev. ed. London: Verso.

Arze Aguirre, René Danilo. 1987. *Guerra y conflictos sociales: El caso rural boliviano durante la campaña del Chaco*. La Paz: CERES.

Attali, Jacques. 1985. *Noise: The Political Economy of Music*, trans. Brian Massumi. Minneapolis: University of Minnesota Press.

Barragán, Rossana. 1992. "Entre polleras, lliqllas, y ñañacas: Los mestizos y la emergencia de la *tercera república*." In *Etnicidad, economía, y simbolismo en los Andes: II Congreso internacional de etnohistoria, Coroico*, comp. Silvia Arze, Rossana Barragán, Laura Escobari, and Ximena Medinaceli. La Paz: HISBOL/IFEA SBH-ASUR, 85–127.

Bigenho, Michelle. 2002. *Sounding Indigenous: Authenticity in Bolivian Music Performance*. New York: Palgrave Macmillan.

de la Cadena, Marisol. 2000. *Indigenous Mestizos: The Politics of Race and Culture in Cuzco, Peru, 1919–1991*. Durham, N.C.: Duke University Press.

Gill, Lesley. 1997. "Creating Citizens, Making Men: The Military and Masculinity in Bolivia." *Cultural Anthropology*, vol. 12:527–50.

Grossberg, Lawrence. 1991. "Rock, Territorialization, and Power." *Cultural Studies* 5, no. 3:358–67.

Guillermoprieto, Alma. 1990. *Samba*. New York: Vintage.

Gutmann, Matthew C. 1996. *The Meanings of Macho: Being a Man in Mexico City*. Berkeley: University of California Press.

Hobsbawm, Eric, and Terence Ranger, eds. 1983. *The Invention of Tradition*. Cambridge: Cambridge University Press.

Malloy, James. 1989. *Bolivia: La revolución inconclusa*. La Paz: CERES.

McClary, Susan. 1991. *Feminine Endings: Music, Gender, and Sexuality*. Minneapolis: University of Minnesota Press.

Meisch, Lynn. 2002. *Andean Entrepreneurs: Otavalo Merchants and Musicians in the Global Arena*. Austin: University of Texas Press.

Montenegro, Carlos. 1943. *Nacionalismo y coloniaje: Su expresión en la prensa de Bolivia*. La Paz: Ediciones Autonomía.

Nelson, Diane. 1999. *A Finger in the Wound: Body Politics in Quincentennial Guatemala*. Berkeley: University of California Press.

Parker, Andrew, Mary Russo, Doris Sommer, and Patricia Yaeger. 1992. "Introduction." In *Nationalisms and Sexualities*, ed. Andrew Parker, Mary Russo, Doris Sommer, and Patricia Yaeger. New York: Routledge, 1–18.

Poole, Deborah. 1997. *Vision, Race, and Modernity: A Visual Economy of the Andean Image World*. Princeton: Princeton University Press.

Radcliffe, Sarah, and Sallie Westwood. 1996. *Remaking the Nation: Place, Identity, and Politics in Latin America*. New York: Routledge.

Ranaboldo, Claudia, and Unidad de Investigación SEMTA. 1987. *El camino perdido; chinkasqa ñan; armat thaki: Biografía del dirigente campesino kallawaya Antonio Alvarez Mamani*. La Paz: SEMTA.

Rappaport, Joanne. 1994. *Cumbe Reborn: An Andean Ethnography of History*. Chicago: University of Chicago Press.

Rivera Cusicanqui, Silvia. 1986. *Oprimidos pero no vencidos: Luchas del campesinado aymara y qhechwa de Bolivia, 1900–1980*. Ginebra: United Nations.

———. 1993. "La raíz: Colonizadores y colonizados." In *Violencias encubiertas en Bolivia I*, coordinadores Xavier Albó and Raúl Barrios. La Paz: CIPCA/Aruwiyiri, 27–139.

Rose, Tricia. 1994. *Black Noise: Rap Music and Black Culture in Contemporary America*. Middletown, Conn.: Wesleyan University Press.

Salmón, Josefa. 1997. *El espejo indígena: El discurso indigenista en Bolivia 1900–1956*. La Paz: Plural Editores-UMSA.

Sánchez Canedo, Walter. 1988. "El proceso de creación musical en el norte de Potosí." *Boletín*, vol. 7:1–18. Cochabamba: CENDOC-MB-PORTALES.

Savigliano, Marta. 1995. *Tango and the Political Economy of Passion*. Boulder, Colo.: Westview Press.

Stephenson, Marcia. 1999. *Gender and Modernity in Andean Bolivia*. Austin: University of Texas Press.

Stevens, Evelyn. 1973. "Marianismo: The Other Face of Machismo in Latin America." In *Male and Female in Latin America: Essays*, ed. Ann Pescatello, 89–102. Pittsburgh: University of Pittsburgh Press.

Stobart, Henry. 2001. "La flauta de la llama: Malentendidos musicales en los Andes." In *Identidades representadas: Performance, experiencia, y memoria en los Andes*, ed. Gisela Cánepa Koch, 93–115. Lima: Pontificia Universidad Católica del Perú.

Stoller, Paul. 1997. *Sensuous Scholarship*. Philadelphia: University of Pennsylvania Press.

Taller de Historia Oral Andina and Silvia Rivera Cusicanqui. 1990. "Indigenous Women and Community Resistance: History and Memory." In *Women and Social Change in Latin America*, ed. Elizabeth Jelin, 151–83. London and New Jersey: Zed Books/United Nations Research Institute for Social Development.

Tamayo, Franz. 1944 [1910]. *Creación de una pedagogía nacional*. La Paz: Editoriales de "El Diario."

Taussig, Michael. 1993. *Mimesis and Alterity: A Particular History of the Senses*. New York: Routledge.

Taylor, Diana. 1994. "Performing Gender: Las Madres de la Plaza de Mayo." In *Negotiating Performance: Gender, Sexuality, and Theatricality in Latin/o America*, ed. Diana Taylor and Juan Villegas, 275–305. Durham, N.C.: Duke University Press.

Taylor, Julie. 1998. *Paper Tangos*. Durham, N.C., and London: Duke University Press/Public Planet Books.

Turino, Thomas. 1984. "The Urban-Mestizo Charango Tradition in Southern Peru: A Statement of Shifting Identity." *Ethnomusicology* 28, no. 2:253–70.

———. 1993. *Moving Away from Silence: Music of the Peruvian Altiplano and the Experience of Urban Migration*. Chicago: University of Chicago Press.

Vila, Pablo. 1991. "Tango to Folk: Hegemony Construction and Popular Identities in Argentina." *Studies in Latin American Popular Culture*, vol. 10:105–39.

Waksman, Steve. 1999. *Instruments of Desire: The Electric Guitar and the Shaping of Musical Experience*. Cambridge: Harvard University Press.

Weismantel, Mary. 2001. *Cholas and Pishtacos: Stories of Race and Sex in the Andes*. Chicago: Chicago University Press.

Discography

Cooder, Ry. 1997. *Buena Vista Social Club*. Wea/Atlantic/Nonesuch.

Música de Maestros. 1998. *ReCanTanDo*. La Paz: Dayan Records.

Vives, Carlos. 1993. *Clásicos de la Provincia*. Mexico: Polygram Discos.

Interviews

Camacho Villegas, María Luisa. August 2000. La Paz.

Camacho Villegas, Norah Julieta. August 2000. La Paz.

Rea Nogales, Chela. August 2000. La Paz.

Tejada, Elsa. August 2001. La Paz.

Tejada, Esperanza. August 2001. La Paz.

Vásquez, Irma. August 2000. La Paz.

4

The Choreography of Territory, Agency, and Cultural Survival

The Vicuña Hunting Ritual "Chuqila"

Marcia Stephenson

Recent studies on the nation have called attention to the importance of the performative as a way of understanding how national narratives generate meaning and self-legitimation. Drawing from Judith Butler's work on the performance of gender norms, Joanne P. Sharp argues that the nation is not founded on a single "originary moment or culturally distinct essence" (1996:98). Instead, the nation is created through the process of reiteration of its symbols and narratives. Through ritualized repetition, narratives of the nation become both normative and "natural." They can be mobilized to incorporate sameness and exclude otherness by fixing the limits of a particular signifying space and transforming the "difference of space" into the "Sameness of Time," "Territory into Tradition," and the "People into One" (Sharp 1996:98; Bhabha 1990:300). Counternarratives performatively intervene in and disrupt this specular relationship between the nation's self-authorizing narratives and the people who are figured in and of its image when they evoke and interrogate the nation's totalizing boundaries at the same time as they mobilize alternative histories and agencies (Bhabha 1990:299–300).

Homi Bhabha describes the nation-space that results from this process as the "barred Nation," which he designates as "*It/Self*," because it has become alienated from its self-generating representations to become instead a space that is "*internally* marked by cultural difference and the heterogeneous histories of contending peoples, antagonistic authorities, and tense cultural locations" (299; emphasis in the original). The performative therefore also introduces the question of embodiment and location, to foreground the ways that narratives mobilize particular representations of gender, race, ethnicity, sexuality, and class, among others. Individual and collective bodies participate in competing and often contentious ways of nation-making as they negotiate the liminal spaces of cultural and political borderlands.

The Andean region is one example of a space where hegemonic and resistant narratives of national identity are mobilized in myriad conflicting ways. Indeed, the essays in this volume point to the variety of engagements that take place as individuals and collectives generate meaning at the limits of dominant narratives of the nation. In the performative context of nation-making in Andean Bolivia, the struggle for alternative narratives of nationhood has fundamentally structured indigenous mobilization. Aymara activist-intellectuals engaged in the decolonial movement for human rights, social justice, and gender equality push hegemonic nationalist discourses to a point of crisis because they link this struggle to the demand for territory and self-determination. They argue that the ethno-political struggle for the right to autonomous material and symbolic spaces of cultural reproduction and representation is a struggle for survival itself. Throughout the twentieth and twenty-first centuries, the native movement for territory and autonomy has exposed the ragged edges of prevailing national narratives, which, in response, have set into motion hegemonic nation-making in its most violent forms.

There are perhaps few examples of competing forms of "nation-making" more stark than the events that took place throughout the Bolivian *altiplano*, or highland plateau, in the years preceding the Chaco War (1932–1935). During these years, the indian movement to reclaim autonomy and self-determination, known as the movement of the *caciques-apoderados*, was based on the search to recover land titles indian communities had purchased during Spanish colonial rule. Due to the increasing encroachment on indigenous lands by large landholders or *hacendados* during the 1910s and 1920s, Aymara leaders used these titles to engage in a legal struggle to protect their communities' boundaries. The government upheld the claims of the hacendados in most instances and deployed battalions in the indigenous communities to seize agitators and quell the violence. Throughout the altiplano, indian leaders were arrested or killed as a result of the actions they undertook to safeguard their communities. Once the Chaco War started, indians labeled as instigators were forcibly conscripted and sent off to carry out their "patriotic duty" at the front lines, from where few returned (Mamani Condori 1991). For those engaged in the study of nation-making at the margins, there is no mistaking one of the ironies of this undeclared war against Bolivia's indigenous peoples. The battalions deployed in the countryside for the purposes of occupying indigenous communities, pursuing "troublemakers," and protecting hacendados from the threat of violence were named for some of the most prominent heroes and founding fathers of the republic: Bolívar, Sucre, Murillo, and Abaroa. Once the Chaco war was under way, moreover, mestizo townspeople and urban elites could avoid going to war against Paraguay by volunteering instead for the Civic Legion, a military unit formed expressly to subdue organized indigenous movements inside the country. This illustration brings to light some of the ways in which nationalist discourses violently reinscribe themselves when faced with a crisis situation. Moreover, it unequivocally shows how in Bolivia indigenous peoples still remain disenfranchised from the imagined community, the borders of which are policed by very real armed forces.

This chapter examines how narratives are deployed performatively by different groups to make very distinct claims about the nation. It argues that the movement to reconstitute native territory and restore traditional forms of governance mobilizes alternative, subaltern histories that resist the modern imperative to forget the past. The revitalization of native ways of knowing, as Carlos Mamani Condori so eloquently argues, serves as a vital cultural and political matrix that enables indigenous peoples to imagine a future (2000).

Indigenous Peoples Reclaiming the Past and Mobilizing Alternative Knowledges

Over the past quarter century, the indigenous struggle for autonomy and self-determination in the Bolivian Andes has been increasingly linked to the critical reexamination of prevailing nationalist and historiographic paradigms. As early as 1969, for example, with the publication of *La revolución india*, Fausto Reinaga, the influential theorist of decolonizing *indianista* discourse, argued that the indigenous struggle for power and knowledge must necessarily be tied to the recuperation of native historical memory. The groundbreaking work of Aymara historian Roberto Choque Canqui documenting the trajectory of native historical memory as expressed through the ongoing movement to retain colonial territorial boundaries has impacted greatly on decolonizing methodologies of struggle.[1] Choque Canqui's important publications and those of other Aymara intellectuals underscore the relationship between alternative epistemologies and the formation of a contestatory Andean cultural politics. Native peoples reclaim the past, challenging dominant accounts of national history through the retelling of ancient stories (Smith 1999:33–34). The persistence of these stories in the present counters normative histories that attempt to marginalize indigenous peoples by positioning them as a dogged obsolescence that threatens the coherence of the modern nation-state. Indeed, these stories of survival establish a crucial link between the past and the present, a link that affirms the fact that in spite of the ongoing history of colonialism and repression, indigenous historical memory, conveyed performatively through oral history, dance, weaving, and song, among other ritual forms, has persisted for more than five hundred years. The aim of these stories is not to bring back a utopian past, but instead to see how the past is being articulated and mobilized for the deployment of specific identities and representations in the present (cf. Shohat 2000:136).

Maori cultural critic Linda Tuhiwai Smith has argued that "coming to know the past has been part of the critical pedagogy of decolonization. To hold alternative histories is to hold alternative knowledges. The pedagogical implication of this access to alternative knowledges is that they can form the basis of alternative ways of doing things" (1999:34). Writing about indigenous oral narratives from the Canadian Yukon Territory, Julie Cruikshank similarly contends that alternative histories are complex constructions of the imaginary grounded in the material conditions of local practices (2002:20). Therefore, oral histories "have social histories, and they acquire meanings in the situations in which they emerge, in situations where they are used, and in interactions between narrators and listeners." Even though many of the stories told by indigenous peoples are rooted in ancient traditions, "their telling emerges at the intersections of power and ideas where larger forces impinge directly on local experience" (20–21).

In the case of the Bolivian Andes, one way to understand the narrativized relationship between the past, present, and the future is through the phrase *qhip nayra* or "future-past," whereby the Aymara community looks to the past as a model for future action. Reflecting on the significance of native historical interpretation, Aymara historian Carlos Mamani Condori explains that the word *nayra* literally means "eye," but it also refers to the past, as with the expression *nayray ukhamax* ("this is the way it used to be") (14). The past, in other words, can be perceived or envisioned from the perspective of present circumstances. In contrast, Mamani Condori continues, the word *qhipa*, literally the "back," is used to convey that which comes afterward, the future. The phrase *qhiparu nayraru uñtas sartañani*, "looking back [to the past] we will move forward [into the future]" suggests that the past informs and is a part of the present and the future (1992:14). Mamani Condori's analysis points to a spatial relationship between the action of recounting native histories and the construction of alternative epistemologies. Indeed, this notion of time expressed in "qhip nayra" cannot be separated from the Aymara concept of space, or *pacha*. *Pacha* has many nuanced meanings, including, for example, the spatial relationship between agricultural practices that are linked to the changing seasons and to the community's distribution of lands in diverse ecological systems (12). It also conveys symbolic meaning, referring to life and death, here and now, fertility, nourishment, and protection (13). Mamani Condori explains that pacha brings together history and society in the space of the ayllu community (14). The communities, even though they have been fragmented by colonialism, continue to be a dynamic, performative space for Aymara social, cultural and juridical practices (9–10).

This relationship between the retelling of alternative histories in the context of the contemporary, material circumstances of the community and the forging of an alternative forum independent from the Euro-hegemonic nation-state, suggests that stories play a vital role in the mapping of spatial or territorial boundaries (see de Certeau 1984:126). These narrative rituals, in Stephen Muecke's words, set up this struggle for space, "both in terms of real space (for instance, land rights) and the more metaphorical space of representation (whose 'image' will count?)" (1992:2).

Historian Thérèse Bouysse-Cassagne and anthropologist Olivia Harris similarly emphasize the relation between the struggle for metaphorical and territorial spaces of representation when they point to the importance of physical space for shaping native narratives. In Andean Bolivia, the Aymara "read" the geographical contours that surround them: mountain peaks, territorial boundary markers, crossroads, and merging rivers. In their reading of these geographic landmarks, the Aymara also emphasize their relationship to their ancestors, neighbors, and deities. Performative forms of memorization such as the *ch'allas*, or oral litanies prompted by alcohol, can last for many hours as participants enumerate the reality of the world around them. According to Bouysse-Cassagne and Harris, the early Spanish evangelizers were not incorrect when they identified these telluric rites as some of the most egregious forms of idolatry. By attempting to abolish those practices that involved alternative spatial and temporal relationships, the Spanish tried not only to eliminate certain heretical rites but also to suppress native ways of knowing and thinking, both at the individual and collective levels (Bouysse-Cassagne and Harris 1987:12–13).

If the narrativization of the struggle for native epistemologies takes on spatial implications, prevailing nationalist discourses, historically, have also attempted to plot the geopolitical spaces of cultural identification by deploying particular representations of race, gender, sexuality, and class, as Andrew Canessa so clearly demonstrates in the introduction to this volume. In a recent study of nationalism, colonialism, and spatiality in late-nineteenth-century Bolivia, Seemin Qayum argues that colonialist discourses depended on the fueling of particular imaginative geographies and histories in order to appropriate the so-called blank spaces on the map (2002:277). Colonialist discourses structured nationalist ideologies of race and ethnicity as well as geographic and territorial demarcations, including the all too familiar dichotomy between metropolitan center and rural periphery that marks the divide between civilization and barbarism: "Just as colonialism formed a geographical nexus between metropolis and periphery, the internal colonial hierarchies were also present spatially in the distinction between the capital, La Paz, and its hinterland, the town (*pueblo de vecinos*) and surrounding indian countryside, and the nation and its frontiers—all of which had their specific colonial derivation" (279–80). Qayum draws on René Zavaleta Mercado's study of seigneurial space, the feudally organized, inward-looking enclaves of the hacienda-landholding elite: "For Zavaleta, Bolivian regionalism, the sort of regional factionalism that led to the Federal War in 1899, signified nothing more than the incapacity to imagine, to conceptualize and to construct *national* space. . . . By contrast, Zavaleta distinguishes Andean space as having been integral, collective and all-encompassing" (285; emphasis in the original). Indeed, in sharp contrast to seigneurial space, deeply rooted in the Andean imaginary and fundamental to the successful exchange of diverse goods and services, is an understanding of space and national territory that encompasses a variety of ecological systems, including the flat lands of the Pacific coast, the high plateaus and valleys of the Andes, and the Amazonian plains (cf. Choque Quispe and Mamani Condori 2002).

Qayum's analysis confirms the idea that Bolivian nationalist discourses have been unable to convey the sense of "deep, horizontal comradeship" that is fundamental to Benedict Anderson's depiction of the nation as an imagined community (1991:7). As Javier Sanjinés puts it, "At the present time, La Paz is the best example of a dominant culture that does not *transculturate* with the Aymara or mestizo culture. The dominant culture is historically responsible for this situation. Due to its exclusivity, it has been incapable of generating creative and *transculturating* individuals from within. For this reason, Bolivia never had a José María Arguedas, someone capable of becoming a nexus between two worlds: the western and the indigenous" (Chávez 2001:8; emphasis in original). The ambivalence or impossibility of a unified people underlying Bolivian national narratives is further evident in their inability to construct a consensual genealogy of origin. Thus, while urban elite and mestizo cultures honor Simón Bolívar as the founding father of the nation-state, Bolivia's Andean indigenous peoples look to the eighteenth-century Aymara insurgents Túpak Katari and Bartolina Sisa, embodied symbols of the overturning of colonial order.[2] The tenacity of Andean contestatory genealogies of origin disturbs the elite culture's bid for "cultural supremacy and historical priority" (Bhabha 1990:307), and instead gives precedence to alternative historical narratives.

It is to these contentious, narrativized spaces that the essay now turns, to focus on the traditional Aymara dance known as *chuqila* that depicts an ancient vicuña hunting ritual.

Performative Narratives and Counternarratives of Nation-Making

While there is not an abundance of information about the dance, this discussion pieces together details from written sources such as colonial chronicles, *visitas de idolatrías*, histories, and more contemporary studies, as well as from two video recordings of the dance, including John Cohen's 1986 version from Peru and the version filmed in 1993 at Puerto Pérez, Bolivia, by the Aymara nongovernmental organization known as the Taller de Historia Oral Andina (THOA). Analysis of the chuqila ritual reminds us that cultural productions and expressions achieve meaning when they are perceived through, or performed in, a particular ideological framework. They do not carry an essential or innate signification outside of these frames of reference.[3] In the pages that follow, I examine the ways that the dance has been used to consolidate different forms of nation-making. With the exception of Cohen and THOA's video recordings, chuqila signifies a primitive aesthetic in hegemonic accounts. During the colonial period, chroniclers' descriptions of the dance confirm the idea of the indian as an idolatrous savage, while, during the republican period (late nineteenth and twentieth centuries), accounts of the dance corroborate other writings of the time that declare indians to have figured importantly in a remote past that is prior to national history. In the present, their continuing existence holds the nation back from attaining modernity. These accounts ultimately stage the disappearance of indigenous peoples from the national imaginary.

Yet, the dance clearly exceeds this normative ideological frame; certainly it has never been incorporated as a cultural symbol of national authenticity into easily consumable urban folkloric performances. THOA's interest in the chuqila ritual highlights an alternate framework of interpretation that counters hegemonic nationalist representations. For this group of Aymara activist-intellectuals involved in the movement to reconstitute native territory during the 1980s and 1990s, the chuqila ritual choreographs sustaining narratives about exchange and reciprocity between different ethnic communities. Through dance, the community forges a spatial arena where the topographical and temporal complexities of indigenous agency are visibly rooted between the struggles of the past and the circumstances of the present. This arena, or *locus proprius* maintains, in Michel de Certeau's words, "a difference rooted in an affiliation that is opaque and inaccessible to both violent appropriation and learned cooptation. It is the unspoken foundation of affirmations that have *political* meaning to the extent that they are based on a *realization of coming from a 'different' place* (different, not opposite) on the part of those whom the omnipresent conquerors dominate" (1986:229; emphasis in original). The mobilization of participation in this way suggests that for indigenous projects of nation-making, the organizing principles of the chuqila dance exceed Emilio Vásquez's observation that Andean choreography is simply a harmonious landscape of man and mountains, earth and soul, set in motion (1944:68). In the context of the native movement to reconstitute territory and self-determination, the importance of the chuqila ritual resides in the way that the dance enacts social, gendered, political, and economic identities that profoundly disorder the dominant narratives of western modernity and nationalism and the systemic violence of colonial and modern state institutions. The chuqila ritual performs an alternative understanding of community and territoriality, one that emphasizes the rich bio- and cultural diversity of the area, and is expressed in community ritual and storytelling (cf. Choque Quispe and Mamani Condori 2002).

Archaeological evidence indicates that the dance, which represents the ritual hunt or *chaku* of wild camelids, predates the Inca empire (Lavallée et al. 1995). In the chaku, a community of hunters, or chuqilas, pursued their quarry by forming an enormous circle that could extend as far as several miles. The hunters all carried different kinds of weapons and traps that they employed as they slowly moved inward toward the center of the circle. In this way they were able to catch vicuñas, guanacos, deer, birds, and other prey as the circle became smaller and smaller. As a communal form of hunting, the chaku represented the mobilization of the exchange of goods and services in the cooperative practice known as *ayni* (Vásquez 1944:69). Vásquez identifies four parts or movements to the dance. The first is that of the farewell, as the dancers enact the melancholic moment of departure. The second movement pertains to the exultant carrying out of the hunt itself, and the third performs the solemn moment wherein the noblest animals captured are sacrificed and buried. The fourth movement is that of the successful return home. This point marks a kind of transition whereby the rewards of the hunt are linked to the complementary efforts of the harvest. According to Vásquez, the music of the fourth movement implicitly draws attention to the convergence of different ecosystems (71). Chuqila performs this moment when the members of pastoral and agricultural communities come together to exchange their goods, thereby guaranteeing the survival of both communities for another year.

Most studies of the chuqila dance underscore that it is one of the oldest dances still performed in the Andean region. Emilio Romero noted in 1929 that "from among the multitude of indigenous dances . . . one of the oldest and most pure, is the one known by the name of *chokelas*" (1929:107), while Vásquez made the similar claim in 1944 that "without a doubt, the chokelas is the oldest dance of Peru; it probably comes to us from very remote times" (1944:68). These comments fix indigenous peoples in what Jane C. Desmond refers to as a "'primitive' aesthetic," because they present a ritual like chuqila as timeless and, hence "outside of time" or history. "If the dances cannot be contemporary, then neither, we are to assume, are the people who perform them" (1997b:47). From the earliest reports of the Spanish chroniclers, the dance was described as depicting primitive and semi-savage times and peoples. For example, Juan de Matienzo, in his *Gobierno del Perú* (1567), identified the "chuqilas" as idolatrous hunters: "Of these there are only a few—and the ones living understand only how to kill wild cattle—and in their idolatrous practices they are sorcerers" (1910 [1567] part 2: 179–80), and Ludovico Bertonio noted in his *Vocabulario de la Lengua Aymara* (1612), that the "vicuña hunter who makes a living from the hunt in the *punas*" is "choquela, lari lari" (1984 [1612]:107/1) and that he is a "wild person" (89/2). Bertonio defines "lari lari" as "Wild men, people from the puna who recognize no Authority" (191/2). *Lari*, as will be examined in greater detail below, also signifies "the brother of the mother" and, by association, most of the male relatives of the female line are referred to as lari (191/2). Verónica Cereceda reminds us that one word for "wild," *cimarrón*, is etymologically linked to *cima* (summit or top), the highest part of the mountain, precisely the area where the chuqila hunters lived (1990:79). Thus, for the early Spanish evangelizers, the chuqila hunter who obeyed no law personified a form of primitive wildness and animality that consolidated the idea of heresy and a specific landscape, in this case, the high mountains.[4]

With the campaigns of extirpation, the Spanish worked actively to suppress Andean ceremonial rituals such as chuqila. During the sixteenth century, for example, the inspector general for the extirpation of idolatries, Cristóbal de Albornoz, underscored the vital relationship between dance and native historical memory when he called for the prohibition of ritualized indigenous expression. In particular, he found dances in which the participants wore animal masks and used conch shells to be most dangerous because they celebrated the *wak'as*, or Andean sacred deities, and helped keep fresh in mind pre-Columbian rituals: "They use many types of dances to celebrate their *guacas* [wak'as]. In particular, one should be forewarned of the dances where the dancers are done up with seashells called *mollos* and musical figures using animal heads and clothing made from the animal skins of tigers, lions, *ozcollos*, deer, and serpents, and other animals from the mountains. These dances should be destroyed, even if they are of value, because when they are seen, the memory of past rituals comes to mind" (cited in Duviols 1967:21–22). The colonial chronicles thus foreground the significance of a dance like chuqila as a performance of savagery that is dangerous precisely because it functions as a mnemonic bridge between the past and the present.

In spite of the efforts on the part of the Church to eliminate native rituals, many survived nonetheless. In 1913, the prominent folklorist M. Rigoberto Paredes, called his readers' attention to the persistence of many Bolivian indigenous dances, which even in the case of those that have undergone transformation, resist disappearance (1981:11). As a member of the Geographic Society of La Paz, Paredes belonged to an elite creole institution that was engaged in the civilizing project of nation-building. As was typical of the role played by geographic societies of the time, the Geographic Society of La Paz joined national and international debates on issues related to the development of culture, geography, the sciences, and the economy (Qayum 2002:281–84). Qayum observes that "geographical societies served as vehicles for exploration and inventory of exploitable and extractable natural resources and, in similar fashion, the categorization and attempted assimilation—or eradication—of indigenous human groups; territorial delimitation and consolidation; and, not least, national and patriotic self-definition and identity formation" (282–83). One of the primary folklorists of the group, Paredes published extensively on the region surrounding La Paz, covering indigenous history and culture, as well as prominent native myths and folklore practices (284).

In an essay first published in 1913 in the society's journal, the *Boletín de la Sociedad Geográfica de La Paz*, and later in *El arte folklórico de Bolivia*, Paredes claimed that Bolivia's indigenous peoples had a great passion for dance, and that as a result they willingly spent vast sums of money to celebrate their many festivals. Paredes supported his argument by citing from the 1827 Spanish edition of William Robertson's *Historia de América*. Robertson argued that, for indigenous peoples, dance was much more than a favorite pastime; rather, it constituted a fundamental part of life: "It is true that among them dance should not be called a diversion; rather it is a serious and important occupation that blends in with the circumstances of public and private life" (Robertson, cited in Paredes 1981:10). In keeping with the geographical mind-set of the society, which was to compile detailed information, statistics, and other kinds of descriptive categorization, Paredes classified Bolivian dances according to three types, distinguishing among those that are "authentically indigenous," those introduced or imposed by the Spanish, and those brought by black slaves (10). According to the folklorist, dances that are autochthonous can be differentiated from other dance traditions because of the combined use of feathers and animal skins worn with the clothing (11). Among the dances he includes in this category is the chuqila ritual. Because dance is a "discourse of the body," as Desmond notes, it can be subject to interpretations that attempt to associate racial difference with biological difference (Desmond 1997b:36–37). In his description of indigenous dances, Paredes locates racial difference in the native, who essentially embodies a timeless, natural world of animal skins and feathers. Paredes observes in his essay that in the past, native dances served as performative bodily narratives that pointed to alternative histories and memories. The dance's "objective was to remember the past and worship the suffering gods" (1981:37). The use of the imperfect verb tense in the original Spanish suggests that while this objective was a motivating force in the past, it is so no longer. Instead, he suggests that in contemporary times the relationship between ritual dance performance and historical memory has been ruptured, with performances continuing primarily as colorful spectacles that have been emptied of any larger cultural significance. His descriptions depict the present-day dance practitioners within the autonomous frame of a festive, folkloric image of indianness (cf. Brady 2002:151), that is ultimately inoffensive because it has been separated from its historical context. In a somewhat offhand remark, however, Paredes does note that during his time there had been renewed efforts to put a stop to these performances: "It seems that recently there are efforts to wipe them out by means of municipal ordinances that would make their representation onerous, or would prohibit them from taking place at all" (11). In spite of Paredes's observations to the contrary, these dances apparently caused enough concern to justify ordinances discouraging their continued performance.

How does a dance like chuqila produce anxiety in hegemonic nationalist discourses? What are the dynamics of mobilization elaborated in this cultural performance? An alternative reading of chuqila proposes an interpretation radically different from a spectacularized depiction that focuses on the authenticity of structure, costume, and movement, but overlooks how the performance mobilizes alternative epistemologies. Sabine MacCormack, for example, has observed that, unlike imperial ceremonies that soon lost their relevance once the Inca had been defeated, Andean rural celebrations survived "because they gave voice to the ecology of the Andes and to Andean concepts of humanity. Every year the crops were planted and harvested, and every year they were exposed to the same natural hazards" (MacCormack 1991:180). Writing on the significance of communal, ritual performance, Mary Douglas comments that "the rituals enact the form of social relations and in giving these relations visible expression they enable people to know their own society. The rituals work upon the body politic through the symbolic medium of the physical body" (Douglas 1992:128). A ritual dance like chuqila, therefore, that rallies the entire community, is key to the mobilization of particular social identities that are culturally, spatially, and historically situated. Not surprisingly then, at the turn of the twentieth century when Paredes was writing his article, these rituals clearly still produced enough anxiety to warrant renewed efforts prohibiting their performance. Paredes's essay suggests, in fact, that far from serving as a colorful image of the Bolivian nation-state (cf. Shay 2002), a dance such as chuqila produced anxiety as late as the beginning of the twentieth century precisely for the reasons stated above, because it engages alternative understandings of community and territoriality that are not necessarily rooted in prevailing nationalist discourses (see Brady 2002:151; Foster 1998:9). It is undoubtedly not a coincidence therefore that at the time efforts were stepped up to prohibit dances such as chuqila during the late nineteenth and the early twentieth centuries, the Bolivian state and the landholding elite were aggressively engaged in the fragmentation and seizure of indigenous lands.[5]

Recent studies on dance theory can enhance the understanding of how meaning is performed in the embodied narrativization of the dynamic between spatiality or territoriality and the mobilization of alternative epistemologies in the Andean region. In the introduction to her edited volume *Corporealities: Dancing, Knowledge, Culture, and Power*, Susan Foster argues that dance theory enables us to see the role of the body in the production of collective and individual social relations, human agency, gendered narratives, and history and memory (1996:xv). Desmond has similarly observed that dance is a product *and* a process that foregrounds relationships between "the public display of bodily motion and the articulation of social categories of identity, of their transmission, transformation, perception, and enactment" (1997a:3). The study of dance as both product and process allows us to "trace historical and geographic changes in complex kinaesthetic systems and study comparatively symbolic systems based on language, visual representation, and movement" (1997b:29–30). Randy Martin suggestively claims that through dancing it is possible to situate mobilization as a dynamic mediating between process and product. The process is dance's "capacity for movement," while the product "is not the aesthetic effect of the dance but the materialized identity accomplished through the performativity of movement" (1998:4). Just as identity is materialized through the performativity of movement, so too is the terrain constituted as it is traversed by the dancing bodies.

Susan Foster's essay "Choreographies of Gender" is a useful source for thinking about the choreography of alternative narratives in the Andean region. Foster reads Judith Butler's theory of gender performance through dance theory to introduce the concept of choreography, or "the traditions of codes and conventions through which meaning is construed in dance" (1998:6). By bringing choreography into discussions of corporeality and materiality, attention is drawn to bodily gestures and movement, which, as with speech, play a vital role in the social construction of gendered and racialized identities (6–7). Foster's discussion bolsters this essay's claim that a dance ritual such as chuqila choreographs particular economic, gendered, and racialized identities that are accomplished individually and collectively as they traverse a given territory. Each ritual performance follows a choreographic idea of biodiversity, exchange, and reciprocity between different communities.[6] As a ritual dance, chuqila is particularly significant because it enacts the moment of convergence between communities, the threshold space where differences become blurred. From the point of view of the early twenty-first century, we can say that chuqila choreographs dancing bodies across the contested terrain that delineates the margins of the modern Bolivian nation-state.

THOA's film version of the ritual performance emphasizes the ways that chuqila articulates what Richard Schechner has referred to in another context as a "paradigm of liminality" (Schechner 1985:295). The opening camera shots pan across the landscape that marks the meeting point between Lake Titicaca and the surrounding hills, and includes a few close-ups of llamas. The Aymara voice-over, translated in subtitles on the screen, tells the viewer that "the importance of the chuqila ritual is that it is one of the oldest rites that the Aymara culture preserves." As the shot continues to move across the landscape, the subtitles provide the following description of chuqila: "The myth of chuqila refers to the relationship between the unhunted vicuña (*wari*) and the llama, the virgin maiden and the married woman, the uncultivated field with the cultivated, the fish never caught. The wild plant, the light at dusk and bright sunlight, in this way becoming a ritual." This script, emphasizing movement and transition rather than stasis and fixity, is quoted almost directly from Thérèse Bouysse-Cassagne and Olivia Harris's essay "Pacha: En torno al pensamiento aymara." This pioneer study meticulously analyzes colonial texts to cull from them fundamental concepts of Aymara thought and their relationship to the idea of space and time as expressed in traditional myths. The reference to Bouysse-Cassagne and Harris's text in THOA's video points us suggestively to the epistemological paradigm described above as *qhip nayra* or "future-past." THOA's project looks back to the past to recover native agency and an alternative model of nation-making.

Written sources from the colonial period on Aymara mythology link chuqila to the ancient temporal division known as the second age, the age of *puruma* or *purunpacha*. According to Joan de Santacruz Pachacuti Yamqui's *Relación de antigüedades deste reyno del Pirú*, in purunpacha a particular time and space converge (1950 [1879]: 210). Purunpacha has two meanings, the first of which alludes to a wild or savage and barbarous time, while the second refers to a space that is uninhabited, uncultivated, or without culture, *inculto*, a barren wilderness (Duviols 1993:21). Also drawing from Santacruz Pachacuti's *Relación*, Bouysse-Cassagne and Harris associate puruma with diffused light and nightfall, a twilight space where borders become blurred and ambiguous (Bouysse-Cassagne and Harris 1987:22). The dark, desertlike and wild space known as puruma symbolizes a society without a state, a world of hunters called chuqila.

This twilight space is also associated with lightning. Chronicler Bernabé Cobo notes that the indians had three names for lightning or thunder, the first and foremost of which was *chuquiila*, "which means a golden resplendence" (1956:160). Because of its association with lightning and the high mountains, puruma is additionally related to the wak'as, or ancestors located in the lofty mountain peaks. The chuqila hunter is thus one who embodies various intersecting borders, including that between man and the gods, and between the savage state (chuqila) and that which is civilized (Aymara culture). As described by Bouysse-Cassagne and Harris and later punctuated by THOA's video, chuqila marks the place of convergence or the moment of transition between binary opposites: "its relationship to the Aymara is like that of the unhunted vicuña in reference to the llama, the virgin maiden with the married woman, the barren land (puruma) with the cultivated, the light at dusk and bright sunlight" (Bouysse-Cassagne and Harris 1987:27). In those spaces that border this world of strange forces, shapes and colors become blurred (27). Cereceda has found the same characteristic with certain woven bags called *talegas*. The border design is composed of a subtle gradation of colors, creating at the edges of these bags a diffused hue (1987). According to Bouysse-Cassagne and Harris, this textile design reproduces the same cultural code as puruma. In contrast to the first age, known as *taypi*, where opposites merge in a central point, the power of puruma occurs at the borders, where that which is normally one becomes divided into symmetrical and sometimes monstrous pairs or doubles (Bouysse-Cassagne and Harris 1987:26–27). Yet, chuqila suggests that these binary opposites are neither fixed nor still; rather they are already in motion, traversing space, in a "mutual displacement of forces" (Martin 1998:3). This flow of motion is best visualized in the figure of the vicuña.

Most studies of the role of camelids in the Andean region distinguish between the domesticated animals, such as the llama and the alpaca, and undomesticated animals, such as the vicuña and the guanaco. During pre-Columbian times, for example, all of the animals were valued for their meat, skins, wool, and excrement, but the vicuña and the guanaco in particular were directly linked to the supernatural world, often acting on behalf of the gods, or in their service (López Rivas 1976:52; Dedenbach-Salazar Sáenz 1990:40). Guamán Poma notes, for example, that under the rule of the Inca, vicuñas and guanacos were referred to as "yntipllaman" or "llamas of the Sun" (1980 286[288], vol. 1:203).

The relationship between the vicuña and the divine is clarified somewhat in recent publications. For example, Carlos Condarco Santillán, in his study of the Uru peoples, offers a detailed description of the god Wari, known simultaneously as the god of fire and of the nether world (1999:32–33). As the god of fire and thunder, Wari figured as a fundamental element of the cosmos, probably around 20,000 to 10,000 B.C., during the period of hunting and collecting represented in the altiplano region of Lake Titicaca by the Viscachani culture. As the culture became increasingly sedentary, Wari came to be known as the god of agriculture (Condarco Santillán 1999:50). Pierre Duviols's research similarly indicates that Wari, or Huari, was the god who created the universe, one who was capable of many physical transformations and who was also a kind of cultural hero (1973:156). In some oral narratives, Wari represented a mythic creature, a light-haired man with the body of a vicuña (Enrique Oblitas Poblete, cited in Duviols 1973:154).[7] Indeed, the vicuña was also referred to by the name Wari. For Condarco Santillán, this designation was not arbitrary: "Analogies can be made between the reddish-brown wool of the vicuña and its speed when running and the attributes of fire. For the imagination and mythopoetic understanding of the ancient Andeans, the vicuña, streaking across the endless pampa, would seem like an errant flame carried by the wind" (1999:52–53). As a symbol of the perpetual motion of fire and lightning, the vicuña traverses the boundary between light and dark, the divine and the terrestrial, culture and savagery, the Aymara, and the chuqila hunters.

Pierre Duviols has studied the ritual significance of the meeting of closely linked opposites, including sky/earth, fire/water, high lands/low lands, hunting/cultivation, male/female, self/other in his work on colonial inquisition documents, wherein the narratives of the ancient Huari (or Wari) and Llacuaz ayllus were violently extracted from the indigenous peoples of Cajatambo, Conchucos, and Huaylas during the early-seventeenth-century campaigns of extirpation (1973:155; see also 1986). Whereas the Huari were more sedentary peoples from lower, agriculturally rich lands, the Llacuaz, or children of the lightning bolt, were associated with the so-called masculine traits of untamed nature and hunting. In ancient times, the two ayllus warred with each other until they finally declared a treaty that was observed annually during the autumn solstice in June. Under the new relations of the treaty, the Llacuaz offered the Huari food from the hunt as well as textiles woven from the fiber of the camelids, while the Huari provided corn, corn beer, and potatoes. This complex annual ceremony personified the complementarity of two different groups coming together for the purposes of exchange and reciprocity, even as it articulated and affirmed the distinct cultural identity of each (Duviols 1986:lx–lxi). Although the groups existed first as two autonomous and self-supporting communities, they eventually reached certain agreements regarding coexistence and cooperation, going so far as to establish common settlements and decision-making places at the boundary line where the two bio-ethnically diverse communities intersected (Duviols 1973:184). One way to comprehend this socioeconomic dynamic is through the spatial and temporal lens of the three pre-Columbian mythic periods of the region, taypi, puruma, and auca, whereby difference is continually recovered and mobilized through combination, contrast, and rejection.[8]

The Choreography of Cultural Survival

A closer reading of the chuqila dance provides insight into the cultural and political implications of the temporary merging of two bio-ethnically diverse communities and the broader discussion of nation-making. Aymara communities in Peru and Bolivia still perform the dance today, most notably in areas around Lake Titicaca. Not coincidentally, this is the area generally considered to be the "locus of domestication" of the llama and the alpaca, and the place where the largest number of wild and domesticated species of camelids were to be found (Murra 1965:187). According to Harry Tschopik, although the dance represents the ritual hunt of the vicuña, its purpose is to celebrate the harvest and to produce abundant crops the following year (Tschopik 1946:567). This is the time of year that the Pleiades appear in the sky, and, while this cluster of stars is linked to the cultivation of corn, it is also believed to ensure the health and fertilization of animals, including the camelids (Bauer and Dearborn 1995:56). Chroniclers of the dance note that it begins at dusk and continues throughout the night and on into the next day. In some instances the festivities span two or three nights and days. Dancing is periodically interrupted as community members take breaks to eat and socialize. In the version of chuqila filmed by THOA, one of the most important moments of the ritual takes place when adolescent girls sing and dance the "Canto de las doncellas al wari (vicuña)" to lure the vicuña down from the high puna so that it can be hunted. In other versions, a chorus of women dance and sing, carrying long poles that represent a fence for capturing the vicuña (Tschopik 1946:567; Cohen 1986). This ritual symbolically brings together the chuqila hunters from the mountains and the young girls from the agricultural community who are ready to find husbands. The words to the song as translated into Spanish by THOA are:

Canto de las doncellas al wari

> bajando, bajando de la
> cumbre estoy entrando
>
> bajando, bajando de los
> cerros estoy bajando
>
> bajando chuqilay
>
> de los cerros estuve bajando
> la "charque de Taruja"
> se me ha terminado
>
> de los cerros estuve bajando
> estiércol se me ha terminado
>
> chuqilay
>
> guía punta, lanza
> tropezando en tus pies
>
> cáete al suelo
> cría punta, lanza

habían sacrificado, en la
víspera de nuestro creador

cría de wari habían sacrificado
chuqilay

The words to the song depict this age-old alliance based on trade and exchange between the hunters and herders who lived in the high mountains and the Aymara agricultural communities inhabiting the more fertile valleys. Thus, the ritual maps out a series of clearly demarcated territorial and economic relations.

The fundamental narrative of chuqila choreographs both a past *and* a present relationship to a specific material and social space. The mobilization of these interdependent social, spatial, and economic relations is foregrounded through the dancing and singing. Returning to the song "Canto de las doncellas al wari," the words, as they appear on the screen of THOA's version, subtitled in Spanish, employ an abundance of verbs in the present progressive tense, thereby emphasizing movement through space. This movement is reiterated through the eye of the camera that follows the dancers across the landscape. The voice-over in John Cohen's video version of the dance also calls attention to the mobilization of bodies through space: "In the altiplano of Peru this ritual has been performed by peasant communities for centuries. The song describes travel across the landscape, through mountains and villages that are a part of the ritual. It uses names whose meanings have been forgotten. Some are places of female power; others have lunar, masculine references. The final villages named are the actual communities near Muqaraya." Cohen's narrative suggests that there is also movement through time, spanning early mythical places whose names are no longer remembered, to more familiar, local landscapes rooted in the present.

As the dancing bodies traverse the landscape, identities are mobilized in different ways. According to Cohen, "the men become masked clowns. They are hunters who are supernatural beings." In the version filmed by THOA as well as in other written accounts, men carry stuffed vicuñas or wear them draped across their backs. The male performers are men, and yet not men, themselves and yet not themselves. Melding into the figures of the animals, clowns, and gods, they dance through what Schechner refers to as the liminal spaces of "'characterization,' 'representation,' 'imitation,' 'transportation,' and 'transformation'" (Schechner 1985:4). Thus, chuqila enacts the temporary convergence both of different spaces, including the human, the animal, the divine, the savage, and the cultured, and different times, including the mythical past and the material present (see also Gutiérrez C. 1992:121).

Because one of the high points of the chuqila ritual is enacted by the young girls during their song and dance "Canto de las doncellas al wari," it is imperative to examine further how the performance of particular gender relations fundamentally structures the mobilization of identities and the constitution of this liminal space. The girls' song sets into motion economic and social relations that are mutually beneficial to two different groups as they invite the chuqila hunters to come down from the mountains and join them. Their physical union becomes a metaphor of the joyous moment of two communities coming together. As mentioned earlier in the essay, the chuqila hunters were designated as lari lari, meaning someone who is a barbarous outsider—barbarous, because they know no law—and uncle. In an essay on women and structures of power in the context of the Andes, Silvia Rivera Cusicanqui analyzes the term *lari* to show the implications of its effects within the context of such an ethnically diverse region as was the area around Lake Titicaca during pre-Columbian and early colonial times. Within their distinct kinship groups, men's and women's social, economic, and ritual roles differed in complementary, if not egalitarian, ways. While the men defended the ethnic lines of the community, the women were integral to a system of interethnic alliances through which the stranger/outsider could be incorporated into the group. In this context, lari, with its double meaning of outsider/uncle, suggests that difference did not necessarily imply a direct threat to the integrity of the community, nor signify the other's lack of humanity (1997:18): "Any stranger or outsider could become integrated at various levels into the culture of the stronger group by changing one's condition from stranger to that of a relative, even to the point of sharing power and the inheritance of the collective's cultural assets. Nonetheless, this was only possible through women, who could thus hold any group back from achieving absolute dominion over another" (18–19). Women were crucial to the performance of this liminal space of mediation between self and other. The adolescent girls' song of invitation to the vicuña hunters sets into motion the moment of transition where opposites begin to merge, where the other becomes recognizable as both other *and* same.[9]

In 1532, with the advent of new outsiders—the Spanish—the choreography of difference and recognition was dealt a severe blow. According to Rivera Cusicanqui, Andean indigenous peoples attempted at first to incorporate these strangers into the existing structure of socioeconomic relations by creating alliances through the offering of women. However, the arrival of the Spanish turned the world on its head (*pachakuti*), and the new conquerors initiated a heretofore unknown form of othering when they treated the indian as a brute form of nature, someone or something less than human. Furthermore, the systematic rape and abuse of indigenous women linked colonialism unambiguously to new forms of patriarchal violence (Rivera Cusicanqui 1997:19). The ongoing history of colonialism has transformed the vexed, heterogeneous legacy of mestizaje into a polarized world divided along gendered and racialized lines, whereby the woman articulates the indigenous heritage and the man articulates the legacy of acculturation and subordination to the creole and foreigner (23; see also Stephenson 1999, and Van Vleet and Canessa this volume). This gendered divide is further manifested by urban indigenous women who maintain an identity characterized through difference, a difference that is linked historically to the struggle for territory and self-determination. Rivera Cusicanqui contends that this cultural resistance carries the promise of a pluralistic, decolonizing democracy that embraces equality in difference, as well as the risk of closing off this avenue of change for one of accommodation and personal gain (1997:23).

What, then, is the importance of chuqila to alternative forms of nation-making? As a ritual performance of memory, chuqila mobilizes identities that are based on historical rather than biological experience (cf. Foster 1998:23). In this sense, chuqila conveys an alternate interpretation of modernity that underscores the significance of native historical memory and political agency as they are actuated and transmitted through embodied narratives. Paul Connerton suggests that rituals convey an alternative interpretation of modernity because, through their repetition, they establish a continuity rather than a break with the past. Commemorative rites, however "do not simply imply continuity with the past but *explicitly claim* such continuity" (Connerton 1989:45; emphasis added). Ritual reenactments that refer to prototypical persons or events, whether perceived as having a historical or a mythological basis, play a vital role in the shaping of communal memory (61). Through ritual performance, Connerton explains, the community "is reminded of its identity as represented by and told in a master narrative" (70). In the case of chuqila, this ritual reenactment underscores the importance of the community's territorial extension and its role in sustaining traditional Andean nutritional regimes through exchange and reciprocity with other peoples. Chuqila thus figures as an important counternarrative to hegemonic nationalist discourses that still call for the homogenization of the body politic and the suppression of native memory. In contrast to normative discourses of nation-making that perform the elimination of indigenous peoples, chuqila dares to imagine a national space wherein ethnic differences can coexist and one group does not require the suppression of another. Read in this way, chuqila takes on resonance as an important narrative of decolonization because it performs the suppressed history of Andean bio-ecological diversity and it reauthorizes the agency of women in that history. In this struggle for alternative narratives of the nation, chuqila choreographs what is most unique about the cultural politics of survival in the Andean region: the notion of equality in diversity as it is directly linked to the land.

Acknowledgments

I would like to acknowledge Andrew Canessa and the University of Arizona Press's two anonymous readers for their thoughtful evaluation of this essay and for their valuable suggestions for revision.

Notes

1. See for example, Choque Canqui (1986, 1993); Choque Canqui et al. (1992); and Choque Canqui and Ticona (1996). On memory and the long-standing struggle for territory, see also Rivera Cusicanqui (2003 [1984]).

2. In his discussion of the conflicting identity politics between indigenous peoples and *populares* that emerged at the 1991 Xela Conference in Guatemala, Charles R. Hale also calls attention to the ethnic and political divide epitomized by the references to different and even competing national heroic figures such as Bolívar and Katari (1994:18).

3. For example, in John Cohen's 1986 video, *Choqela Only Interpretation*, meaning is sought in the text and visual images of the dance, but never found. The inability on the part of the film crew to make sense of the ritual is underscored throughout the video. The final voice-over states: "The villagers had invited us to their ritual; although they told us what it meant, the meaning was only clear to them. There was no further explanation given. For them, Choqela is always done this way. The villagers checked out our tape recordings. But they gave us no translation. The translations we made later were very different from each other . . . the past meanings are buried and the present ones don't make any sense. Our need for structured facts got in the way. All that remains is Interpretation."

4. On wildness and spatiality see White 1978:150–60.

5. See, for example, Mamani Condori 1991; Choque Canqui 1986, 1993; Choque Canqui et al. 1992; Choque Canqui and Ticona 1996.

6. Foster argues that the choreographic idea should not be understood as an unchanging essence: "Choreography is not a permanent, structural capacity for representation, but rather a slowly changing constellation of representational conventions. Both choreography and performance change over time; both select from and move into action semantic systems, and as such they derive their meaning from a specific historical and cultural moment" (1998:17).

7. On the many meanings of *huari* collected from oral interviews and its significance for pan-Andean culture, see Duviols 1973.

8. Bouysse-Cassagne and Harris describe the process in the following way: "The first age [*taypi*] is that of the center; puruma, is that of the borders, and auca is that of opposite elements. To the balanced equilibrium of taypi, responds the inversion of auca, or the centrifugal movement of puruma: seduction, war, rejection" (1987:33).

9. For more on the same/other divide in the Andean context, see Cereceda (1990).

Bibliography

Anderson, Benedict. 1991. *Imagined Communities: Reflections on the Origin and Spread of Nationalism.* New York: Verso.

Bauer, Brian S., and David S. P. Dearborn. 1995. *Astronomy and Empire in the Ancient Andes: The Cultural Origins of Inca Sky Watching.* Austin: University of Texas Press.

Bertonio, Ludovico. 1984 [1612]. *Vocabulario de la lengua aymara.* Cochabamba: CERES; IFEA; MUSEF.

Bhabha, Homi K. 1990. "DissemiNation: Time, Narrative, and the Margins of the Modern Nation." In *Nation and Narration*, ed. Homi K. Bhabha, 291–322. London and New York: Routledge.

Bouysse-Cassagne, Thérèse. 1987. *La identidad aymara: Aproximación histórica (Siglo XV, Siglo XVI).* La Paz: HISBOL.

Bouysse-Cassagne, Thérèse, and Olivia Harris. 1987. "Pacha: En torno al pensamiento aymara." In *Tres reflexiones sobre el pensamiento andino*, ed. Javier Medina, 11–59. La Paz: HISBOL.

Brady, Mary Pat. 2002. *Extinct Lands, Temporal Geographies: Chicana Literature and the Urgency of Space.* Durham, N.C.: Duke University Press.

Cereceda, Verónica. 1987. "Aproximaciones a una estética andina: De la belleza al tinku." In *Tres reflexiones sobre el pensamiento andino*, ed. Javier Medina, 133–231. La Paz: HISBOL.

———. 1990. "A partir de los colores de un pájaro. . . ." *Boletín del Museo Chileno de Arte Precolombino* 4:57–104.

de Certeau, Michel. 1984. *The Practice of Everyday Life*, trans. Steven Rendall. Berkeley: University of California Press.

———. 1986. *Heterologies: Discourse on the Other*, trans. Brian Massumi. Minneapolis: University of Minnesota Press.

Chávez, Walter. 2001. "De Tamayo al Mallku." Interview with Javier Sanjinés. *El Juguete Rabioso* 2, no. 38 (Aug. 12–25): 8–9.

Choque Canqui, Roberto. 1986. *La masacre de Jesús de Machaca*. La Paz: Chitakolla.

———. 1993. *Sociedad y economía colonial en el sur andino*. La Paz: HISBOL.

Choque Canqui, Roberto, and Esteban Ticona. 1996. *Sublevación y masacre de 1921*. Vol. 2 of *Jesús de Machaqa: La marka rebelde*. La Paz: CIPCA; CEDOIN.

Choque Canqui, Roberto, et al. 1992. *Educación indígena: ¿Ciudadanía o colonización?* La Paz: Aruwiyiri.

Choque Quispe, María Eugenia, and Carlos Mamani Condori. 2002 (spring). "Andean Traditions of Giving: A Vocabulary of Generosity." *ReVista: Harvard Review of Latin America*.

Cobo, Bernabé. 1956. *Obras*. Vol. 2. Madrid: Biblioteca de Autores Españoles. Tomo 92.

Cohen, John. 1986. *Choqela Only Interpretation*. Video. Berkeley, Calif.: University of California Extension Center for Media.

Condarco Santillán, Carlos. 1999. *La serranía sagrada de los urus: Ensayo Antropológico*. Oruro: Latinas Editores.

Connerton, Paul. 1989. *How Societies Remember*. Cambridge: Cambridge University Press.

Cruikshank, Julie. 2002. "Oral History, Narrative Strategies, and Native American Historiography: Perspectives from the Yukon Territory, Canada." In *Clearing a Path: Theorizing the Past in Native American Studies*, ed. Nancy Shoemaker, 3–27. New York: Routledge.

Dedenbach-Salazar Sáenz, Sabine. 1990. *Inka Pachaq Llamanpa Willaynin: Uso y crianza de los camélidos en la época incaica. Estudio lingüístico y etnohistórico basado en las fuentes lexicográficas y textuales del primer siglo después de la conquista*. Bonn: Bonner Amerikanistische Studien.

Desmond, Jane C. 1997a. "Introduction." In *Meaning in Motion: New Cultural Studies of Dance*, ed. Jane C. Desmond, 1–25. Durham, N.C.: Duke University Press.

———. 1997b. "Embodying Difference: Issues in Dance and Cultural Studies." In *Meaning in Motion: New Cultural Studies of Dance*, ed. Jane C. Desmond, 29–54. Durham, N.C.: Duke University Press.

Douglas, Mary. 1992. *Purity and Danger: An Analysis of the Concepts of Pollution and Taboo*. New York: Routledge.

Duviols, Pierre. 1967. "Un inédito de Cristóbal de Albornoz: La instrucción para descubrir todas las guacas del Pirú y sus camayos y haciendas." *Journal de la Société des Américanistes* 56, no. 1:7–40.

———. 1973. "Huari y Llacuaz: Agricultores y pastores. Un dualismo prehispánico de oposición y complementaridad." *Revista del Museo Nacional* 39:153–93.

———. 1986. *Cultura andina y represión: Procesos y visitas de idolatrías y hechicerías*. Cajatambo, siglo xvi. Cuzco: Centro de Estudios Rurales Andinos "Bartolomé de las Casas."

———. 1993. "Estudio y comentario etnohistórico." In *Joan de Santacruz Pachacuti Yamqui Salcamaygua: Relación de Antigüedades deste Reyno del Perú*. Edición facsimilar y transcripción paleográfica del *Códice de Madrid*. Cuzco: Institut Français d'Etudes Andines; Centro de Estudios Regionales Andinos "Bartolomé de las Casas."

Foster, Susan Leigh. 1998. "Choreographies of Gender." *Signs* 24, no.1:1–33.

Foster, Susan Leigh, ed. 1996. *Corporealities: Dancing, Knowledge, Culture, and Power.* New York: Routledge.

Guamán Poma de Ayala, Felipe. 1980. *Nueva corónica y buen gobierno*, ed. Franklin Pease. Vols. 1 and 2. Caracas: Biblioteca Ayacucho.

Gutiérrez C., Ramiro. 1992. "Chacu representación simbólica de la caza de la vicuña: El caso de los sikus choquelas de Belén." *Reunión Anual de Etnología.* Tomo II, 121–33. Serie: Anales de la Reunión Anual de Etnología. La Paz: MUSEF.

Hale, Charles H. 1994. "Between Che Guevara and the Pachamama: Mestizos, Indians and Identity Politics in the Anti-Quincentenary Campaign." *Critique of Anthropology* 14, no.1:9–39.

Lavallée, Danièle, Michèle Julien, Jane Wheeler, and Claudine Karlin. 1995. *Telarmachay: Cazadores y pastores prehistóricos de los Andes*, trans. Denise Pozzi-Escot. Tomo 1. Lima: Instituto Francés de Estudios Andinos.

López Rivas, Eduardo. 1976. *Cultura y religión en el altiplano andino.* La Paz: Los Amigos del Libro.

MacCormack, Sabine. 1991. *Religion in the Andes: Vision and Imagination in Early Colonial Peru.* Princeton, N.J.: Princeton University Press.

Mamani Condori, Carlos. 1991. *Taraqu, 1866–1935: Masacre, guerra, y "renovación" en la biografía de Eduardo L. Nina Qhispi.* La Paz: Aruwiyiri.

———. 1992. *Los aymaras frente a la historia: Dos ensayos metodológicos.* Chukiyawu: Aruwiyiri.

———. 2000. "El intelectual indígena hacia un pensamiento propio." Paper presented at the Latin American Studies Association, Miami.

———. 2001. "Memoria y política aymara." In *ARUSKIPASIPXAÑASATAKI: El siglo XXI y el futuro del pueblo aymara*, ed. Waskar Ari Chachaki, 47–65. La Paz: Editorial Amuyañataki.

Martin, Randy. 1998. *Critical Moves: Dance Studies in Theory and Politics.* Durham, N.C.: Duke University Press.

de Matienzo, Juan. 1910 [1567]. *Gobierno del Perú.* Buenos Aires: Compañía Sud-Americana de Billetes de Banco.

Muecke, Stephen. 1992. *Textual Spaces: Aboriginality and Cultural Studies.* Kensington, Australia: New South Wales University Press.

Murra, John V. 1965. "Herds and Herders in the Inca State." In *Man, Culture, and Animals: The Role of Animals in Human Ecological Adjustments*, ed. Anthony Leeds and Andrew P. Vayda, 185–215. Washington, D.C.: American Association for the Advancement of Sciences.

Paredes, M. Rigoberto. 1981. *El arte folklórico de Bolivia.* 2d ed. La Paz: Popular.

Qayum, Seemin. 2002. "Nationalism, Internal Colonialism and the Spatial Imagination: The Geographic Society of La Paz in Turn-of-the-Century Bolivia." In *Studies in the Formation of the Nation State in Latin America*, ed. James Dunkerley, 275–98. London: Institute of Latin American Studies.

Reinaga, Fausto. 1969. *La revolución india.* La Paz: Ediciones Partido Indio de Bolivia.

Rivera Cusicanqui, Silvia. 1997. "Mujeres y estructuras de poder en los Andes: De la etnohistoria a la política." *Escarmenar: Revista Boliviana de Estudios Culturales* 2:16–25.

———. 2003 [1984]. *"Oprimidos pero no vencidos": Luchas del campesinado aymara y qhechwa de Bolivia, 1900–1980*. La Paz: HISBOL; CSUTCB.

Romero, Emilio. 1929. *Tres ciudades del Perú*. Lima: Torres Aguirre.

de Santacruz Pachacuti Yamqui Salcamaygua, Joan. 1950 [1879]. "Relacion de antigüedades deste reyno del Pirú." In *Tres relaciones de antigüedades peruanas*, comp. Marcos Jiménez de la Espada, 205–81. Asunción: Editorial Guarania.

Schechner, Richard. 1985. *Between Theater and Anthropology*. Philadelphia: University of Pennsylvania Press.

Sharp, Joanne P. 1996. "Gendering Nationhood: A Feminist Engagement with National Identity." In *Bodyspace: Destabilizing Geographies of Gender and Sexuality*, ed. Nancy Duncan, 97–108. New York: Routledge.

Shay, Anthony. 2002. *Choreographic Politics: State Folk Dance Companies, Representation, and Power*. Middleton, Conn.: Wesleyan University Press.

Shohat, Ella. 2000. "Notes on the 'Post-Colonial.'" In *The Pre-Occupation of Postcolonial Studies*, ed. Fawzia Afzal-Khan and Kalpana Seshadri-Crooks, 126–39. Durham, N.C.: Duke University Press.

Smith, Linda Tuhiwai. 1999. *Decolonizing Methodologies: Research and Indigenous Peoples*. London and Dunedin: Zed Books; University of Otago Press.

Stephenson, Marcia. 1999. *Gender and Modernity in Andean Bolivia*. Austin: University of Texas Press.

Taller de Historia Oral Andina (THOA). 1993. *Chuqila*. Video.

Tschopik, Harry, Jr. 1946. "The Aymara." In *Handbook of South American Indians*, ed. Juliana H. Steward. Vol. 2: The Andean Civilizations, 501–73. Washington, D.C.: Government Printing Office.

Vásquez, Emilio. 1944. "Coreografía Titikaka: Los chokelas." *Revista del Museo Nacional (Perú)* 13:65–83.

White, Hayden. 1978. "The Forms of Wildness: Archaeology of an Idea." In *Tropics of Discourse: Essays in Cultural Criticism*, 150–82. Baltimore: Johns Hopkins University Press.

5

Dancing on the Borderlands

Girls (Re)Fashioning National Belonging in the Andes

Krista Van Vleet

Notions of modern citizens and national identities are typically built on unmarked categories of masculinity, "whiteness," urban residence, and adulthood, yet those others—women, nonwhites, children—are also citizens, both in the formal sense of having the "right to carry a specific passport" (Yuval-Davis 1997) and in the practical sense of actively negotiating their belonging to national collectivities. As Andrew Canessa points out in the introduction to this volume, the ways in which women and ethnic minorities are materially and symbolically crucial to the construction and maintenance of borders between places and categorical distinctions between "kinds of" people have, in recent years, been explored by scholars from a variety of disciplinary and regional perspectives.[1] Much of this work, drawing on Foucault's theoretical framework (1972, 1978), demonstrates the ways in which colonial and national states engage in and depend on establishing not only new political and economic organizations but also social actors able to function within them. Although often relegated to the margins of political publics, "women," "natives," and other subalterns participate in the nation and are crucial to the production of national identities.

It is also from a Foucauldian perspective that anthropologist Sharon Stephens (1995:6) asks further, "In what respects are children—as foci of gender-specific roles in the family, as objects of regulation and development in the school, and as symbols of the future and of what is at stake in contests over cultural identity—pivotal in the structuring of modernity?" In the highland region of Sullk'ata (Province of Chayanta, Department of Potosí), Bolivia, where I have conducted fieldwork since January 1995, as in other areas of the Andes, children and young adults come into contact with urban hegemonic notions of national identity and become integrated into national arenas through education in rural public schools (Larson, this volume; Luykx 1999; Stephenson 1999); migration to urban areas for work (Gill 1994); consumption and production of commodities (Colloredo-Mansfeld 1999; Parker et al. 1992) and popular culture (Bigenho, this volume); and mandatory military service (Canessa, this volume; Gill 1997). But if people's subjectivities are partially shaped through state and civil institutions, they are also inextricably intertwined with personal experiences and local conceptions of childhood and youth, gender and family (Stephens 1995:16; Stoler 1995).[2]

Moreover, children and youth are not simply *objects* of regulation or symbols of future identities. Children imagine themselves and enact themselves as gendered, ethnic, national, and transnational subjects. They are themselves social actors, agents, who in their ordinary lives do not simply take on the nation's politics as their everyday psychology (Coles 1986; Stephens 1995:3). I draw on Laura Ahearn's (2001:112) definition of agency as the "socioculturally mediated capacity to act" in order to bring attention to performances and interactions that cannot be understood simply as either resistance or free will. Agents are produced within certain sorts of social and historical regimes, according to specific cultural frames of meaning and style, and through particular languages. Yet as Desjarlais (1997:201) has suggested, the question of "how" is often neglected in the discussion of agency: "How do people act? What are the means of action specific to a person, a group, an institution, or a social setting?" Gendered, racial, cultural, and linguistic relationships of power shape any individual's capacity to act; how youth navigate social, economic, and political constraints even as they enact themselves as citizens remains a question. At the same time, youth have their own material necessities and personal desires.

In this chapter, I explore how the consumption of clothing may be a site for understanding how Sullk'ata youths experience the possibilities and constraints of their own "belongingness" in Bolivia at the turn of the twenty-first century. I use the term *youth* throughout this paper to refer to unmarried Sullk'atas who are generally between the ages of eleven and twenty-two, and often in school. The age corresponds to Quechua categories of *sipas* and *jovencita*, which along with cholita, are used most often by Sullk'atas to refer to girls transitioning between child and adult status. Although Sullk'atas perceive youth as incompletely socialized, as I describe further below, they also recognize that children and young adults are socially, politically, and economically capable of acting for themselves.[3] My emphasis on Sullk'ata youth, and on girls in particular, decenters the notion of "citizenship" by focusing on categories of identity not typically assumed to be significant to "the nation." Born and raised in a rural region of the Bolivian Andes, the girls who dance through these pages migrated to urban areas of Bolivia as teenagers. In different contexts and among various interlocutors, the girls identify themselves as modern and civilized, rejecting the label of "india" yet identifying themselves as Sullk'atas. My emphasis on these girls' words and actions also highlights the significance of everyday experiences and interactions in the production of national, racial, and gendered identities and refigures the nation by analyzing practices, such as buying and wearing clothes, not typically assumed to be political.[4] Finally, I forefront girls in order to analyze the processual aspect of claiming belonging to multiple identities or collectivities.

The ethnographic episodes I discuss are drawn from twenty-two months of research primarily conducted in rural communities of Sullk'ata (Department of Potosí), Bolivia, in 1995–1996 and more recently with Sullk'ata migrants in the cities of Sucre and Cochabamba in 2001 and 2003. In the first episode I describe how Reina skips school the day after her teacher calls her an "india" or indian.[5] "Indio" is a derogatory term in Bolivia, carrying connotations of dirtiness, stupidity, laziness, and dullness (see also Abercrombie 1991, 1992; Luykx 1999; Stephenson 1999; Weismantel 1997, 2001). Reina returns to school only after buying a new pair of shoes. In the second episode I introduce Marisa, a teenager who loves to buy new polleras, the full, gathered skirts iconic of native Andean women (see Femenias 1997; Weismantel 2001), to dance during Carnival. One of Bolivia's most important national holidays, Carnival is celebrated every year for ten days in February, before the Catholic season of Lent. On a daily basis, however, Marisa wears only pants, even in the rural community. In both cases, commodities index racial and gendered positionalities, and are used by girls to identify with familial, ethnic, and national collectivities. Rather than reflect essential and isolable identities, I argue that these episodes reveal processes of identification that occur simultaneously and are embedded in particular contexts and interactions.

Reina's New Shoes

Reina and her younger brother used to come to my room early in the morning or late in the afternoon, to lean on my desk and watch me write or sit on my bed and drink the cups of cocoa that I sometimes provided. If they visited in the morning, Reina's older sister would eventually arrive to remind Reina, who was eleven years old, that it was time to go to school. They would depart together when it was still quite early in order to walk more than an hour to the school in a nearby community. For this reason, late one morning when I went to get water from the river, I was surprised to see Reina, sitting on the cement base of the flagpole in the center of the community's otherwise featureless plaza. Reina had left my room hours before wearing her school uniform and carrying her notebook.

I asked her why she was still hanging around and told her she should hurry up and get to school. "Your mother will scold you if she sees you sitting here."

"No, she won't scold me," she replied.

After a few more minutes of trying to convince her to hurry up and go to school, I returned to my room, going around to the back of the house. Not ten minutes later, I heard her father's shouts and Reina's cries, "Mama, Mama!" as her father scolded her. I stepped out of my room to see Reina's mother, standing by her back gate, listening to her daughter's cries but making no move to intervene. Later that morning, Reina told me that her father had begun yelling and hitting her the moment she entered the house through the front door.

After her father calmed down, the girl explained to her parents that she did not go to school because her teacher had called her "india" the day before. "'India, why have you come to school?' the teacher said to me."

I asked Reina why the teacher might have said that.

"Maybe because I'm wearing sandals," she replied, indicating her sandals made from retreaded tire rubber.

Later in the afternoon Reina's father washed his hair and face, put on his best clothes, and went to town "to scold the teacher." He arrived back a few hours later and squatted down to accept a bowl of boiled corn and fava beans (*mut'i*) and fresh onion salad from his wife. We waited while he ate. Finally, he said that the teacher told him that Reina had not been coming to school in the afternoons. "Maybe she showed up late," he said, "and that's why the teacher said, 'Why are you here? Why did you come?'" The teacher had made no excuses and offered no apologies for calling Reina an india.

The next afternoon, Reina showed off her new shoes to me—blue canvas slip-on shoes with bright white rubber soles. "My mother gave me the money this morning," she said as she did a little dance on the concrete floor of my room. "I bought them on my way to school!"

When the teacher calls Reina an indian, she draws on a hegemonic discourse that maintains a binary distinction between "indians" and "whites," powerfully organizing how people imagine the world and interact with each other (Wade 1997; Weismantel 2001). Although the Bolivian state has not officially used the term "indio" since 1952, replacing the term with campesino, or peasant, republican governments have maintained an ideological and institutional separation between the "modern nation" and the "indian nation" (Canessa 2004; de la Cadena 2000; Mannheim 1998, 1991; Mayer 1991; Weismantel 2001). I heard this distinction reiterated by Bolivians living in provincial towns as well as urban Bolivians when they alternately valorized a romantic vision of ancient civilizations in the Andean region and disparaged the linguistic and ethnic diversity of their nation—the large numbers of native Andeans and lowland indigenous tribes—as a primary reason why Bolivia remains "backward" and "undeveloped."

In spite of more recent attempts to recognize the "multicultural" character of the nation in rural public school curricula, this racial discourse pervades schools. Indigeneity is both marginalized to the interstices of the curriculum and linked to folkloric dances and typical dishes that do little to reflect the lived experiences of most Bolivians (Luykx 1999). For example, children perform "national dances" during Independence Day, but much like the museum exhibits of national ethnicities of Ecuador that Weismantel (2001:83–95) describes, these dances publicly enact the racial and ethnic diversity of the nation, and of political ideologies that reaffirm Bolivia as a multicultural nation, at the same time that they obscure the structuring of power that enables blatant discrimination against campesinos. Thus, Reina's teacher's insult manifests the racialized boundaries of everyday life in Bolivia, which are structured in part by a long history of colonization and extractive capitalism, and reaffirms the ground rules of participation in the Bolivian nation by suggesting that indios may as well not bother coming to school at all.

Reina rejects her teacher's attribution of indianness and turns to her parents and the gringa anthropologist to protect her from the teacher's insults. Nevertheless, she has a ready explanation for her teacher's insult. Drawing on a potent symbol of racial distinction in the Andes, she points to her shoes or, rather, her sandals. As other anthropologists of the Andean region have noted, hands and feet as well as clothing and shoes, are signifiers of class and race as well as gender (Weismantel 2001:188–90; also Colloredo-Mansfeld 1998:187). Sandals made from retreaded tire (*abarcas de goma*) are worn by people throughout the Bolivian country-side; the sandals are readily available, cheap, comfortable, and durable. Whether they dressed *de pollera*—in full-skirted polleras, shawls, and bowler hats—or *de vestida*—in "western," usually secondhand, clothing, most women and girls (including Reina) wore a style of tire sandals with thinner soles and straps rather than the less expensive, thick-soled, slip-on version with wide straps preferred by men and most elderly community members. Whether a person chooses the thick- or thin-soled style of the sandal, wearing the sandals exposes feet to the environment and marks the body of the wearer (Weismantel 2001:198). By buying canvas shoes, then, Reina identifies herself with a more modern and civilized collectivity at the same time that she acquiesces to the racial categorization that distinguishes indian and white, rural and urban, backward and modern, uncivilized and civilized.

The "Civilized" and "Uncivilized" in Sullk'ata

Although the people with whom I lived and worked referred to themselves most often as Sullk'atas, or occasionally as campesinos, they never called themselves indios. Primarily Quechua speakers, living in small rural communities in one of the poorest provinces of Bolivia, Sullk'atas are marginal to, but not isolated from, the national and international society and political economy. Sullk'atas depend on both wage labor and subsistence agriculture and herding for survival. Subsistence agriculture is organized through kinship relationships and a gendered division of labor and embedded in relationships of reciprocity—both exchanges between human and supernatural beings and exchanges of labor among networks of individuals are necessary for production (e.g., Allen 1988; Sallnow 1987; Mannheim 1991).

Sullk'atas have also been integrated into market economies for hundreds of years. In recent decades neoliberal economic reforms and a stagnant economy have reconfigured patterns of migration and labor. In the mid-1980s, the Bolivian economy was plagued by a debt crisis of massive proportions, rampant inflation, and unemployment; subsequent fiscal policies imposed by the International Monetary Fund exacerbated the already severe economic conditions. The government closed down mines in highland regions in the 1980s, leaving tens of thousands of miners and their families without work or housing. Coca production increased in the eastern lowland regions of Bolivia in the mid-1980s, but steadily decreased throughout the 1990s from increased U.S. pressure to eradicate coca. In the mid-1990s job opportunities in urban areas were more favorable for single young women than for young men but mostly as poorly paid domestic servants or market vendors. More recently, severe economic conditions throughout South America combined with the seemingly endemic problems of land scarcity and lack of educational and economic opportunities have resulted in increasing levels of migration of entire families from rural areas to urban centers in Bolivia and in other parts of the world, including Spain and the United States.

In this context of increasing migration and wage work in a global capitalist economy, the sensibilities of reciprocity and sociability that inflect the rural subsistence political economy are intertwined with national discourses of modernization and progress. In their evaluations of themselves and others, Sullk'atas draw on an opposition between "civilized" and "uncivilized," imbricating access to commodities (including money) with language (Spanish or Quechua), residence (urban or rural), clothing style, and level of education. Sullk'atas at once speak of themselves as campesinos who do not partake of a more advanced life in Bolivian cities—where electricity and running water make streets, clothing, and people cleaner; where one might buy electronics and clothes; and where people speak Spanish rather than Quechua—and as *bolivianos* (or Bolivians) who lag behind the United States, unable to develop industry and technology.

The opposition between civilized and uncivilized draws on racial and gendered ideologies as well as material inequalities. For example, most married women in Sullk'ata tend to remain in rural communities while their husbands migrate seasonally for work in eastern lowland regions of Bolivia or urban centers in Bolivia or elsewhere. Married men have greater access to commodities, including money, than their wives. As in other Andean contexts, Sullk'ata women are sometimes said to be "more indian" than men and men said to be "more advanced" than their wives (de la Cadena 1995; Crain 1996). I particularly remember a community meeting during which one man, using the metaphor of running a race, said, "We always say that we men have won, we have beaten our wives, because we go to the cities. We earn money." Although the broader context of the meeting was to acknowledge the significance of the work that women do on a daily basis for the welfare of the community, the gendered shape of the discourse of progress, which subordinates the value of subsistence work, also emerged.

W.E.B. DuBois (1903) has used the phrase "double consciousness" to refer to a splitting of subjectivity through which a marginalized group may see itself from the perspective of a dominant group, from the outside, as well as from the inside "as those whom the dominant group misapprehends or ignores and who are challenged to survive in a context of jeopardy" (Millones and Pratt 1990:21).[6] The discourse through which Quechua speakers construct and construe others as more civilized or more advanced than themselves reflects such a double consciousness, which laminates the racial and gender ideologies particular to the Andes with a more local conception of "civilized." Sullk'atas, like other Quechua speakers in Peru and Bolivia, also take note of the immoral and improper relationships of others through an opposition between human and animal worlds.[7] Animals are used to represent "uncivilized" human beings, those who do not live according to relationships of reciprocity and sociality but who take advantage of others. Animals are also used to talk metaphorically about different stages in the life cycle of human beings (Urton 1985).

The position of youth in Andean communities partially overlaps the distinctions between civilized and uncivilized.[8] First, Sullk'atas perceive youth as incompletely socialized at the same time that they recognize that youth are socially, politically, and economically capable of acting for themselves. Urton argues that adolescents occupy an ambiguous position between worlds, and in this way they are understood to be like bears (Urton 1985). Bears are "on their way to becoming human beings" (Urton 1985:271): they can walk on two legs, they eat wild and domesticated animals, and corn and squash. Bears are also considered boisterous and unruly, destructive and sexually aggressive. In the region of Q'ero, Peru, Quechua speakers tell stories that describe women being raped by bears or having sex with bears and giving birth to bear-human children (Morote Best 1957–58:137–49, cited in Urton 1985:271; also see Allen 1983:39). Bears are commonly represented in dances in Andean communities, and the dancers are typically boys between the ages of nine and eighteen (Urton 1985:270–72; Allen 1983). At least from the perspective of the adults in the community, the dancers are also on the way to becoming fully human beings—adults. Part of this process of maturation is getting married and having children, and eventually taking on responsibilities in the household, community, and ayllu that depend on maintaining relationships of reciprocity.

Second, children are not only exposed to competing notions of civilized practices and desired sociality, but they also move through several differing contexts in the course of a day as well as over the course of many years. Youth may rely upon a variety of practices to negotiate interactions and make sense of relationships and events. From early childhood, Sullk'atas at the end of the twentieth century grow up being educated in public schools and speaking Spanish as well as Quechua. Although girls often drop out of school at a younger age than boys, they also tend to migrate to Bolivian cities for work. Both girls and boys sometimes live with relatives or friends to attend schools in the city. Though raised in rural communities and influenced by locally specific understandings of childhood, gender, race, and family, many Sullk'ata youths spend years living and working in cities—in Argentina, Spain, and the United States as well as Bolivia.

I encountered Reina again not in the rural community but at the celebration of a baptism in the city of Sucre in February 2003. We talked of our memories of the year that I had lived in Sullk'ata, of her family's migration to the city of Sucre in 1998, her experiences attending high school, and her dreams for the future. Just beginning her senior year, she told me that she was thinking of attending a university ("I don't want to become a domestic servant") and studying physics ("I can really understand that subject the best") or perhaps languages ("If only I could come to the United States to learn English"). By then seventeen years old, Reina was, in the words of one of her relatives, "no longer a little girl (*imilla*); she has become a teenager (*joven*)." The modern look of her bell-bottomed blue jeans and blue-and-red striped sweater was enhanced by her black platform shoes. Her hair was worn straight and loose, not confined in a ponytail or braids, and hanging almost to her waist.

I teased her about the ways she used to avoid studying and doing her chores by visiting me, and then asked if she remembered the time that she skipped school because the teacher had called her an india. "Oh yeah," she answered, laughing. "Those teachers were always calling us indios. They always acted superior to us. And when you don't have an understanding of things, you feel really badly about it. You remember *profesor* Martínez? He was always calling me a cry baby (*llorona*). But now that I understand things a little better, I feel proud. They say that people from our region are the best dancers and singers. So when someone asks me where I'm from I say the Norte de Potosí, the ayllu Sullk'ata.

Although she does not wear clothing that marks her as "native," Quechua-speaking, or from a rural community on a daily basis, Reina identifies herself with her community and with indigeneity in particular contexts. In Reina's recounting, the teacher calling her an india was not particularly unusual. She emphasizes that now, rather than feeling badly, she is proud of being from Sullk'ata. Reina told me that she usually goes back to the community only during Carnival. Reina and her sister, Marisa, love to return to the community to dance for Carnival and have done so almost every year since they migrated. Her sister works as a domestic servant in Santa Cruz and is usually able to buy more polleras than can Reina, who is a student. Reina buys at least one new pollera each year and borrows additional polleras so she can dance all week during the festival.

Marisa's Polleras

The most well-known celebration of Carnival in Bolivia occurs in the city of Oruro, where the parading dancers and musicians number in the tens of thousands, and onlookers number in the hundreds of thousands. In May 2001, UNESCO named the Oruro Carnival as one of the nineteen "Masterpieces of the Oral and Intangible Heritage of Humanity," and the fiesta is an integral part of many Bolivian's conceptions of their national patrimony (Abercrombie 1992; Gifford and Hogarth 1976). Sullk'atas, like many other Bolivians, celebrate Carnival not with a parade of costumed dancers in a city but with visits to the homes of friends, neighbors, and relatives within their own rural communities. In Sullk'ata, Carnival is a time of rest, enjoyment, and, especially, consumption marking the transition between rainy and dry seasons. Sullk'atas bless their houses, solicit and celebrate the fertility of animals and fields, and remember their male ancestors, especially the men who have died in the past year. The constellation of activities during this annual celebration—getting drunk, eating ritual food, singing local and regional folk songs, and dancing—is considered an offering to the supernatural forces of the universe. Unlike most other fiestas in Sullk'ata, youth—unmarried young women and men—play a significant role in the ritual success of the fiesta by dancing and singing in other communities while the married adults dance and sing within their own community.

Displays of fashion, consumer consumption, and ritual prowess (including singing and dancing) are significant facets of what cholitas do during Carnival, and significant to what people remember and tell each other about Carnival. In the weeks before Carnival, Sullk'atas speculate about the cholitas who will return to rural communities from their jobs as domestic servants or high school classes in Bolivian cities to dance, bringing huge bundles of clothing with them. "They will bring different skirts. A different pollera for every day that they dance." In this particular context the term *cholita* is used by Sullk'atas to refer to unmarried teenage girls, usually those who are returning to the rural community from jobs in urban centers of Bolivia rather than the more usual association with market women (cf. Albro 2000; Weismantel 2001). Often, Sullk'atas interchange the term *cholita* with *sipas*, Quechua for adolescent girl, or jovencita, a Spanish term for youth with both a diminutive and female gendered ending. Cholitas return to the community to participate in the dancing, singing, eating, and drinking, and at the same time they demonstrate their belongingness to the modern nation through their consumption and display of commodities.

Dancing requires a significant outlay of capital by young women. Most significant is the cost they undertake for their displays of fashion through which the cholitas distinguish themselves from the girls who do not have the material or social resources for this conspicuous consumption. For Carnival, cholitas dance for seven days. The girls returning from the city not only bring polleras made from the most fashionable cloth, each costing between sixty and eighty U.S. dollars, but they also carry with them the specialized clothing to complete their outfits: blouses made of eyelet lace; straight slips also trimmed with lace; bowler hats, shawls, sandals or slip-on shoes; and sometimes even nylon stockings. By wearing their new clothes, the cholitas are displaying their success, their ability to consume commodities, attain a higher standard of living, speak Spanish, and become more educated (or at least more cosmopolitan, living in a city with electricity, television, cement floors and running water). Girls also, however, often go into debt in order to buy or borrow polleras. In contrast to the cholitas returning from the city, the girls living in the rural community—even those of the same age—do not typically buy new clothes.

During Carnival in 1996, Marisa was a girl of fifteen. I knew that she had returned to the community to visit her family. I was surprised, however, when I saw Marisa dancing in a pollera. I had known Marisa for almost a year by then and had *only* seen her wearing pants—never a skirt or dress, much less a pollera. Besides Marisa, and occasionally myself, no other girl or woman in Sullk'ata wore pants, although in the provincial towns and cities some women chose pants over skirts at least occasionally. Many Sullk'atas commented to me that Marisa had male energy (*qhari kallpa*) from the time she was a little girl. Not only did she wear pants, but she also knew how to ride a bike and even to plow with oxen, a thoroughly masculine practice in the region. Marisa had been wearing her usual attire when she arrived in the community, but the next day she braided her hair and slicked back her bangs. She put on a pollera, blouse, and shawl and went with her brothers, sisters, and community mates to dance.

Later that week, I learned from her cousin that Marisa had put on a pollera for the first time on her way to the city of Santa Cruz. In October, just a few months before, Marisa traveled with her cousin to Santa Cruz. Her cousin had been working as a cook in a wealthy household and told Marisa that her employer (*patrona*) needed another servant to clean the house. En route to Santa Cruz, her cousin informed Marisa that the woman would hire only a domestic servant who was de pollera, or who wore native Andean dress. Marisa changed into a pollera in the back of the truck, arriving at the house looking like the urban Bolivian woman's categorical image of a highland native woman. Had she arrived wearing her usual attire of jeans and a T-shirt, she might not have been hired. After just two weeks of working as an *empleada*, however, Marisa quit. She did not like the way the woman treated her. She left Santa Cruz, went to live in Cochabamba with her aunt, and found work as a vendor in the market.

Although Marisa's bodily movements and facial expressions suggested that she was not completely comfortable in her new clothes during Carnival 1996, when I visited her family five years later, Reina told me that Marisa danced every year for Carnival. Marisa was supposed to have gone to Spain, she said. "Our brother is already there and sent word that she should come because work for women is much easier to come by. But Marisa decided instead to go to Santa Cruz." When I asked her sister why this might be so, she said, "She wouldn't miss her Carnival! She loves buying polleras." Although I do not know what she wears when in her current job as a domestic servant, Marisa had not stopped wearing jeans and T-shirts on an everyday basis when I saw her in 2001. She usually buys her clothes from vendors of secondhand U.S. clothing in the large market of Cochabamba. Marisa also buys and wears polleras, at least according to her sister, enjoying the interactions and relationships that radiate from both these practices.

Fashion as well as ritual participation may be an arena or a medium for communicating a particular gender, ethnic, and class position, as anthropologists of the Andean region and elsewhere have pointed out.

Although I emphasize these practices as performative (as in Butler 1990, 1993; Morris 1995), I do not want to suggest that gender, race, or ethnicity is simply "chosen" outside of a system of constraints, put on or taken off like polleras or pants. Rather, I accent the ways in which people may negotiate their connection to others at the same time that they may be identified according to particular categories. As Brubaker and Cooper (2001:6–7) point out, the notion "that 'nations,' 'races,' and 'identities,' 'exist' and that people 'have' a 'nationality,' a 'race,' an 'identity'" obscures the material and symbolic processes through which those relationships and collectivities emerge and evolve. Although some cholitas habitually wear polleras, others may put on their slacks and comb out their hair after Carnival, shifting gracefully between the two. Moreover, certain contexts—such as Carnival or an employer's household—or particular confluences of events may constrain or enable people in different ways just as certain items of clothing may more forcefully mark the body of the wearer.[9] The ways clothing marks the body as well as the structural inequalities that shape perceptions of fashion is also evident in Bigenho's discussion (this volume) of elite mestiza performers who don polleras to sing Aymara songs. For Sullk'atas, the clothes indicate not an either/or distinction between mestiza and india, or jovencita and cholita, but a synthesis in which girls identify themselves *both* as modern and as Sullk'ata through their interactions with others as well as through the things that they buy.

Practicing Multiple Citizenships

Rather than being "in process," then, girls might be understood as participating in multiple "communities of practice" (Eckert and McConnell-Ginet 1995) that are situated in a borderland zone (Anzaldúa 1987). The concept of communities of practice, developed by linguistic anthropologists Penelope Eckert and Sally McConnell-Ginet, emphasizes the agency of individuals and the simultaneity of people's participation in various collectivities. Defining the concept, Eckert and McConnell-Ginet write:

> During the course of their lives, people move into, out of, and through communities of practice, continually transforming identities, understandings, and worldviews. Progressing through the life span brings ever-changing kinds of participation and nonparticipation, contexts for "belonging" and "not belonging" in communities. A single individual participates in

a variety of communities of practice at any given time, and over time. (1995:469–507)

Sullk'ata youth participate in various communities of practice—their natal families as well as the families of employers, rural and urban communities, schools, nation, and ayllu—simultaneously negotiating belongingness in these multiple and partially overlapping arenas and at the same time constituting those communities through their practices. Social, economic, and political institutions also, however, structure peoples' relationships and experiences. Gloria Anzaldúa's (1987:3) conception of the borderlands as an open wound "where the Third World grates against the first and bleeds" with "the lifeblood of two worlds merging to form a third country—a border culture" contributes a sense of the trenchant inequalities of power that configure different communities of practice and the relationships among those communities.

Understanding Sullk'ata girls' participation in the nation, as a community of practice, then requires analysis of the ways that particular practices constitute belongingness or "citizenship" in other collectivities as well. In the incident with which I began this chapter, Reina actively identifies herself with various "imagined communities" (Anderson 1983), negotiating differing ideologies of what constitutes civilized behavior, that overlay her connectedness to the modern nation and to her Sullk'ata family. Reina's emphasis on shoes takes up the hegemonic discourse that categorizes people into a racial group based on not only their physical attributes but also their material possessions (Weismantel 1997, 2001). However, buying shoes in this context is not only about whiteness and modernity. Commodities and consumption are also linked to kinship as well as to notions of modernity, race, and national identity in Bolivia. Anthropologists have long recognized that the circulation of goods also produces and sustains social relationships (Colloredo-Mansfeld 1999; Douglas and Isherwood 1979; Mauss 1950; Weismantel 2001). Recent research on kinship in the Andes (Harvey 1998; Weismantel 1995; Van Vleet 2002) has demonstrated the ways in which habitual everyday practices such as sharing food and work and living spaces and "buying material goods with scarce funds" (Weismantel 1995) continuously re-create kinship in the Andes.

Reina thus actively negotiates both the objectified system of categorization of the Bolivian state that links race, modernity, and citizenship with the hierarchies of respect that constitute kinship and sociability in

Sullk'ata families. In the Andes, as Harvey (1998:69) notes, successful kinship relationships are relationships in which a hierarchy remains intact, in which respect is given to the appropriate individuals. Children are positioned in a relationship of dependence on and subordination to parents when they receive food and other gifts (Harvey 1998:74–75; Weismantel 1995; Van Vleet 2002). In return, children are expected to respect their parents and older siblings—expressed by carrying out tasks readily, watching over younger siblings, or addressing adults in a proper manner. A parent may meet a child's defiance with varying degrees of reprimand and may scold or hit the child to reinforce physically the understood hierarchy between parents and children (Harvey 1998:74–75; Van Vleet 2002).

Reina is caught between her father's anger, as he asserts a hierarchy of authority in the family, and her teacher's abuse as she asserts the racialized hierarchy of the school, region, and nation. Reina's father reacts with violence when he interprets her absence from school as a sign of disrespect within the family. Reina's gamble, that her parents' potential anger at her disobedience will be outweighed by their anger at her teacher, pays off only after the emotional and physical affront of being hit with a strap. Her father turns his anger toward her teacher, articulating his intent to "scold the teacher." Although I do not know to what extent Reina's father was able to voice a critique of the teacher's racial insult, he does succeed in demonstrating to his daughter his concern for her welfare. Moreover, by giving her money to buy shoes, shoes that are both more expensive and less durable than the sandals she already owns, both of Reina's parents at once reestablish relatedness and hierarchy between themselves and Reina and identify themselves as participants in a modern nation and global economy.

Although adult actions are crucial in establishing and maintaining kinship relationships, children are not simply passive recipients of relatedness. As Sullk'ata adolescents increasingly leave rural communities to work in cities, temporarily or permanently, their means of maintaining relatedness shift. Rather than contribute labor on the family agricultural plots, herd sheep, or cook meals, children carry home gifts of sweaters and jeans, radios and blankets, and food such as bread, fruit, and rice. One of the most prominent times when Sullk'ata youth return to communities bearing gifts for family members as well as displaying their own commodities is Carnival. In fact, it is primarily from their children rather than their husbands that Sullk'ata women expect these gifts, as expressions of relatedness and affection. The adolescents who participate in Carnival actively demonstrate their belongingness to the modern nation through their consumption and display of commodities, and they simultaneously reinstate their citizenship in family and community.

The layering of practices is also contradictory, however. Sullk'atas recognize that during adolescence children not only become less dependent on and connected to parents but also identify themselves with urban ideologies of sociality and modernity, creating contradictions in the structural relationship of hierarchy between parents and children (Colloredo-Mansfeld 1999; Van Vleet 1999:160–71). Often older Sullk'atas express sadness when talking about their children who bring gifts. Anacleta cried when she told me of her daughter bringing her sweaters and polleras and telling her that she should not wear ragged clothes, even in the *campo*, countryside. Sebastian also cried when he told me of his children who were "no longer Sullk'atas but Sucreños and Cochabambinos" because they had lived since adolescence in those cities. Through these gifts as well as their preferred residences, the things that they own and use, their life experiences and attributes (such as their ability to speak Spanish, education in public schools, access to amenities such as television, radio, electricity, and running water), children and grandchildren may also position themselves or be identified by others as urban Bolivians, Sucreños or Cochabambinos rather than Sullk'atas.

As practices of identification carried out in particular contexts, wearing, buying, making, lending, and repairing certain kinds of clothes may also have specific meanings for youth that only partially overlap the meanings of similar practices for adults. Even the more habitual performances of girls as cholitas intertwine femininity with production and consumption *outside* the arena of subsistence. Sullk'atas thus associate girls (in comparison to boys) more closely with commodities, the urban sphere, and displays of fashion, inverting the notion of women as "more indian" (de la Cadena 1991, 1995). At the same time, a cholita who has accumulated a number of polleras, displayed during Carnival dancing, may also be perceived as a lively, hard worker who owns property necessary for life as part of a married couple, and as a generous and civilized companion should she share her polleras. Girls do not only buy but also borrow polleras, creating relationships of debt and obligation with other girls or with urban market women. Historian Carolyn Steedman has suggested for a very different cultural context that girls may come to understand that they possess themselves through these activities. From this perspective, marriage is less a process in which girls are exchanged as objects by groups of men as a process in which girls may exchange themselves for *something else*, for the ability to buy new clothes or for a particularly conceived of future (Steedman 1987:68). Sullk'ata girls' performances as "cholitas," whether habitual or extraordinary, might be understood as productive labor by which they attempt to maintain and transform themselves (as consumers, natives, friends, modern citizens, adults, and Sullk'atas) even as they are themselves translated by others.

Sullk'ata girls move through places just as do Marcia Stephenson's chuqila dancers (discussed in this volume)—mapping relationships with space, learning the relationships that inhere in particular places, and creating certain kinds of "civilized" arenas through their practices. If we conceive of the nation as a community of practice overlapping other such communities of practice that people move in and through over the course of a lifetime, or even a day, isolating and essentializing "family," "ethnic group," and "nation" becomes more obviously problematic. As David Nugent points out, much scholarship on the making of national cultures has taken an oppositional stance, assuming that national cultural values and institutions are "inherently alien and threatening to the many pre- and non-national populations who live within state boundaries" (Nugent 1998:8). Nugent shows that among Chachapoyas in northern Peru of the 1920s, modernity was viewed as liberating and a national culture as "autochthonous and real rather than artificial and imposed" (1998:10). Although frames of reference, such as the definition of "civilized" and "uncivilized," within different communities of practice may be opposing or contradictory, how individuals negotiate those values, practices, and discourses becomes a question to be asked rather than an answer assumed.

Conclusion

Girls contribute to imagining and constituting their identifications with national, ethnic, and familial collectivities through their everyday and ritual actions more often than through explicit commentaries on the "nation." In this chapter I have analyzed how the consumption of clothing is a window onto Sullk'ata youths' experiences of the possibilities and constraints of living as Bolivians at the turn of the twenty-first century. Consuming fashion is not a straightforward claim to any particular identity or to a constant relationship within a community of practice. Reina's struggle with how to claim a position as Bolivian and as Sullk'ata, at the same time that others may name her as simply "india," resonates in her desires for shoes and for recognition as being somehow desirable, as belonging in school and in the nation. Although Marisa may have been reluctant to don a pollera in 1996, by 2003 Marisa's love of buying polleras and dancing during Carnival shaped—or at least was used as an explanation for—her decision to remain in Bolivia rather than migrate to Spain. Her ambiguously gendered practices, of wearing pants and plowing, are laminated upon less frequent practices iconic of indian women, such as wearing polleras. If buying polleras and shoes, giving gifts, meeting friends, going to school, and dancing during Carnival can be counted as national cultural practices, then Reina's and Marisa's experiences and understandings of themselves as Sullk'atas are intimately intertwined with their experiences as Bolivianas.

Wearing polleras may in certain contexts enable girls and women to identify themselves with the nation, but at least for Sullk'ata girls, identification with the nation is not straightforward or simply claimed. Their experiences of national belonging are embedded within broader gendered and racial power hierarchies. Gendered and racial discourses of modernity and asymmetries of power are consistent undercurrents to Sullk'atas' construction of national citizenship. The inclusive nation-state does not exist in Bolivia. Elites continue to struggle with the "indian problem" even as the political rhetoric, supported by funding from nongovernmental organizations, shifts to incorporate notions of "interculturalism" (*interculturalidad*). Teachers, often not far removed from living as campesinos themselves, may berate children for their footwear or laziness and link these to moral failings that undermine national progress (also see Larson, this volume). Youth recognize their exclusion from the nation at the same time that they claim belonging to the nation.

Integrating multiple aspects of identity and the changes and continuities that may occur in a person's life and perspectives over time is, thus, crucial to understanding individuals' experiences as national subjects and actors. Years after the teacher calls her an india, Reina insists that she is proud of being from Sullk'ata, and she explains that this is because "people say that we are the best dancers and singers." Reina's words reflect the late-twentieth-century rhetoric of public schools that valorizes native Andean cultures and practices through "national" dances. At the same time, Reina's words voice a personal discovery. Attending to the specificities of subaltern Andeans, and the transformations that occur in any person's life, enhances understanding of what belonging to the nation might mean. Analyzing the ways that one may "identify with" multiple collectivities, in addition to being "identified as" a particular kind of person, complicates understanding of girls, and others, as citizens.

Acknowledgments

An earlier version of this chapter was published as "Adolescent Ambiguities and the Negotiation of Belonging in the Andes" in *Ethnology* (42, no. 4:349–63). I am grateful for permission to reprint an expanded version here. Research for this chapter was carried out under the auspices of a Fulbright-Hays Dissertation Research Abroad Fellowship in 1995 and further supported by a 2001 Faculty Travel Grant from Bowdoin College. Thanks to Andrew Canessa for his insightful comments on earlier drafts of this chapter and to the anonymous reviewers at the University of Arizona Press. The chapter was originally presented as a paper at the 2001 American Anthropological Association meetings. I am grateful to Andrew Canessa and Elayne Zorn for organizing the panel "Ñustas, Natives, and the Nation: Gender, Indigeneity, and the State in Highland South America" and to the discussant Mary Weismantel for an insightful commentary that generated a lively discussion among panelists and participants. Of course, I remain solely responsible for the ideas presented in this essay.

Notes

1. Among others see Albro 2000; Kaplan et al. 1999; de la Cadena 2000; Collins 1998; de Grazia 1996; Layoun 2001; Luykx 1999; McClintock 1995; Nugent 1998; Parker et al. 1992; Radcliffe and Westwood 1996; Stephenson 1999; Stoler 1995; Weismantel 2001; Yuval-Davis 1997.

2. For recent research on children also see, among others, Amit-Talai and Wulff 1995; Bucholtz 2002; Eckert and McConnell-Ginet 1995; Luykx 1999; Stephens 1995.

3. As Mary Bucholtz (2002) points out, the category "youth" is not as closely associated with an assumed universal and biological life stage as "adolescence"; I use the term *youth* to acknowledge the variability in social and cultural conceptions of childhood. Youth is, thus, difficult to define and may be best understood as a word that depends for its significance on the context of its use (Bucholtz 2002). Transitioning from youth to adult in Sullk'ata, for example, typically requires getting married and having children. When a man in his late fifties died, his younger sister told me that he was an "old joven." He had no wife or children and had never been married.

4. The Bolivian government has, however, recently begun to demonstrate an interest in youth and is considering a series of proposed laws on issues salient to youth, including labor and social services. In February 2003, Sucre was the site of the first of a series of conferences to be held in each of the major Bolivian cities concerning youth issues. Although hundreds of youth participated, many complained that the conference was not a successful forum for youth views and concerns because the events were so dominated by politicians.

5. All names are pseudonyms. All subsequent foreign language terms are in Quechua, unless indicated otherwise.

6. Also see Anzaldúa 1987; Collins 1998; Pratt 1999.

7. On conceptions of civilized and uncivilized from the perspective of an Andean moral universe, see, for example, Allen 1983; Mannheim and Van Vleet 1998; Urton 1985.

8. On polleras and identity, see Buechler and Buechler 1996; de la Cadena 1995; Crain 1996; Femenias 1997, 2004; Weismantel 2001. See Weismantel 2001:83–135 for an excellent discussion of cholitas and the material attributes of performances.

9. In fact, Carnival, more than any other time of year, highlights the ambiguities of "identity," particularly among youth, for on the final night of the fiesta young men also dress as cholitas (Bolin 1998; Van Vleet 1999; Weismantel 2001). In Sullk'ata in 1996 four teenage boys dressed up as cholitas—wearing polleras, bowler hats, and shawls—and performed an exaggerated rendition of the interactions between "cholitas" and "jóvenes" with other teenage boys. The young men did not solely borrow and wear the clothing of women but also altered their voices, using a higher pitched register, and mimicked the dancing movements of women. To the amusement of many appreciative onlookers, the "cholitas" are also alternately aggressively sexual with or deflecting the advances of the "jóvenes." Although the aggressive sexuality of both the "cholitas" and the "jóvenes" is most closely associated with mountain spirits and male ancestors, Carnival is also a time of "stealing women" (*warmi suway*)—a phrase that references a range of interactions from elopement to rape—the most common way for marriages to begin. The gendering of the "cholitas" is doubled, for audience members see both the character of a cholita and the young man playing her. The sexually explicit performances of "jóvenes" and "cholitas" may be seen as at once transgressive, an inversion typical of Carnival, and reconfirming the heterosexual contract of marriage (Van Vleet 1999).

Bibliography

Abercrombie, Thomas. 1992. "To Be Indian, to Be Bolivian." In *Nation-States and Indians in Latin America*, ed. Greg Urban and Joel Scherzer, 95–130. Austin: University of Texas Press.

———. 1992. "La fiesta del carnaval postcolonial en Oruro: Clase, etnicidad y nacionalismo en la danza folklorica." *Revista Andina* 10, no. 2: 279–352.

Ahearn, Laura. 2001. "Language and Agency." *Annual Review of Anthropology* 30:109–37.

Albro, Robert. 2000. "The Populist Chola: Cultural Mediation and the Political Imagination in Quillacollo, Bolivia." *Journal of Latin American Anthropology* 5, no. 2: 30–88.

Allen, Catherine. 1983. "Of Bear-Men and He-Men: Bear Metaphors and Male Self-perception in a Peruvian Community." *Latin American Indian Literatures* 7, no. 1: 38–51.

———. 1988. *The Hold Life Has: Coca and Cultural Identity in an Andean Community*. Washington, D.C.: Smithsonian Institution Press.

Amit-Talai, Vered, and Helena Wulff. 1995. *Youth Cultures: A Cross-Cultural Perspective*. New York: Routledge.

Anderson, Benedict. 1983. *Imagined Communities: Reflections on the Origin and Spread of Nationalism*. New York: Verso.

Anzaldúa, Gloria. 1987. *Borderlands/La Frontera*. San Francisco: Aunt Lute Book Company.

Bolin, Inge. 1998. *Rituals of Respect: The Secret of Survival in the High Peruvian Andes*. Austin: University of Texas Press.

Brubaker, Rogers, and Frederick Cooper. 2000. "Beyond 'Identity.'" *Theory and Society: Renewal and Critique in Social Theory* 29, no. 1: 1–47.

Bucholtz, Mary. 2002. "Youth and Cultural Practice." *Annual Review of Anthropology* 31: 525–52.

Buechler, Hans, and Judith-Maria Buechler. 1996. *The World of Sofia Velasquez: The Autobiography of a Bolivian Market Vendor*. New York: Columbia University Press.

Butler, Judith. 1990. *Gender Trouble: Feminism and the Subversion of Identity*. New York: Routledge.

———. 1993. *Bodies that Matter: On the Discursive Limits of Sex*. New York: Routledge.

de la Cadena, Marisol. 1991. "'Las mujeres son más india': Etnicidad y género en una comunidad del Cusco." *Revista Andina* 9, no. 1:7–29.

———. 1995. "'Women Are More Indian'": Ethnicity and Gender in a Community Near Cuzco." In *Ethnicity, Markets, and Migration in the Andes: At the Crossroads of History and Anthropology*, ed. Brooke Larson and Olivia Harris, with Enrique Tandeter, 328–48. Durham, N.C.: Duke University Press.

———. 2000. *Indigenous Mestizos: The Politics of Race and Culture in Cuzco, Peru, 1919–1991*. Durham, N.C.: Duke University Press.

Canessa, Andrew. 2004. "Reproducing Racism: Schooling and Race in Highland Bolivia." *Race, Ethnicity and Education* 7, no. 2:185–204.

Coles, Robert. 1986. *The Political Life of Children*. Boston: Atlantic Monthly Press.

Collins, Patricia Hill. 1998. "It's All in the Family: Intersections of Gender, Race, and Nation." *Hypatia* 13, no. 3:62–82.

Colloredo-Mansfeld, Rudi. 1999. *The Native Leisure Class: Consumption and Cultural Creativity in the Andes*. Chicago: University of Chicago Press.

Crain, Mary. 1996. "The Gendering of Ethnicity in the Ecuadorian Andes: Native Women's Self-Fashioning in the Urban Marketplace." In *Machos, Mistresses, and Madonnas: Contesting the Power of Latin American Gender Imagery*, ed. Marit Melhuus and Kristi Ann Stølen, 134–83. London: Verso.

Desjarlais, Robert R. 1997. *Shelter Blues: Sanity and Selfhood among the Homeless*. Philadelphia: University of Pennsylvania Press.

Douglas, Mary, and Baron Isherwood. 1979. *The World of Goods*. New York: Basic Books.

DuBois, W.E.B. 1903. *The Souls of Black Folk: Essays and Sketches*. Chicago: A. C. McClurg.

Eckert, Penelope, and Sally McConnell-Ginet. 1995. "Constructing Meaning, Con-

structing Selves: Snapshots of Language, Gender, and Class from Belten High."
In *Gender Articulated: Language and the Socially Constructed Self*, ed. Kira Hall
and Mary Bucholtz, 469–507. New York: Routledge.

Femenias, Blenda. 1997. *Ambiguous Emblems: Gender, Clothing, and Representation
in Contemporary Peru*. Ph.D. diss., University of Wisconsin, Madison.

Foucault, Michel. 1972. *The Archaeology of Knowledge*, trans. A. M. Sheridan. New
York: Harper Colophon.

———. 1978. *The History of Sexuality*, vol. 1, *An Introduction*, trans. Robert Hurley.
London: Allen Lane.

Gifford, Douglas, and Pauline Hoggarth. 1976. *Carnival and Coca Leaf: Some Traditions of the Peruvian Quechua Ayllu*. New York: St. Martin's Press.

Gill, Leslie. 1994. *Precarious Dependencies: Gender, Class, and Domestic Service in
Bolivia*. New York: Columbia University Press.

———. 1997. "Creating Citizens, Making Men: The Military and Masculinity in
Bolivia." *Cultural Anthropology* 12, no. 4:527–50.

de Grazia, Victoria. 1996. "Nationalizing Women: The Competition between Fascist
and Commercial Cultural Models in Mussolini's Italy. In *The Sex of Things: Gender and Consumption in Historical Perspective*, ed. Victoria de Grazia with Ellen
Furlough, 337–58. Berkeley: University of California Press.

Harvey, Penelope. 1998. "Los 'hechos naturales' de parentesco y género en un con-
texto andino." In *Gente de carne y hueso: Las tramas de parentesco en los Andes*, vol.
2, ed. Denise Y. Arnold, 69–82. La Paz, Bolivia: CIASE/ILCA.

Kaplan, Caren, Norma Alarcón, and Minoo Moallem, eds. 1999. *Between Woman
and Nation: Nationalisms, Transnational Feminisms, and the State*. Durham, N.C.:
Duke University Press.

Layoun, Mary N. 2001. *Wedded to the Land: Gender, Boundaries, and Nationalism in
Crisis*. Durham, N.C.: Duke University Press.

Luykx, Aurolyn. 1999. *The Citizen Factory: Schooling and Cultural Production in
Bolivia*. Albany: State University of New York Press.

Mannheim, Bruce. 1991. *The Language of the Inka since the European Invasion*. Austin: University of Texas Press.

———. 1998. "A Nation Surrounded." In *Native Traditions in the Post-Conquest
World*, ed. Elizabeth Boone and Tom Cummins, 381–418. Washington, D.C.:
Dumbarton Oaks.

Mannheim, Bruce, and Krista Van Vleet. 1998. The Dialogics of Southern Quechua
Narrative. *American Anthropologist* 100, no. 2:326–46.

Mauss, Marcel. 1990 [1950]. *The Gift: Forms and Functions of Exchange in Archaic
Societies*, trans. Ian Cunnison. New York: W. W. Norton.

Mayer, Enrique. 1991. "Peru in Deep Trouble: Mario Vargas Llosa's 'Inquest in the
Andes' Reexamined." *Cultural Anthropology* 6, no. 4:467–504.

McClintock, Anne. 1995. *Imperial Leather: Race, Gender, and Sexuality in the Colonial Contest*. New York: Routledge.

Millones, Luis, and Mary Louise Pratt. 1990. *Amor Brujo: Images and Culture of Love
in the Andes*. Syracuse, N.Y.: Maxwell School of Citizenship and Public Affairs.

Morris, Rosalind. 1995. "All Made Up: Performance Theory and the New Anthropology of Sex and Gender." *Annual Review of Anthropology* 24:567–92.

Nugent, David. 1998. "The Morality of Modernity and the Travails of Tradition: Nationhood and the Subaltern in Northern Peru." *Critique of Anthropology* 18, no. 1:7–33.

Parker, Andrew, Doris Sommer, and Patricia Yaeger, eds. 1992. *Nationalisms and Sexualities*. New York: Routledge.

Pratt, Mary Louise. 1999. "Apocalypse in the Andes." *Americas* 51, no. 4:38–47.

Radcliffe, Sarah, and Sallie Westwood. 1996. *Remaking the Nation: Place, Identity, and Politics in Latin America*. New York: Routledge.

Sallnow, Michael J. 1987. *Pilgrims of the Andes: Regional Cults in Cuzco*. Washington, D.C.: Smithsonian Institution Press.

Steedman, Carolyn. 1987. *Landscape for a Good Woman: A Story of Two Lives*. New Brunswick, N.J.: Rutgers University Press.

Stephens, Sharon. 1995. "Children and the Politics of Culture in 'Late Capitalism.'" In *Children and the Politics of Culture*, ed. Sharon Stephens, 3–48. Princeton, N.J.: Princeton University Press.

Stephens, Sharon, ed. 1995. *Children and the Politics of Culture*. Princeton, N.J.: Princeton University Press.

Stephenson, Marcia. 1999. *Gender and Modernity in Andean Bolivia*. Austin: University of Texas Press.

Stoler, Ann. 1995. *Race and the Education of Desire*. Durham, N.C.: Duke University Press.

Urton, Gary 1985. "Animal Metaphors and the Life Cycle in an Andean Community." In *Animal Myths and Metaphors in South America*, ed. Gary Urton, 251–84. Salt Lake City: University of Utah Press.

Van Vleet, Krista. 1999. *"Now My Daughter Is Alone": Performing Kinship and Embodying Affect in Marriage Practices among Native Andeans in Bolivia*. Ph.D. diss., University of Michigan, Ann Arbor.

———. 2002. "The Intimacies of Power: Rethinking Violence and Affinity in the Bolivian Andes." *American Ethnologist* 29, no. 3:1–35.

Wade, Peter. 1997. *Race and Ethnicity in Latin America*. Chicago: Pluto Press.

Weismantel, Mary. 1995. "Making Kin: Kinship Theory and Zumbagua Adoptions." *American Ethnologist* 22, no. 4:685–709.

———. 1997. "White Cannibals: Fantasies of Racial Violence in the Andes. *Identities* 4, no. 1:9–35.

———. 2001. *Cholas and Pishtacos: Stories of Race and Sex in the Andes*. Chicago: University of Chicago Press.

Yuval-Davis, Nira. 1997. *Gender and Nation*. London: Sage.

6

The Indian Within, the Indian Without

Citizenship, Race, and Sex in a Bolivian Hamlet

Andrew Canessa

On a recent trip to the village of Pocobaya[1] in the highlands of Bolivia I found myself sitting in a friend's kitchen whilst she prepared one of my favorite dishes. As she busied herself preparing the guinea pig and I peeled vegetables, we chatted about my goddaughter, Alicia, who had just left her husband because of his violence. We commiserated with Alicia and then I asked, "Do you fight?"[2] She nodded matter of factly and explained yes they did; her husband even beat her up once with the metal tube she uses to blow on the fire, she said with a laugh. We talked on and I asked her what kinds of things her husband said when they "fought." She said he often shouted in Spanish and said "carajo" (damn!) as well as phrases such as "india sucia" (dirty indian woman) and "maldita india" (accursed indian woman). I was not surprised, as I had heard people recount similar things before, and Bonifacia simply shrugged when I asked her why her husband spoke to her in this way.

Pocobaya is an indian village several hours' walk from the nearest road. Everyone in the village speaks Aymara; all the women dress in the mode that currently typifies indian dress in Bolivia, and all the residents would certainly be considered indian, indigenous, Aymaras, campesinos, or whatever term outsiders use to characterize the ethnically distinct peasant communities of the highlands. So why then would a man from this community bark insults in Spanish to his wife and call her an "indian"?

The Community and the Nation

Pocobaya, at an altitude of 3,000 meters above sea level, is a hamlet of approximately two hundred persons (INE 1992) in the province of Larecaja (La Paz). No road leads to Pocobaya, but it is a few hours' walk from the provincial capital of Sorata (pop. 2,000), which is the most important market town in the region. Sorata is on the road that connects the Bolivian highlands to the tropical lowlands. Thus, even though Pocobaya is at some distance from the metropolitan centers, it is not difficult to travel to the mines and cities of Bolivia; indeed, many Pocobayeños travel with some frequency to the gold mines. Pocobaya furthermore has a school that teaches children up to the sixth grade (until recently only to third) and many adults listen to Aymara language radio. Thus Pocobayeños, even those who rarely leave the community, are quite aware of life beyond their small village.

Nevertheless, the experience of Pocobayeños of the life beyond the village is by no means homogeneous: some spend a good deal of their time away from home and consequently have views on the world beyond that differ from those who remain. The people of Pocobaya may all be indians as far as Bolivian society is concerned, but within the community some symbolize indianness more than others: namely the monolingual women who rarely move beyond the ambit of the Aymara-speaking world. Many of the men, in contrast, speak Spanish, do seasonal work in mines and large agricultural concerns, and have done military service, which gives them a familiarity with the country most women do not possess. Men are generally the only ones able to obtain cash, which is virtually unobtainable in Pocobaya.[3] Due to increasing population in recent decades, the fertility of the land has decreased as a result of shorter fallow periods and erosion. This leaves little surplus for the market; and when Pocobayeños do take their produce to market, rates of exchange are generally quite disadvantageous. As a result, and as is the case in many indian communities in Bolivia (Rivera Cusicanqui 1996:75), men are obliged to leave the community to acquire the resources to satisfy the demands of the community. That is, Pocobaya, as is the case with most similar communities, is dependent on the society and economy beyond it.

In terms of the household economy, men and women agree, when asked, that they have complementary roles, and many household tasks require the labor of men and women to be performed properly (Canessa 1997). For example, plowing requires a man to lead the team and a woman to drop the seeds. These tasks are deemed "male" and "female," respectively. The positive value of complementarity is clearly stated by both men and women. Women strongly assert their position and dominance in their households and sometimes speak of their husbands as "pasiri," visitors who come and go. Many men are quite frank that important decisions, especially financial ones, are equally shared. I once asked one of my neighbors what would happen if, without consulting his wife, he bought a cow with the money he brought back from the mines. He gave me a horrified look and shook his head, insisting he would never do that because he would get all the blame if it were a wrong decision.

Men will frequently speak with high regard for their wives and in many contexts talk positively of their productive activities. One of the most important values for men and women is labor, and men value their wives' labor highly; in contrast, manual labor is not valued highly in metropolitan discourse. In the Andes, the proximity to earth has particular racialized meanings as urban people contrast their "clean" lives with the lives of peasants who are in contact with earth through their hands and feet and the houses in which they live (Orlove 1998). A white man whose family used to have a hacienda in the highlands not far from Pocobaya and now lives in La Paz explained to me how indians labored crouched and animal-like for hours, with their heavy hands working the soil in all weathers. "They don't feel cold or pain like you or I." He illustrated his point by bending over and opening his hands and making a digging motion with a brutish grimace on his face.

The metropolitan culture, however, devalues not only indian labor but rural indian culture in general. In Bolivia the dominant national discourse values urban, mestizo,[4] Spanish-speaking culture over rural, indian, Aymara, or Quechua-speaking cultures. This is most starkly evident in media representations: in a country wherein the vast majority of the population is of indigenous origin, the absence of indian faces on television and posters is quite striking.[5] This is true of all the posters that appear in Sorata, the market town closest to Pocobaya. From beer posters featuring pouting women to the posters of the various churches, it is abundantly clear that "Bolivians" are imagined as white or light-skinned mestizos by the people who produce the posters.[6]

There is something of an irony in the absence of any indian-looking person in these representations, for throughout the country's history indians have certainly been very present in the imagination of Bolivia's elites: they have constantly drawn on images of indians to illustrate their own sense of superiority. To some extent the absence of indians in public images is testament to their ambivalent presence in the imagination of dominant groups: the indian and rural aspect of the Bolivian experience is an essential part of the metropolitan discourse, and in some sense can be seen to have been created by it (Abercrombie 1992). By the same token, indian identity is historically contingent and does not exist sui generis, outside of colonial and neocolonial cultural, economic and political structures. The dominant Bolivian national imagining, as indeed that of many other American nations, is founded on a series of mutually implicating dyads that contrast urban, Western-oriented, modern culture with a rural, anachronistic, indian one. As a consequence, indian "otherness" is at the very heart of the elite national imagination: the more it is repressed, the more it is reified.

Although the categories of indian and rural versus hispanic and urban are mutually implicating, they are not equally so: the dominant metropolitan discourse is clearly hegemonic in that it is produced and reproduced in a wide range of social, political, and cultural contexts by whites, mestizos, and indians. As is noted in the introduction to this volume, indian identity is also internalized by many urban mestizos and whites (even if only to localize or repress it) (cf. Salomon 1981); but it is equally true that indian identity is read off as a reflection of the dominant discourse in the few spaces allowed for such an identity; for even those discourses that challenge dominant ideas about race and identity do so using a very occidental language around indigeneity, identity, and difference. To borrow Laura Lewis's (2003) phrase, ethnicity and identity in Latin America are a "hall of mirrors" with an infinite number of reflections as difference and identity constantly rebound on each other. If "the indian" is at the very center of elites' imagination of themselves (see Bigenho, Larson, this volume), it is also the case that whiteness and metropolitan values lie at the very center of how indians think of themselves.

More White, More Indian: Men and Women in Pocobaya

The question arises, however, how notions of what is white and what is indian become salient in a community such as Pocobaya. As with all successful hegemonic processes, the ways such ideas spread is not always even or coherent. There are three areas of life, however, where it is clear that Pocobayeños are exposed to ideas that are at variance with broadly held views in Pocobaya about identity and gender. If in most contexts Pocobayeños are in agreement that they share an ethnic or racial identity and that men and women have different but complementary roles in life, it is also the case that there are other occasions wherein people say things and behave very differently. Women and men negotiate these values in multifarious ways according to their own circumstances and personalities, but it seems clear that all have to deal with the tension between the values that are dominant in the society beyond the community and those that are largely held within it. For many people such conflicting values are, at best, temporarily resolved (Canessa 1997).

Schools and Schooling

Silvia Rivera Cusicanqui (1996:78) notes that it was one of the paradoxes of the 1952 Revolution that "in extending formal 'citizenship' to indians and women it opened the doors to hegemonic representations of gender at the very heart of communities that were previously isolated from the national political fabric." One of the key ways in which citizenship was extended after the Revolution was through education, which certainly went to the heart of every community, with the school replacing the church as the most prominent building. As Roberto Choque Canqui et al. (1992) have argued, education since the Revolution has been primarily aimed at Bolivianizing, rather than educating, indians—a powerful form of colonization.

I have dealt with racism in the school in Pocobaya at length elsewhere (Canessa 2004), but it is worth looking at some key aspects and how they relate to gender relations and ethnic identity in Pocobaya, namely, how indian culture is feminized and marginalized. Central to this process is the concept of civilization: in Pocobaya, the word *civilización* is one often heard in school lessons, be it in mathematics, history, or in the speeches given by teachers as children line up to enter the school. "Civilización" is something the children do not have but should aspire to, and it is interesting to note the kinds of things which, according to their teachers, mark them as uncivilized. Recalling Larson's discussion in her chapter, one may not be surprised to learn that personal hygiene figured high on the list; but teachers also regularly point out a wide range of things such as food, rural architecture, footwear, the lack of machinery, and language use to exemplify the children's lack of "civilización." The clear message to schoolchildren is that their rural indian existence is profoundly uncivilized and in sharp contrast to the images of clean, white urban people in many of their textbooks.

The teachers themselves, however, are by no means unambiguously white. All the teachers in Pocobaya and surrounding villages are from Aymara-speaking communities from the high plain around Lake Titicaca. These communities are a good day's walk away from Pocobaya and have better roads, more schools, and better communication with the capital city. The teachers are great believers in the power of education to civilize, but they are faced with a bitter irony: they have worked hard to raise themselves from the indian peasantry but find themselves in communities more "backward" than the ones they left. The indian origin of teachers is elided; the barbarous indianness of their pupils accentuated. So, even as some of them perm their hair for a more European look, they are deeply ambivalent about the people among whom they live and veer from effusive comments about "our peasant brothers" to vituperative speeches about their lack of civilization.

In the last fifty years the role of schools has been to eradicate indian culture through its civilizing mission, so it is not surprising that it is only in the past few years that indians have been widely represented in schoolbooks. When they are depicted, however, they are invariably in the mountains or forest in a rural and "traditional" setting. People are very much depicted as "indigenous" in the literal sense of the word, that is, of being of and belonging to the dramatic landscape, and the timelessness of these images further underlines their lack of modernity.

Indians have, however, long been depicted in history books. The cover of one schoolbook recently used in Pocobaya shows a blue-eyed boy dressed as a conquistador accompanied by an indian girl smiling coquettishly at him (dressed, incidentally, in contemporary, not colonial, indian dress). This image is a very succinct summary of Bolivian political and social history: white males conquering a feminized indian race; white men taking indian women as partners and creating a new mestizo race. The Conquest is represented as a union of Europeans and indians, which resulted in the mestizo nature of the current Bolivian nation. The violence, and in particular the sexual violence, that accompanied the Conquest is conveniently elided.

Throughout history it has principally been European men who have had relationships with indian women rather than the other way around (Weismantel 2001:155). These relationships have always been hierarchical and not always consensual (Dore 2000:154). One of the clearest images of indians through history then is as the wives and concubines of Europeans, and this is reflected in the history books used in Pocobaya.

Indians as a whole were seen as embodying feminine characteristics in the early decades after the Conquest (Lewis 2003; Silverblatt 1987); at times, indeed, the entire continent was seen as feminine (Mason 1990). The image of two children looking at each other dressed as conquistador and indian girl (above) is a clear illustration of what Ashis Nandy (1983:3) has called the "homology between sexual and political dominance," which, in the context presented here, is also racialized.

This homology is at the center of why indian women so epitomize indianness in a way that men do not, since conquest and dominance are so racialized and gendered. This begins to explain some of the paradoxes inherent in the anecdote that opened this chapter: in the broader national context indianness is gendered, and in that gendering are encoded the tropes of violent conquest.

Schooling offers children citizenship in the nation by giving them access to metropolitan mores and language but at the price of introducing them to hegemonic representations of race and gender. It proves, moreover, to be an ever-elusive citizenship in which they are expected to leave their communities and change their lifestyles in order to be accepted into the wider Bolivian mestizo-creole society. In practice, it is chiefly men who leave Pocobaya; but, men or women, they are never quite accepted because people have great difficulty in hiding their rural, indian roots even when they try: they will never speak Spanish well enough; they will never be white enough.

Masculinizing Spaces: The Army and the Mines

The Bolivian army, as with every "people's army" since Napoleon, has a social function, which is to create a sense of national purpose and identity among its recruits. In this it is very similar to the school, which also has had as one of its key goals the creation of a national and homogenous culture and extending citizenship to indians. Here, too, are hegemonic representations of gender introduced.

The Bolivian army, as is the case with every other public institution, gets whiter as one moves closer to the top. Indian men heavily dominate as conscripts, and the officers are almost exclusively mestizo or white. Zenobio from Pocobaya told me that one had to change one's name to become an officer, from, for example, "Condori to Cortés." "Condori" (a typically indigenous surname), in Zenobio's words, indicates poverty (nombre de pobreza es), and such names are not acceptable, he said, in universities and the high ranks of the army. One of the things that many Pocobaya ex-soldiers remembered about their military experiences is the almost ritual humiliation and occasional violence meted out to indian recruits. They recalled being ridiculed for their stupidity, clumsiness, and inability to speak Spanish. Many Pocobayeños recall seeing soldiers ordered to bend over and being beaten for speaking Aymara or Quechua.

Bolivian boot camps are no different from others around the world where new recruits are accused of being homosexuals or women. In some cases soldiers are made to parade around the base in women's clothing for infractions (Gill 1997:536); and there is a very clear homology between citizenship and masculinity that military service is expected to confer.

It is in the army, above all, that young men learn to speak Spanish, and it is in the army that they learn the extent and nature of their country. Military service in the Andes "provides the structured and 'patriotic' means through which male citizens take part in movement around their country, meeting co-nationals and re-imagining their community" (Radcliffe and Westwood 1996:124), and it is through military service that men become citizens (Fraser 1989:125). Writing about Guatemala, the other Latin American country with a majority indigenous population, Diane Nelson notes that "reports of the brutal barracks training suggest that internalized racism is a tool used to break the boys down so they can be remade as soldiers, in part by promising them marks of the ladino [mestizo] . . . and of masculinity" (1999:91). In Guatemala, as in Bolivia, the army service simultaneously offers citizenship and masculinity and, in both cases, the boundaries between one and the other are ambiguous.

In the words of Lesley Gill, "Military service is one of the most important prerequisites for the development of successful subaltern manhood, because it signifies rights to power and citizenship" (1997:527). Through military service men obtain the *libreta militar*, the military booklet, which is a requisite for a national identity card. These two documents are essential for obtaining a passport, a job in a government agency, or a degree in the state university (ibid.: 537). For many Pocobayeños, military service is their only opportunity for seeing distant regions and, as Benedicto, one of my neighbors in Pocobaya, told me, it was in the army that he really understood what Bolivia was. This imagining of the nation occurs in a highly masculine, hierarchical, and racialized context.

It is not, however, only the "imagined community" (Anderson 1983) of the nation, the patria that is experienced during military service, but the local community of personalized relationships is reimagined too, the *patria chica*, the "little" homeland. Through military service young men come to see their homes, their families, their language and culture in a powerfully different light. It is true that they have been exposed to these kinds of imaginings through their school education, but being exposed to these ideas in an all-male, Spanish-speaking environment far from home in a total institution has a profound effect. Military service and the acquisition of the libreta militar structure the relationship of a man with the state on the basis of his new citizenship. Such service also has an important impact on his membership in his home community. Returning soldiers are patriotically fêted under a specially made arch on their return from military service. Zenobio commented to me that when one leaves military service one feels "as if one has come close to the Presidency" (como si acercaste la presidencia). This illustrates well how military service is considered in terms of approaching the top of the nation, the pinnacle of political power and social status. A returning soldier is a full citizen almost to the point of being presidential.

Military service not only confers membership of the nation state but has implications for membership in the indian community too. Whereas in the recent past it was through marriage that indian men became full members of their community, now military service is increasingly performing this role. For women full adulthood continues to be achieved through marriage, and women prefer marrying someone who has undergone military service. Men are therefore frequently proud to undertake their national service. As my friend Pastor put it to me: "It is a requirement as a Bolivian; it is to fulfill a duty";[7] and Zenobio told me that young men entered military service because they come out "macho": "'You are a man now' is what people say."

Some men avoid military service, but they are consequently likely to be functionally monolingual in Aymara.[8] They are also therefore likely to have difficulty finding better jobs and not be very good marriage prospects. These men lack the masculinizing experience of military service, and their poor or inadequate Spanish forces them to inhabit more closely the world of women.

One area of life that is affected, as men become citizens in the nation-state, is their sexuality. One of the key features of army life mentioned by many Pocobayeños is the regular visits to prostitutes. Every garrison has its prostitutes who are easily available, and they are apparently a standard feature of army life. It is not only during their twelve months of army service that Pocobayeños purchase sex. Most spend extended periods in the gold mines, and it is quite common for men to spend several years in such work before returning to their community to get married. The work is hard, hot, wet, and dangerous and they relax in bars, cinemas, and with prostitutes. A visit to a prostitute costs "one gram of gold, for a 'quickie,' five to spend the night."[9] As one friend put it, "They take a lot of gold. 'Bring gold!' they say and a little later we just give it to them."[10]

Where military service allows Pocobayeños to travel and see their country in its variety and lay claim to his citizenship, prostitution serves a similar function. One friend beamed proudly as he told me he had slept with white (*rinka*), black (*nigra*), and indian (*chulita*) women, "all the women of Bolivia." His clear sense of accomplishment at having spanned sexually the three most recognizable racial groups in Bolivia is significant in the context of Bolivia as a mixed nation.

This mixing occurred through sexual relations hinted at on the cover of the textbook mentioned above. Although in Bolivia the African contribution is rather more muted, the country shares a discourse with many other Latin American countries of being a product of the mix of European, African, and indigenous peoples (e.g., Placido 2001). Historically in Bolivia and elsewhere in Latin America the social advance that mestizaje implies has been seen in terms of white men having sex with nonwhite women (e.g., Nelson 1999; Freyre 1946; Wright 1990). Indeed the degenerative (and often putatively predatory) sexuality of lower-class and darker men has been seen as particularly problematic in twentieth-century Latin American discourse, which was concerned with "improving" the race (Stepan 1991:93). My friend's evident pride in having slept with this variety of women must be seen in this context, a laying claim to his nation not only through military service and travel but through sex with racial and ethnic "others," a prerogative more generally seen as belonging to creole males (Condarco Morales 1983:311; Nelson 1999:221) and even a civilizing mission (Stephenson 1999:38). The politics of citizenship are not only gendered but sexualized; and these kinds of multiracial sexual experiences may have a political dimension whether or not the individuals involved explicitly recognize it.

Aside from consorting with prostitutes, Pocobayeños and other miners regularly go to see pornographic films and through these are exposed to different sexual practices. These small cinemas showing video films run all day and all night so they can be visited whatever shift one is on. The various men I spoke to about this said that they watched many of these videos, which are clearly described as being illicit, but that is quite possibly part of the thrill. Various aspects fascinated these men, such as having sex naked and the length of time sex acts take in these films, which, it was suggested to me, indicates the white people are very slow to reach orgasm. In contrast, sex in Pocobaya typically takes place in the dark, whilst clothed, and is over much quicker. Pocobayeños talk about lesbian sex (*siñurax panini ikanti*),[11] anal sex (*chinajat ikasipxi*), fellatio (*lakata pichilumpi apantaña*), and a variety of other sexual practices, which, according to men,[12] women in Pocobaya have little taste for, since they prefer to have sex on their sides in a ventral-dorsal position.

It is not just practices but particular aesthetics that men are exposed to through films and brothels. Porn actresses and prostitutes often have shaven pudenda (*jan tarwani*), and many men believe that this makes women "horny" and eager for sex.[13] These experiences develop aesthetics and produce desires that cannot easily be met in Pocobaya, and, in fact, men say that such practices do not occur in Pocobaya (indeed they are described as *prohibido*, forbidden), although this is, of course, difficult to ascertain. One man, however, did claim to have anal sex with his wife, stating the added pleasure and contraceptive value of the practice; other men expressed a desire to have anal sex but were ambiguous about whether they did so with their wives.

Pocobayeños return from their military service and stints in the mines with a very different view of the world than that with which they left. They have proudly served their country and can consider themselves true citizens who have fulfilled their patriotic duty; they have learned to speak Spanish, which, even though they have not done so very well, is as much a marker of Bolivian citizenship as an identity card; and they have experienced a very different sexuality to the one prevalent in Pocobaya. They have traveled across the nation and made it theirs; they have slept with numerous women of various racial and ethnic groups. They will also have experienced the widespread racism against indians in Bolivia and know that however well they speak Spanish it is not well enough. This experience of the promise of inclusive mestizaje proving ever elusive is shared by many migrating groups in the Andes as Radcliffe (1990) has noted for female indian domestic workers in neighboring Peru. With these deeply ambivalent experiences, they return to Pocobaya with conflicting ideas and imaginations, which they in some form pass on to their wives as indeed they sometimes pass on their venereal diseases.

Young men, however, rarely settle permanently in the village after military service; the exigencies of life in a community with population growth and land erosion necessitates seasonal migration. Whatever the length of time away and whatever job they manage to find, indian men receive very low wages when they leave the community and enter into the capitalist economy. They receive low wages because as indians, any labor defined as indian labor is low-status labor. So in the markets and towns indians get paid a pittance for carrying loads, and in the lucrative cocaine industry the poorly paid and dangerous work of stamping the coca leaves in kerosene is reserved for indians (Harris 1995).

Indians are low paid for another reason: they *can* be low paid because their wage does not need to cover the costs of reproducing their labor. Their children and wives are supported principally by the land at home whilst men's wages supplement that subsistence; that is, an indian's wage is not expected to support him and his family. Moreover, when the mine closes, or when men become old or sick, they return to the village, which provides them with a form of social security. Thus, none of the costs of maintaining, reproducing, or protecting the labor supply are borne by the employer (Weismantel 1988:30).

In this important way peasant laborers are fundamental and not peripheral to the capitalist system as these semi-proletarianized laborers (de Janvry 1981) provide the system with a cheap and flexible source of labor, being reabsorbed by the communities in times of unemployment and providing a reserve in times of expansion. De Janvry presents this situation as a function of the post-hacienda condition of rural Latin America, but there is, in fact, a long history of semi-proletarianized indian labor for the colonial and republican economic systems were highly dependent on the temporary (and therefore subsidized) indian migration to mines, the backbone of the Bolivian economy for centuries. Mining continues to be important for Pocobayeños, and when the price of gold fell in the late 1990s Pocobayeños simply returned to their communities or looked for less lucrative (but also less dangerous) work in the rice fields of the valleys (*yungas*).

In this way the peasant household is not marginal to the modern mining and agricultural businesses of Bolivia but intrinsic to it; as many of the other contributions in this volume illustrate, such marginality is an illusion on many levels. The peasant sector cannot survive without cash income, and the capitalist sector is dependent on the cheap labor supplied by the peasantry. The articulation of the two sectors of the economy occurs at the level of the peasant household, which, as Meillassoux (1981) has pointed out, bears the brunt of a double exploitation. More specifically, wider economic structures penetrate right into the level of intimate personal relationships between men and women since it is the men who work in the capitalist sector and the women who almost entirely work in the peasant one: the "dual economy" is articulated at the level of the married couple.

Gender Troubles

Despite what many urban Bolivians believe about highland indian women, women in Pocobaya have a relatively high status within their community (cf. Paulson 1996). There is a strong sense of gender complementarity and people are very aware that it takes two adults to run a household properly. This sense of complementarity goes beyond the economic, for one is not considered a complete and properly social person until one is married. In Pocobaya marriage is often referred to as *jaqichasiña*, which literally means "the making of a person." There is a profound sense in which the married couple, the *chachawarmi* (a singular noun meaning "manwoman"), is a single social and political unit. As a consequence, women's opinions are respected, and all important decisions are made together by the chachawarmi. Moreover, women are considered heads of household even though men represent the household at the community level and beyond. Both men and women I spoke to were explicit about sharing responsibility and important decisions.

Whilst the men are in the army, in the mines, or working in rice fields, the women in Pocobaya are working the fields and taking care of the children and animals. This is hard work and difficult to do alone, particularly since the running of the household is predicated on a gendered division of labor. The absence of men for extended periods also means that women necessarily have to undertake tasks normally reserved for men.

Agricultural and domestic tasks, as in many cultures, are divided into male and female roles. Women, for example, sow, weave, and cook; men plow, break the ground, and fetch firewood. Gender difference is performative rather than essential in that gender distinction is seen as being expressed through the different things men and women *do* rather than a differing sense of what they *are*.[14] Since the absence of men requires women to undertake male tasks, they are masculinized by their labor. So at the same time that men are masculinized by their military service and by navigating the geography of the mestizo-creole nation, women in Pocobaya are masculinized through their agricultural labor. There are, however, important differences in this process of masculinization. Men are "whitened" by this process through their acquisition of citizenship and relative fluency in Spanish; women, on the other hand, are not. Whereas men retain their higher "whitened" status when they return to their villages, women, in contrast, return to their female roles when their partners return, but this is not always a smooth transition, as women are becoming increasingly independent.

In the past, women depended entirely on their husbands to deal with money. Francisca, who is now in her sixties, describes the predicament she found herself in when her husband died: "My husband left me without knowing money. No, my husband just took care of me here. He was the one who knew how to work for money. (When he died) he left me here without any money. I don't know how much things are; I don't know (the value of) a peso. Now that my husband is lost, my children are teaching me a little."[15]

Her granddaughters, however, all speak some Spanish and are certainly more likely to be able to use money even if most purchases are undertaken by menfolk. When men are away for long periods, women will go to market to make necessary purchases, and younger women in particular are becoming, out of necessity, increasingly autonomous. Gaining that autonomy comes easier to some women than others, especially for those women who can earn cash independently by making dolls for sale. In a neighboring community the women have made a successful business of rearing chickens, and a woman has been elected to the leadership post of *secretario general*, a position normally reserved for men. Such an election for a one-year term requires the votes of all householders and would have necessitated the assent and support of a majority of men. The people of Pocobaya met this news with a mixture of shock, amazement, and admiration.

It is clear, even though the parameters of women's lives are constrained by geography and language, that they nevertheless do not live in some rural idyll far removed from the gendered nationalist imaginings of their menfolk. Women from Pocobaya will also have learned a clear sense of their racial and ethnic inferiority from their visits to the market town when they are spoken to abruptly and rudely in Spanish, for mestizo traders as well as mestizo teachers always give their commands in Spanish. Very few Pocobayeñas speak Spanish, even those who have gone to school; and although many will have made brief visits to La Paz, they very rarely travel beyond the Aymara-speaking world. As a consequence, they have little claim to the kind of "whitened" Spanish-speaking militarized citizenship their menfolk can claim.

"Whiteness" is therefore not simply the color of one's skin but a complex of social and cultural attributes that confer membership of the dominant cultural group. In speaking Spanish, undergoing military service, working in the mines, men are closer to the white urban ideal than women. When they are present in the (increasingly female) village they reproduce the racialization of cultural values and difference along gendered lines, which are, in any case, values that are gendered to begin with. Because the metropolitan discourse on nation is as gendered as it is racialized, indian women are twice removed from what is valued in nationalist terms in Bolivia.

In the village context these gendered and racialized imaginings of nation are reproduced with different signifiers. Away from the community, in contrast, Pocobayeño men are relatively powerless and even feminized indians. A simple case illustrates the point. One day I traveled to Sorata with two friends to deliver some dolls for sale, destined for the United States and Europe. These dolls are sold as "traditional," "indigenous," and "Aymaran" crafts; and so the indian identity of my friends is central to their participation in a global market, illustrating that their "indianness" has an international as well as local significance.

We entered the store by the rear entrance and the couple I was with was berated in Spanish (even though the agent spoke fluent Aymara) for being late and not having finished the work. They were ordered to sit down on the floor in the corner of the patio to work on the dolls. The agent who knows me well, greeted me respectfully, and quickly brought a chair for me to sit on. In Pocobaya women sit on the floor and men sit on benches or stools. This is the case in any public gathering but also in private when, for example, a family is assembled in the kitchen for a meal. My female friend speaks very little Spanish, a fact known to the agent, and so the agent's use of Spanish in her barked commands and complaints served to underline the status difference between them. The meek and submissive way my male friend responded to the agent differed sharply with the way he acts in Pocobaya, where he is a respected member of the community. In Sorata he is merely an indian who is supposed to be meek and submissive (behavior considered appropriate to women and children in Sorata) and instructed to sit on the floor like the women in his own community.

In Pocobaya the same kind of language and the same abrupt manner of speech used by the agent are also used by the schoolteacher as well as men when they berate their children or scold their wives. Spanish, therefore, functions in the same way within the community as without: to mark status difference and assert authority by invoking an association with the metropolitan culture. The same strategy used against indian men when they travel beyond the community is used by them when they return.

When I asked people in Pocobaya about language use, men and women alike often told me that women spoke a more pure and sweeter (*muxsa*) Aymara, in contrast to men who use many Spanish words. Speaking sweetly is a positive quality, but in a context where languages are hierarchized, the ability to speak Spanish obviously has greater status. So, for example, on one occasion a man told me his wife was "like a dog" (*anujamawa*) because she could not speak Spanish. It is common in the Andes to use animals to represent "uncivilized" human beings (van Vleet, this volume); and the ability to speak is one of the key markers between humans and animals for many Andean peoples (Harris 1980). In this instance the implication is that it is the ability to speak *Spanish* which is most important.

In likening his wife to a dog, this man was doing more than simply comparing monolingual women to animals in general. As Laura Lewis (2003:54 and passim) has noted, there is a long history of associating indians with dogs, which goes back to the early colonial period, and this was used to justify their beatings as much as it was to command their faithful and servile "nature." In contrast to sheep, dogs are shown little affection in Pocobaya; instead, they are regularly cursed and have stones thrown at them, sometimes for no apparent reason. The idea that women are somehow incomplete men, lacking intellectual faculties and moral strength is *not* typical of what men and women in Pocobaya generally say about women; it does, however, resonate with long-standing European ideas about the status of women and, in the American context, the justification of the domination of indians on the grounds that they possessed the moral and intellectual qualities of women, children, and domestic animals. This argument was most clearly and famously stated by Sepúlveda in the mid-sixteenth century (Lewis 2003:59; Pagden 1982) and has clear echoes today. In this particular ethnographic context, the very human status of a woman is questioned because of her lack of Spanish, but the man himself implicitly accepts that speaking Aymara and being indian is clearly inferior to speaking Spanish and being white; by underlining his wife's inferior status, however, his status as a Spanish-speaker is implicitly elevated.

Peppering their language with hispanicisms is a way in which men underline their association with the metropolitan culture; men are "whitened" by this association and can contrast themselves with their Aymara-speaking and unambiguously indian womenfolk.[16] Over the years I have heard a number of men talk to me of their aspirations to move to town, where they will be civilized. Almost invariably a mark of this newly acquired "civilization" is that their wives and children will speak Spanish and that the womenfolk will wear dresses (as opposed to the full skirts indian women wear). There can be no doubt that social and racial mobility is most clearly inscribed in the dress and bodies of women (Stephenson 1999; van Vleet, this volume; Weismantel 2001). These deeply ambivalent experiences of being part of the metropolitan culture whilst simultaneously rejected by it sometimes have violent consequences.

Domestic violence is quite prevalent in Pocobaya, but unevenly so. Although many, perhaps most, men do not beat their wives (and there are many women as well as men who say this is so) others do so frequently and severely. People speak readily about domestic violence in Pocobaya, and it is often a topic of conversation.[17] I evidenced little sense of shame or guilt about domestic violence, but it is widely regretted, if not always condemned, by the beaters, the beaten, and the commentators thereon.

To account for domestic violence is far beyond the scope of this paper, but there are some important features that are worth noting in the context of this discussion.[18] Men beat their wives only when they are drunk, and many women say that the beatings are either totally unprovoked or provoked by something trivial such as the kind of food they have served.[19] Some say that their husbands say very little when they beat them, but others comment that they are abused in Spanish.[20] They spit out words like "ignorante" (ignorant) and "india sucia" (dirty indian), an experience not restricted to Pocobaya (Jiménez Sardon 1998:159).[21] For their part, men say that they remember nothing of what they say and do, and it is the alcohol that makes them beat their wives. To some extent, it seems, women believe them.

There are a handful of men notorious for beating their wives. One of them, Don Andrés,[22] has often talked to me about his desire to move to the town, where his wife would wear dresses and speak Spanish and they would all become more "civilized." In the fifteen years I have known him he has often spoken of this desire but has yet to achieve it. His desire for his wife to speak Spanish and wear a dress (something she says she would feel very uncomfortable doing) clearly indicate a wish for her to "whiten." Her indianness affects his relative whiteness, and, although there are doubtless many reasons for his violence, it is clear that his own frustration at their lack of social and racial mobility are taken out on her. This is perhaps augmented by a sharper sense of hierarchy that men absorb in the army and the mines, a hierarchy that contrasts with the more egalitarian ethos of Pocobaya. Pocobayeños continue to practice fiesta sponsorship in rotation, which has the effect of distributing wealth. More than one person has complained to me that they find it impossible to resist the pressure to become a fiesta sponsor when it is known they have accumulated wealth in the mines; so, although some families are better off than others, there are quite small disparities of wealth.

It would be overdrawn to put domestic violence in Pocobaya simply down to men's frustrations at their inability to move in the world the way they would like and their deep ambivalence at their racial status and condition in Bolivia. Nevertheless I think it is quite clear that the contradiction of being an indian in the world beyond Pocobaya and a "whiter" status within it and all this represents in terms of frustrated desires has a part to play in accounting for domestic violence. Mary Weismantel (1988:183) suggests much more specifically that the reason men beat their wives in the highland community of Zumbagua in Ecuador is because of the increasing demands for goods imposed on a man as he returns from the city. Zumbaguaños and Pocobayeños have different patterns of wage migration and the latter do not come and go as regularly as appears to be the case in Zumbagua. Nevertheless it is true to say that currently defined men's role vis-à-vis their households require them to leave the community for a potentially infinite amount of cash and goods. Men can never earn enough money to satisfy their and their family's demands for goods and the status it buys. Moreover, the more a man aspires to personal progress through whitening by acquiring those goods and status symbols associated with the mestizo metropolitan class, the more likely he is to be frustrated in this elusive goal. It is also the case that the longer a man is away from his family the more accustomed to autonomy his partner becomes. To put it another way, a model of complementarity between two people is increasingly difficult to sustain if they are apart for long periods. This is even more likely to be the case if women have access to their own source of cash and are able to speak at least some Spanish, as is becoming increasingly the case in Pocobaya with an expanded school.

There are other contradictory pressures on women. Whereas women are highly valued for their labor and social responsibility in maintaining the fields, livestock, and household, this very labor roots them ever more solidly into the indian world, which is widely denigrated, even, in certain contexts, by themselves. Women often complain that men leave them for months on end with little money and a lot of work to do, as men are imagined to be cash rich and may even be supporting lovers. Men, when they are far away from home, have considerable demands on their cash income and do not want to be pulled down by responsibilities that simply by association frustrate any social ambitions they may have. Having a family in an indian village is a clear marker of indian status.

Women and men will often express deeply ambivalent feelings on the subject of male migration. Women who bemoan the absence of their husbands will also express a strong desire for men to earn the money to buy goods, whilst men often love their wives and children and are frequently sentimental about their home and land even as they sometimes wish not to be associated with an indian village. These contradictions and tensions, which are ultimately irresolvable, are dealt with in myriad ways by different couples and sometimes with violence. What is clear, however, is that these wider social and economic structures come to be focused onto very intimate spaces.

There is also a clear echo here of the frustration of the schoolteachers in Pocobaya and their ambivalent attitudes toward the community described above. They too appear to be caught between a sense of indian fraternity and their own personal desires to progress and be civilized; they swing from sentimental identification with their "indian brothers" and deep frustration at having to live in and be associated with an indian village; they also use a language imbued with a sense of racial superiority when they berate children, rather like the language men sometimes use when they argue with their wives.

Conclusion

Even though Pocobaya may be marginal in terms of the hegemonic political and social geographies of Bolivia, its people and their labor form a fundamental element in the economic structures of modern, capitalist Bolivia. On the level of ideology, a whole series of national symbols, language, and concepts are produced and reproduced within the community. Communities such as Pocobaya are marginal in terms of national discourses, which favor urban, mestizo-creole, Spanish-speaking culture over rural, indian, and Aymara-speaking culture. They are, however, absolutely central in that they support the center economically whilst long providing a useful contrast for the aspirations to progress of dominant groups: one can always try to be "whiter" and can always justify one's social superiority in terms of being racially or culturally superior. For this powerful system to operate, at least a notional indian "other" needs to exist.

It is clear that there is an important gender difference in how men and women are implicated in and by these discourses, since these national discourses are themselves gendered. Given that men and women are located differently in the national space that these discourses produce, it is not surprising that they are, in turn, differently transfigured as they move through the national geography. In the case of Bolivia, men have a heightened sense of their (inferior) indianness as they move through institutions and spaces whilst at the same time they are "whitened" by this very movement and association. This migration, which supports the nation through military service and by working in the capitalist economy, has important consequences for women in the community. By maintaining the farms and households they, in effect, subsidize the low wages of their menfolk. More striking, though, is the dissonance between the gender model that stresses the equally important contributions of men and women to the household, which makes sense in the village community, and the racialized and hierarchic model men struggle with as part of their own conflictive identities as ethnically marked men. It is important to remember that women and men themselves are not consistent in the values attached to different forms of labor, dress, identity, and so on. A woman may on one occasion bemoan the absence of her husband in the mines but a few weeks earlier may have been encouraging him to leave. A man may comment that he wishes his wife would wear a Western dress and live in the town but later comment approvingly of her ability to work in the fields. People talk disparagingly about the misery of village life, but the same people may talk of the village in maudlin tones. These conflicting desires and aspirations can even be expressed in the same conversation.

Racial hierarchy, the pressures of wage labor in industries that exploit indians, an economy that depends on indian labor even as it denigrates it, feelings of sentimentality about one's home village, an association with which is the source of one's despised racial identity: these and many other tensions and contradictions are articulated at the level of a married couple. It is therefore not difficult to see how a drunken man can see his frustrations quite literally embodied by his wife and take it out on her violently. The arguments presented here do not account for domestic violence, but they do explain some of the context in which it occurs and the particular form it takes.

The bodies of indian men and women are marked and transformed in various ways by the institutions and structures of the nation-state, concerned to turn indians into citizens. Diane Nelson, writing about Guatemala, illustrates through painful and humorous examples how national hegemony comprises discourses of gender, sexuality, and state violence against Maya, all of which are intimately intertwined. This hegemonic process is, however, unstable; it is not only conflictual but contradictory. "Rather than being a solid ground for bodies politic, bodies are produced (and aroused) in complex and often contradictory ways through desire and racial discourses like mestizaje" (1999:209).

Ideas about nationhood, racial hierarchies, and an economic structure that depends on a semi-proletarianized indian labor force are not merely abstract constructs far removed from the realities of people who live at a distance from the metropolitan centers: they are real and immanent and are re-created in remote villages and in the intimate relationships of couples; they inscribe unstable bodies and create often unpredictable desires and frustrations.

Acknowledgments

A version of this chapter was presented at the American Anthropological Association conference in Washington, D.C. (2001). I am grateful to Leonore Davidoff, Elayne Zorn, Michelle Bigenho, and Lucinda Platt for their insightful comments on earlier drafts. Any errors or omissions remain, of course, my responsibility.

Notes

1. Fieldwork has been conducted regularly in Pocobaya since 1989.

2. By far the most common term for domestic violence is "nuwasiña," which is a reflexive and nontransitive verb; that is, when a women says "we fight," she often means "my husband beats me," which, even though the meaning may be quite clear, gives a sense of a phenomenon without a specific agent.

3. It is quite common in towns for indian women to dominate the markets, and even though Aymara-speaking women are much in evidence in the local market of Sorata, the women of the surrounding villages attend the market as buyers rather than as sellers. In any case, it is generally the men of Pocobaya, rather than the women, who travel to Sorata for supplies.

4. *Mestizo* originally meant someone of mixed European/American parentage. It is an ambiguous category defined largely by what it is not (Harris 1995). "White" too, does not necessarily mean someone who is exclusively of European decent. For

aesthetic reasons, I do not put these words in quotes throughout the text, but it should be understood that they are by no means clear and unambiguous categories. This racialized spectrum, moreover, overlays and informs hierarchies of rural vs. urban, small town vs. large city, Aymara language use vs. Spanish, male vs. female, and so on.

5. This is even true of the Paceña beer advertisement, which features "indian" dancers. These "indians," however, are clearly mestizas dressed in folkloric dress. That is, even when indians are represented, they are often done so in terms of colorful folklore by urban mestizos.

6. Until very recently school textbooks featured white, urban people, and some of the books still used in school depict a family life much more resonant of the paradigmatic suburban family of 1950s USA than any Bolivian reality. Since the Sánchez Lozada administration of 1993–97, however, there has been a greater awareness of multiculturalism in Bolivia, after decades of investment in the idea of a single mestizo Spanish-speaking Bolivian culture. Much of this, nevertheless, appears to remain at the level of rhetoric, and there is little evidence of an awareness of multicultural issues in the area around Pocobaya.

7. Mä ordena utji boliviana; ma deberaj phuqañataki.

8. The very few men in Pocobaya under forty who are monolingual in Aymara are those who have not undertaken military service.

9. Mä gramu . . . mä ratuki, mä ora. Arumpaqari pisqha gram munapxi.

10. Wali quri purakawa. Qur apanim siyast mä rat churasaki.

11. "Lesbian sex" is perhaps something of a misnomer: the Pocobayeños I spoke to did not associate two women having sex in a video with what might be understood as "lesbians." They interpreted such sex acts, possibly quite accurately in the case of pornography, as having nothing to do with any kind of relationship between the women involved or a particular sexuality; in fact, people were amazed that such a thing could possibly exist. Women, I was told, could not have (penetrative) sex and nor could they have a relationship, since running a household requires a man and a woman. There is, needless to say, no word for "lesbian" in Pocobaya: there is a word for "manly woman," "urquchi," but this does not refer to sexuality. Similarly, there is no word for male homosexual. "Q'ewsa," which appears to mean male homosexual in other parts of the Andes, in Pocobaya refers to someone who lacks generosity, does not fulfill his social obligations and does not drink "properly" (i.e., heavily) at fiestas. People do use the Spanish word *maricón* to describe those mestizos who have sex with other men. Men in Pocobaya speak of "maricones" with fear, ridicule, and revulsion.

12. In contrast to the theme of domestic violence, Pocobayeños do not talk readily about sexual issues. Although I was able to get some men to talk about sexuality, I have not been able to talk to women in any depth about sexual issues.

13. Jan tarwani uka wali achala; ukat chach munija.

14. Whenever I asked men or women to explain to me the difference between men and women, I always received a list of tasks men and women respectively undertake.

15. Chachajawa jani qullqi uñt'iri jaytawayitu, jani, chachaxa akjarukiwa uywi-

tana pirmiruxa, chachaxa uka aynachanaka rawajt'asiri saraskiri, ukata jani qullqini jaytawayitu chachaxa, janiwa qawqhasa uñt'kthti, janiw milsa uñt'kthti, chachaxa chhaqxi ukata wawanakawa uñañchayaskitu.

16. The use of Spanish flourishes in this way when the speaker may actually have no idea of what he is saying is widespread in Bolivia and, according to Spedding (1999) has its roots in the public education system, which encourages style over content.

17. Conversations I had with women about domestic violence occurred whilst accompanying them around the cooking fire and in other social contexts (where more commonly third parties were discussed). Men discussed domestic violence with me in varying contexts. In general, it took very little effort on my part to initiate discussion on this topic, and in many cases the issue was raised independently. See also Harris (1994:52), and Van Vleet (2002:570).

18. For discussions on domestic violence in the Andes, see Allen 1988; Harris 1994; Harvey 1994; Millones and Pratt 1980; and van Vleet 2002.

19. See also Harris 1994; Harvey 1994; and van Vleet 2002.

20. There is a long history in the Andes of people speaking in Spanish when drunk, as Saignes (1993) and others have well documented. The issue here is not simply that the men speak Spanish when they are drunk but what it is they are actually saying.

21. When being affectionate with their wives, men, in contrast, will most often call them "mamita," a combination of the Aymara respectful form of address for a woman (*mama*) and the Spanish diminutive. It could be translated into English as "little lady," although here the Spanish diminutive is used more to denote affection than as a diminutive strictly speaking. I am grateful to Billie Jean Isbell for suggesting I investigate this.

22. Names have been changed.

Bibliography

Abercrombie, Thomas. 1992. "To Be Indian, to Be Bolivian." In *Nation States and Indians in Latin America*, ed. Greg Urban and Joel Scherzer, 95–130. Austin: University of Texas Press.

Allen, Caterine. 1988. *The Hold Life Has: Coca and Cultural Identity in an Andean Community*. Washington, D.C.: Smithsonian Institution Press.

Anderson, Benedict. 1983. *Imagined Communities Reflections on the Origins and Spread of Nationalism*. London: Verso.

Blom, Ida, Karen Hagemann, and Catherine Hall, eds. 2000. *Gendered Nations: Nationalisms and Gender Order in the Long Nineteenth Century*. Oxford: Berg.

de la Cadena, Marisol. 1995. "'Women are more Indian': Ethnicity and Gender in a Community near Cuzco." In *Ethnicity, Markets, and Migration in the Andes*, ed. Brooke Larson and Olivia Harris, 329–48. Durham, N.C.: Duke University Press.

Canessa, Andrew. 1997. "Chachawarmi: Negociando (des)igualdades de género en una aldea aymara boliviana." In *Nuevas direcciones en los estudios andinos*, ed. Denise Arnold. La Paz: ILCA/CID.

————. 1998. "Procreation, the Person and Ethnic Difference in Highland Bolivia." *Ethnos* 63, no. 2:227–47.

————. 2004. "Reproducing Racism: Schooling and Race in Highland Bolivia." *Race, Ethnicity and Education* 7, no. 2:185–204.

Choque Canqui, Roberto, et al. 1992. *Educación indígena: ¿Ciudadanía o colonización?* La Paz: Aruwiyiri.

Condarco Morales, Ramiro. 1983. *Zarate, el Temible Willka, Historia de la Rebelión Indígena de 1898.* 2d ed. La Paz: Talleres Gráficos Bolivianos.

Crain, Mary. 1996. "The Gendering of Ethnicity in the Ecuadorian Andes: Native Women's Self-Fashioning in the Urban Marketplace." In *Machos, Mistresses, Madonnas: Contesting the Power of Latin American Gender Imagery*, ed. Marit Melhuus and Kristi Ann Stølen. London: Verso.

Dore, Elizabeth. 2000. "Property, Households, and Public Regulation of Domestic Life: Diriomo, Nicaragua, 1840–1900." In *Hidden Histories of Gender and the State in Latin America*, ed. Elizabeth Dore and Maxine Molyneux. Durham, N.C.: Duke University Press.

Fanon, Franz. 1986 [1952]. *Black Skin, White Masks.* London: Pluto.

Fraser, Nancy. 1989. *Unruly Practices: Power, Discourse, and Gender in Contemporary Social Theory.* Minneapolis: University of Minnesota Press.

Freyre, Gilberto. 1946. *The Masters and the Slaves: A Study in the Development of Brazilian Civilization.* New York: Knopf.

Gill, Lesley. 1997. "Creating Citizens, Making Men: The Military and Masculinity in Bolivia." *Cultural Anthropology* 12, no. 4:527–50.

Hall, Catherine, K. McClelland, and J. Rendall. 2000. *Defining the Victorian Nation: Class, Race, Gender and the Reform Act of 1867.* Cambridge: Cambridge University Press.

Harris, Olivia. 1980. "The Power of Signs: Gender, Culture and the Wild in the Bolivian Andes." In *Nature, Culture and Gender*, ed. Carole MacCormack and Marilyn Strathern. Cambridge: Cambridge University Press.

————. 1994. "Condor and Bull: The Ambiguities of Masculinity in Northern Potosí." In *Sex and Violence: Issues in Representation and Experience*, ed. Penelope Harvey and Peter Gow. London: Routledge.

————. 1995. "Ethnic Identity and Market Relations: Indians and Mestizos in the Andes." In *Ethnicity and Markets in the Andes: At the Crossroads of History and Anthropology*, ed. Olivia Harris, Brooke Larson, and Enrique Tandeter. Durham, N.C.: Duke University Press.

Harvey, Penelope. 1994. "Domestic Violence in the Andes." In *Sex and Violence: Issues in Representation and Experience*, ed. Penelope Harvey and Peter Gow. London: Routledge.

Instituto Nacional de Estadística. 1992. *Censo Nacional 1990.*

De Janvry, Alain. 1981. *The Agrarian Question and Reformism in Latin America.* Baltimore: Johns Hopkins University Press.

Jiménez Sardon, Greta. 1998. "The Aymara Couple in the Community." In *The Spirit of Regeneration: Andean Culture Confronting Western Notions of Development*, ed. Frédérique Apffel-Marglin. London: Zed Books.

Lewis, Laura. 2003. *Hall of Mirrors: Power, Witchcraft, and Caste in Colonial Mexico.* Durham, N.C.: Duke University Press.

Luykx, Aurolyn. 1999. *The Citizen Factory: Schooling and Cultural Production in Bolivia.* Albany: State University of New York Press.

Mason, Peter. 1990. *Deconstructing America: Representations of the Other.* London: Routledge.

Meillassoux, Claude. 1981. *Maidens, Meal and Money: Capitalism and the Domestic Community.* Cambridge: Cambridge University Press.

Millones, Luis, and Mary Pratt. 1989. *Amor brujo: Imagen y cultura del amor en los Andes.* Lima: Instituto de Estudios Peruanos.

Mosse, George. 1985. *Nationalism and Sexuality: Middle Class Morality and Sexual Norms in Modern Europe.* Madison: University of Wisconsin Press.

Nandy, Ashis. 1983. *The Intimate Enemy: Loss and Recovery of Self under Colonialism.* Oxford: Oxford University Press.

Nelson, Diane. 1999. *A Finger in the Wound: Body Politics in Quincentennial Guatemala.* Berkeley: University of California Press.

Nugent, David. 1997. *Modernity on the Edge of Empire: State, Individual, and Nation in the Northern Peruvian Andes, 1885–1935.* Stanford: Stanford University Press.

Orlove, Benjamin. 1998. "Down to Earth: Race and Substance in the Andes." *Bulletin of Latin American Research* 17, no. 2:207–22.

Pagden, Anthony. 1982. *The Fall of Natural Man: The American Indian and the Origins of Comparative Ethnology.* Cambridge: Cambridge University Press.

Paulson, Susan. 1996. "Familias que no 'conyugan' e identidades que no conjugan: La vida en Mizque desafía nuestras categorías." In *Ser mujer indígena, chola o birlocha en la Bolivia postcolonial de los años 90*, ed. Silvia Rivera Cusicanqui. La Paz: Ministerio de Desarrollo Humano.

———. 2003. "Placing Gender and Ethnicity on the Bodies of Indigenous Women and in the Work of Bolivian Intellectuals." In *Gender's Place: Feminist Anthropologies of Latin America*, ed. Rosario Montaya, Lessie Jo Frazier, and Janise Hurtig. New York: Palgrave Macmillan.

Placido, Barbara. 2001. "'It's All to Do with Words': An Analysis of Spirit Possession in the Venezuelan Cult of María Lonza." *Journal of the Royal Anthropological Institute* 7, no. 2:207–24.

Platt, Tristan. 1993. "Simón Bolívar, the Sun of Justice and the Amerindian Virgin: Andean Conceptions of the Patria in Nineteenth-Century Potosí." *Journal of Latin American Studies* 25, no. 1:159–85.

Radcliffe, Sarah. 1990. "Ethnicity, Patriarchy, and Incorporation into the Nation: Female Migrants as Domestic Servants in Peru." *Society and Space* 8:379–93.

Radcliffe, Sarah, and Sallie Westwood. 1996. *Remaking the Nation: Place, Identity and Politics in Latin America.* London: Routledge.

Rivera Cusicanqui, Silvia. 1996. "Prólogo." In *Ser mujer indígena, chola o birlocha en la Bolivia postcolonial de los años 90*, ed. Silvia Rivera Cusicanqui. La Paz: Ministerio de Desarrollo Humano.

Saignes, Thierry, ed. 1993. *Borrachera y memoria: La experiencia de lo sagrado en los Andes.* La Paz: HISBOL/IFEA.

Salomon, Frank. 1981. "Killing the Yumbo: A Ritual Drama of Northern Quito." In *Cultural Transformations and Ethnicity in Modern Ecuador*, ed. Norman Whitten. Urbana: University of Illinois Press.

Silverblatt, Irene. 1987. *Moon, Sun, and Witches: Gender Ideology and Class in Inca and Colonial Peru*. Princeton: Princeton University Press.

Skidmore, Thomas. 1993 [1974]. *Black into White: Race and Nationality in Brazilian Thought*. Oxford: Oxford University Press.

Spedding, Allison. 1999. "Investigadores en apuros." *Tinkazos* 2, no. 3:146–61.

Stepan, Nancy. 1991. *The Hour of Eugenics: Race, Gender, and Nation in Latin America*. Ithaca: Cornell University Press.

Stephenson, Marcia. 1999. *Gender and Modernity in Andean Bolivia*. Austin: University of Texas Press.

Stoler, Ann Laura. 1995. *Race and the Education of Desire*. Durham, N.C.: Duke University Press.

Van Vleet, Krista. 2002. "The Intimacies of Power: Rethinking Violence and Affinity in the Bolivian Andes." *American Ethnologist* 29, no. 3:567–601.

Wade, Peter. 1997. *Race and Ethnicity in Latin America*. London: Pluto.

Weismantel, Mary. 1988. *Food, Gender, and Poverty in the Ecuadorian Andes*. Philadelphia: University of Philadelphia Press.

———. 2001. *Cholas and Pishtacos: Stories of Race and Sex in the Andes*. Chicago: Chicago University Press.

Wright, Winthrop. 1990. *Café con leche: Race, Class, and National Image in Venezuela*. Austin: University of Texas Press.

Yuval-Davis, Nira. 1997. *Gender and Nation*. London: Sage.

Yuval-Davis, Nira, and Flora Anthias. 1989. *Woman-Nation-State*. New York: Macmillan.

7

From Political Prison to Tourist Village

Tourism, Gender, Indigeneity, and the
State on Taquile Island, Peru

Elayne Zorn

In 1922, eight years before seizing presidential power in a coup, "The Macho" Luís Miguel Sánchez Cerro was exiled to Lake Titicaca's remote and frigid Taquile Island, 3,800 meters above sea level, following an unsuccessful armed revolt against the dictator Leguía. The sole role of Taquile, reachable only by an arduous trip in a very small reed boat from the Andean highland city of Puno, was as the Peruvian nation's most remote outpost: a political prison. Nearly eighty years later, "The Chino" Alberto Fujimori helicoptered onto Taquile while campaigning for reelection in 2000 and, wearing items of native dress, posed for photographs and television footage with authorities and residents in the community that had become the "poster child" for indigenous Peru.

In the intervening decades between these two Peruvian presidents, many things had changed for the better for Taquileans. Unprecedented success in locally controlling mass tourism from the late 1970s to the mid-1980s had led to generally positive recognition for the island, which is now the key draw in southern Peru on the tourist route from Cuzco to La Paz. Taquilean successes in tourism has led to increased general prosperity but has also led to social change, particularly for women, who now participate more publicly in community affairs.

Taquile has gone from being at the extreme margins of the Peruvian nation to being an iconic representation of it. By the turn of the twenty-first century, Taquile and its colorfully dressed indigenous inhabitants had become visible in the Peruvian nation, through tourism advertisements, publicity from Fujimori's election campaign, and the modest celebrity of Taquileans, who frequently performed at regional and national folkloric events, traveled abroad, and won Peru's highest prize for artisan production: the Grand Master of Peruvian Crafts (1996). At the same time, the Peruvian nation-state was increasingly prominent in Taquileans' lives, solidly manifested in the island's high school and health post, and embodied by Taquileans who performed in crafts and folklore events and sometimes served on regional government committees concerned with tourism. This points to the central paradox of Taquile's position vis-à-vis the nation-state. Taquile's status as the quintessential Andean community (it is a recognized peasant community or *Comunidad Campesina Reconocida*) is partly a function of its remoteness and marginality from the main currents of Peruvian life. At the same time, it is this status that has given it the ability to engage with the nation-state at quite a sophisticated level, negotiating rights and privileges not accorded its more cosmopolitan peasant neighbors.

The increased wealth represented by the growth in tourism, although by no means evenly distributed among Taquileans, has nonetheless also had a significant impact on Taquilean lifeways. Cash income has given Taquileans the ability to travel off-island and obtain goods and materials previously inaccessible, such as cement and tin for house construction, and factory-spun and dyed wools for weaving. It has allowed Taquileans to invest in cooperatively owned and operated motorized boats and a cooperative store, as well as individually owned restaurants (Healy and Zorn 1982–83). In many ways, the wealth brought by ethno-tourism has ironically served to visibly change the Taquilean way of life, the very subject it seeks to freeze in an idealized indigenous "authenticity."

Taquileans themselves have neither been passive bystanders in these processes nor fully autonomous agents, and the development of tourism in Taquile has not been without its conflicts. Whereas the Peruvian state is happy to exploit Taquile's image for tourism and domestic politics, it has done little to help Taquileans in their struggles to retain autonomy over tourism and access to the island. Starting in the mid-1980s, Taquileans faced increasing competition from outside tour agencies over transportation to and from the island, the key to community control of tourism. Governmental policies that occasionally favored Taquileans vanished by the 1990s as the neoliberal Peruvian state refused to intervene in conflicts or concede any special benefits to islanders with regard to controlling transit to and from the island. Occasional favorable decisions or aid obtained by Taquilean male authorities through sympathetic bureaucrats, sometimes through patron-client channels, became increasingly limited.

By the turn of this century tourism had changed, and Taquile's early model of community controlled small-scale tourism hosting adventurous travelers had been transformed in the hands of outsiders into brief stops by tourists rushed up, over, and down the island's mountain, thereby eroding the goodwill of islanders and tourists, as well as Taquilean profits. As Taquileans desperately tried to compete with outside companies that recruited on the Internet and offered package tours, Taquileans became increasingly embittered by the Peruvian state's insistence on Taquile's need to conform to a "model tourist village" without providing any support or assistance for community control or even the modifications that the government and regional businesses demanded. The patron-client model of relations between indians and the state, which never had provided more than occasional handouts, no longer functioned in the neoliberal state. Taquileans continue to struggle to retain autonomy over their lives, balancing the demands of conforming to others' images of their island and indianness with their own desires to develop as individuals and a community in ways they see fit.

What is clear is that the struggle on the part of Taquileans to retain control over the tourist industry and, more broadly, the way in which the island and its inhabitants related to the nation-state was, and continues to be, a highly gendered process. Not only did the economic and social changes have different implications for men and women, but also their strategies for coping with it were different. Indeed, the very images with which Taquileans, and in fact indigeneity in general, are represented are gendered too. Various scholars have noted that gender and indigeneity are conceptually linked and that indian women function as metonyms for a broader indigenous identity (e.g., Canessa this volume; de la Cadena 1995).

In this chapter I explore the delicate interplay of tourism, gender, indigeneity, and the nation in Taquile. I examine gendered differences in women's and men's experiences and actions in the context of efforts to control tourism on their island. I also analyze some of the ways that indian identity is experienced and acted upon. The rise of tourism based on Taquileans' perceived authentic indigenous identity acts to mediate and change many aspects of that identity, which it paradoxically both undermines and strengthens.

Background: Taquile and the Peruvian Nation

In the early twentieth century, Taquile was quite isolated, connected to the mainland only by reed boat, then eventually by wooden sailboats, and recently by motorboats. Taquile is one of several permanent islands on the Peruvian side of Lake Titicaca, South America's highest navigable lake. In addition to the symbolic importance of Lake Titicaca to pre-Conquest civilizations, the lake is also a border between the nations of Peru and Bolivia. Taquileans are poor peasant farmers, primarily growing potatoes on an intensively terraced island 3,800 meters above sea level, and fishing from the lake. Taquile's 1,700 inhabitants speak Quechua (Inca); an increasing number also speak Spanish. Taquile is one of the few communities in Peru where all residents continue to weave and wear ethnic dress on a daily basis. This is important because cloth was the pre-eminent Andean cultural product for three thousand years, and in this region women create the most important textiles. Taquile appears the essence of indian Peru: Quechua-speaking potato farmers wearing beautiful clothing, living in the Andes mountains, with adobe brick homes and no modern conveniences. Until tourism there, Taquile was known outside its region as a political prison, despite the fine studies by Peruvian anthropologists Rosalía Avalos de Matos (1951a, 1951b) and José Matos Mar (1951a, 1951b, 1960, 1964, 1986). Starting in the late 1960s, Taquile also became known to a limited audience as a place to find some of the finest handwoven cloth in Peru.

During the twentieth century, Taquileans were conservative in some ways—they retained many traditional cultural practices, including hand-weaving, and they were late to build wooden sailboats—but innovative in others. In the 1930s, Taquileans began to fight a long court battle to purchase and then legally confirm title to their lands owned by landlords (hacendados). Taquileans had to endure twenty years of legal struggle, and harassment and persecution, but were increasingly successful by the 1940s and gained title to most of their land ahead of any other peasant community on the Peruvian side of Lake Titicaca (they obtained the rest by 1970). Taquilean audacity and predilection for "going straight to the top" dates from a famed audience that Taquileans had in Lima in 1931 with President Sánchez Cerro. Longtime rival of President Leguía, Sánchez Cerro was sent to internal exile on Taquile after an ill-fated coup in 1922. Sánchez Cerro's successful coup in 1930 and elevation to the presidency in 1931 (which resulted in Leguía being exiled to another island, San Lorenzo) coincided with efforts led by Prudencio Huatta and other Taquileans to purchase title to their land from the landlords on the island. That meeting, of former political prisoner turned president with poor Taquilean peasants, could be considered the ultimate patron-client relationship. The results of the meeting were not as significant as perhaps

Huatta and others had hoped, but Sánchez Cerro did help end *pongueaje* on the island, the much hated institution whereby indians were obliged to serve in the homes of landlords in servile and unpaid conditions. Pongueaje was not abolished in the rest of Peru until 1968. This further illustrates the ways that notionally "backward" Taquileans were able to effect changes far in advance of their more "acculturated" brethren.

Despite poor communications (no electricity, no phone or telegraph) and difficulty of access, Taquileans have never cut themselves off from the outside world. Like a thousand other rural peasant communities, Taquile has an elementary school, the quintessential institution of the nation, even though Taquileans still find it difficult to get teachers to stay in "exile" on their island for more than three days a week. Despite the typical conflicts between schooling and peasant life, Taquileans wanted more, repeatedly petitioning for a high school (which they did not get until the 1990s). In the early 1950s, Matos Mar wrote of a new generation of young entrepreneurial men, who rose to power in the community by a nontraditional route: interacting more extensively with outsiders, which included learning Spanish in addition to Quechua.

In Taquileans' first significant interaction with non-Peruvians, in 1968, U.S. Peace Corps volunteer Kevin Healy persuaded the islanders to sell their renowned handmade textiles for the first time, in a U.S.–sponsored cooperative in Peru. In the cash-poor altiplano, this represented an unusual opportunity to earn money, and to literally find value in something the dominant society told them was worthless by virtue of their being created by indians. Their enthusiasm, as Healy puts it, was enough to weather the collapse of the cooperative a few years later (Healy and Zorn 1982–83). To continue sales, a handful of young Taquilean men became textile merchants, selling their extended families' fabrics to foreign exporters, scholars, and tourists in Peruvian cities. Even before tourism became significant in Taquile, many Taquileans had important connections with the national and international handicraft market, as well as experience interacting with foreigners (who buy textiles).

Taquile and Global Tourism

Tourism to Taquile started in 1976 as a result of a few paragraphs in the popular tourist guidebook the *South American Handbook* and rapidly expanded as part of a larger shift in backpacking "hippie" tourism from the Himalayas to the Andes. Taquileans responded very quickly to the initial opportunities presented by tourism, creating various community and family-based enterprises to take care of their new visitors, including an unusual lodging system offering overnight stays in Taquilean homes. Innovations included equipping existing cooperative sailboat groups with motors so as successfully to compete with people from nearby peasant communities and Puno, who initially transported tourists to and from Taquile. The Taquileans' unusual and rapid success in controlling tourism in their community led to Taquile becoming a world model for indigenous, community-controlled tourism.

During this period in the late 1970s and early 1980s, Taquileans forged links with nongovernmental organizations (NGOs); the U.S. governmental agency The Inter-American Foundation; Peruvian national institutions, especially the Ministry of Industry and Tourism (now MITINCI); and individuals from all over the world, some of whom became godparents to Taquilean children (Zorn n.d.). Though not always successful, Taquileans, like many Andeans, have spent enormous amounts of time, energy, money, and legwork sending delegations and presenting documents as they sought help for various problems from many private institutions, including the Catholic Church in Puno and Peruvian national agencies in Puno and sometimes Lima. Despite ongoing factional and generational conflicts, the ability of islanders to put aside differences and sometimes unite as a community was key to many of the successes they achieved in the late 1970s and 1980s (Zorn 2004).

Tourism to Peru weathered various cycles during the 1980s and 1990s, declining primarily due to fear generated as a consequence of Peru's undeclared civil war (1981–1995). By the late 1980s, as the economy in Peru worsened in all regions, tourism became an increasingly important source of income. In the Department of Puno, a stop along the Cuzco-La Paz route where Taquile is located, it was clear by the 1990s that the main draw to the region was the islands in Lake Titicaca—especially Taquile (Gartner and Morton 2000). This can be seen clearly by looking at tourist brochures issued by Puno hotels and the Puno office of the national Ministry of Industry and Tourism.

Competition over Tourism

The economic opportunities represented by tourism were not missed by non-Taquileans. Since the early 1980s, outsiders tried to get a share of tourism to Taquile, initially by trying to put up hotels on the island to compete with Taquile's unique billeting system. Individual Taquileans were approached with offers to buy their land. These offers would certainly have been tempting to many poor families, but the community was successful in presenting a united front, and individuals who considered selling land were threatened with loss of community membership. This would invalidate any sales, since only community members can hold title to land.

The major threat to Taquilean control of tourism came not from aggressive attempts to buy up the island but from attempts to control access to it. The transport sector has several components, primarily the boat travel, but also docking at Taquile's docks, visitors' fees, and the presence and behavior of non-Taquilean guides. Transportation is not only key to direct and indirect economic benefits from tourism, but also to overall control of tourism on the island—numbers, time of arrival and departure, where and when tourists dock, and so on—and thus local loss of control of the transport sector to outsiders is significant.

In 1982 Taquile obtained a Peruvian-sanctioned monopoly of transport. That monopoly was, however, basically ignored, and then revoked. By the mid-1980s, non-Taquileans, initially small tour agencies in Puno, began to seriously compete to transport tourists. Members of the local Puno elite working in the ministry of tourism and the coast guard collaborated with private Puno boat owners and tour agencies to undercut Taquilean collectively owned boats (Healy and Zorn 1994:146). The representatives of private tour agencies sought tourists physically—at the Puno dock and in other tourist spaces, such as the train from Cuzco to Puno, the airport in Lima, at hotels—and eventually virtually through the Internet—outmaneuvering Taquileans without those means of access.

Thus began the "lucha," or struggle, as many Taquileans term it, to retain a monopoly on transportation to the island and some control over tourism. Taquileans attempted to fight non-Taquilean agencies primarily by appealing to Peruvian laws and to institutions for assistance. Many different Taquilean elected officials and delegations did this. All of the Taquilean authorities and delegates were male, and they interacted generally with male outsiders, with the exception of a few female office staff members or bureaucrats. Battling against non-Taquilean Peruvians, Taquileans frequently asked members of NGOs, the local office of the Catholic Church, and individuals who visited the island (some of whom lived there for months or even years) to help press Taquileans' appeals to national and paranational Peruvian government agencies. Particularly in the early years of tourism when Taquilean literacy was limited, outsiders helped islanders prepare and present the multitudinous documents beloved in Peruvian courts: *memoriales, solicitudes, demandas*, and so on. Taquileans thus relied on traditional channels based on patron-client or *compadrazgo* relationships to effect change.

In 1989, Taquileans argued that their island community was entitled to a monopoly of transportation, on the basis of Peru's "Ley de Comunidades" (Law for Communities) that authorizes "absolute control over the soil and subsoil rights (save mineral resources)," which includes Taquile's dock areas (Healy and Zorn 1994:146). With help from a lawyer from a regional branch of the Catholic Church, Taquileans pursued the formidable paperwork necessary to obtain official status as a *Comunidad Campesina Reconocida* required for the community to claim such rights. However, private tour agencies and boat owners argued that these rights are superseded by national laws regulating ownership of waterways, including the massive Lake Titicaca, which belong to the Peruvian state.

Collecting users' fees for docking on the island has been another concern. (It is an enormous effort to build stone docks by hand.) Islanders successfully obtained a decree, granted by the regional authority of the Puno Harbormaster's Office, or *Capitanía del Puerto* (which among other duties regulates fares), that authorized Taquileans to collect a docking fee. Taquileans also obtained the right for its municipal government to charge an entry fee for all visitors to the island. These fees are tiny, averaging US $0.50 per person. These successes were admirable, but enforcement was the problem.

To regain a monopoly over transportation and to gain the right to collect entry fees, Taquileans appealed to the Peruvian nation and its organs as Peruvian citizens and, moreover, as citizens with a particular status as members of a recognized indigenous community. They thus simultaneously affirmed their Peruvianness and indigenous status. This strategy was successful in 1982 but was to prove unsuccessful in the neoliberal Peru of the 1990s and thereafter.

In the 1990s, facing declining tourism and clear loss of transport business to non-Taquilean tour agencies, some Taquileans abandoned collective efforts and tried a "if you can't beat 'em, join 'em" strategy. This sometimes benefited individuals and their families, though at the expense of the community, and ultimately provided little benefit. Individual Taquileans made private arrangements with non-Taquilean tour agencies to transport tourists to the island. Various arrangements were tried. The most common was to rent Taquilean boats and crews to tour agencies. These boats were built, owned, and crewed by some of Taquile's collective boat groups or by the extended family of some of the island's master boatbuilders. Payment agreements varied. None of these individual arrangements lasted very long. According to Taquileans, this was because islanders either were not paid at all, were paid far less than what they had contracted for, or were paid so little that fees didn't even cover the cost of gasoline. Such arrangements left a trail of bitterness, whose echoes can be heard in the consultants' reports that blame opportunistic individuals for the decline in quality of Taquilean tourism (Contorno and Tamayo Flores 2000;[1] Gartner and Morton 2000).

As Peru returned to normal following the decline of its undeclared civil war, tourism increased and became increasingly important as a source of income seemingly to everyone in the region, from tiny Taquile to giant Brazil. By 2001, of eighty-three thousand annual visitors to Puno nearly half, or forty thousand, went to Taquile. This is an astonishing number considering the rustic and mountainous nature of Taquile. A report by private consultants tells us that in 2001 only one-tenth of visitors, or four thousand, spent the night (Gartner and Morton 2000). This is still a very large number considering the size of the island and population, but mass day tourism provides significantly less income to local hosts and provides a diminished experience compared to overnight stays, when hosts and guests have much more interaction.

Tourism was on the rise by the late 1990s, but Taquileans had pretty much lost the battle to transport tourists to and from their community. They appealed directly to the top once again in 2000, sending a delegation to Lima to ask for an investigation by then-president Fujimori of conflicts, and what Taquileans termed abuses (*abusos*), by tour agencies and guides on the island. Taquile's symbolic and economic importance in the Peruvian nation was demonstrated when in March 2000 a delegation of "representatives from the Peasant Community of Taquile Island met with Elena Contorno, a high-ranking advisor to President Fujimori, seeking help in their efforts to regain control of tourism" (Contorno and Tamayo Flores 2000). In their report, the authors appear somewhat sympathetic to Taquileans, but they firmly point out that in the business climate initiated by the Fujimori regime, the state will not grant special or exclusive rights to Taquile; this policy continues under the presidency of Alejandro Toledo. In the neoliberal state, free enterprise is encouraged, with the state merely serving to remind tour agencies to pay local fees. The Peruvian state was, however, unable, reluctant, or unwilling to compel local agencies to pay their dues. This is similar to what Elizabeth Dore and Maxine Molyneux note when they point out that neoliberal states sometimes "regularly" intervene "to guarantee the 'freedom' of the market" (2000:xi). Local people successfully exploit Taquileans' relative powerlessness, often in modes that draw on racialized images of indians as ignorant and submissive, to ignore their legitimate demands.

Gender and Race in Transnational Tourism

Historical racism is a key aspect to both mainlanders' desire and expectation to control Taquile's tourism and to the difficulties Taquileans have in resisting them. The people who live on Taquile overwhelmingly define themselves as indigenous or *runa* (indian), even though much of Peru has been seeking ways to leave behind the status of indian because of widespread discrimination against native people. Mainlanders generally define themselves as mestizo, or Peruvians of "mixed-race," who are culturally non-indian. Both islanders and non-islanders commonly use the language of race to describe their conflicts, as indians versus mestizos. Race also is key to tourism to places like Taquile, because non-indigenous Peruvians and foreign tourists travel to Taquile to see indians.

Tourism on Taquile is gendered as well as racialized. In government and private brochures promoting tourism to Peru, the gender of lower-class mestizas (the erotic chola) is foregrounded, though brochures advertising Taquile are less eroticized. Brochures and videotapes advertising tourism to Taquile commonly depict ruins, young female dancers in pretty clothes, and cute children holding sheep (there are no llamas on the island). Even though the primary textual and visual messages advertise the possibility of seeing both male and female indians, it is women who have preserved in their own dress and weaving styles cultural practices that are considered more "traditional" and consequently more "indian." In their own bodies and textiles, women are often the most visible representations of indianness and, as such, have experienced tourism in distinctively different ways than men.

Elsewhere I discuss gendered aspects of the problems and benefits associated with tourism on Taquile (Zorn 2004). Women do not lead any of Taquile's collective enterprises (boat groups, cooperative store) and still rarely interact with outside organizations. It is well known that women in the Andes who do not hold public office typically exercise power "behind the scenes," discussing decisions and influencing their husbands concerning issues and votes, but not participating publicly. Taquilean women attend the island's weekly assemblies, but generally do not speak in the assembly.

Before the marketing of Taquile textiles in the 1960s and the development of tourism in the 1970s, only Taquilean men interacted with outside NGOs and national and paranational agencies. While few Taquileans attended the community's modest primary schools, as is common in many Peruvian communities, far fewer girls attended than did boys. Early travel was by reed boat, which only men operated. When Taquileans built wooden sailboats, fewer women than men traveled off island, though more women traveled when Taquileans built motorboats, which operate during the day and cut travel time from six to twelve hours, by day or night, to three or four hours by day. Delegations to the Peruvian president in the 1930s to try to obtain title to community lands, court battles to purchase land, and the plethora of intermittent interactions with representatives of Peruvian regional and national agencies consisted entirely of men. Women were active on the island, weaving textiles to sell to raise money, debating involvement, making decisions about risks with the men in their families who represented them in public. Off the island, the public demeanor expected of indians continued to be a submissive shyness that in Peruvian performativity is gendered as female.

When tourism went into full swing by the late 1970s, Taquilean men interacted with tourists more extensively than did women, since men already had the role of dealing with outsiders, and because more men (though still few) spoke Spanish. Monolingual Taquilean women interacted with tourists when taking turns guiding registered guests to homes, and in the evenings when serving meals, but these interactions were far less frequent than those of Taquilean males. The Catholic Church carried out educational programs on the island that had the partial effect of encouraging women to be more assertive in public, to "learn how to speak" as Petrona Huatta remarked to me, by gaining experience through leading these groups. Even though Mothers' Clubs (Club de Madres) have clientalist and assistencialist agendas, Taquilean women found them a training ground for public speech (see Blondet 1990 on Mothers' Clubs in Lima). The many women's organizations and associations, as well as political movements, in Puno city and department do not have branches on Taquile.

By the late 1980s, however, Taquilean women in their twenties and thirties were more publicly assertive, traveling regularly back and forth to Puno, and beginning to participate in the private and public aspects of tourism. I saw women taking passengers' names on boats (indicating women's increased literacy), and on rare occasions, operating the motorboat when out on the lake. Several Taquilean women in their twenties told me they were less fearful of talking in public: "We are no longer afraid like before."

Textile production is the sphere in which gender relations have altered most significantly, because selling textiles brings money, and through the sale of textiles Taquilean women earned money for the first time (the vast majority of Taquile's seasonal migrants are male). Commercializing textiles has become intertwined with tourism, because tourists buy textiles. Because Taquilean women produce the finest and most complex textiles, women potentially earn more than men from textile sales. Cash from textile sales has provided women with a new source of power in their homes and their community, which has led to envy and some family tensions. Apolinar Huatta Marca, a Taquilean man living in Lima, told the anthropologist Matos Mar that "now people, women, know more about money because they make their handicrafts, they have more money than men, because the crafts made by women cost more" (Matos Mar 1986:392).

Textile sales have also led to conflicts, since many of the textiles sold by men were woven for them by their wives; men and women both make clothing for one another, but women weave the finest textiles, commanding the highest prices. I heard spontaneous reports of conflicts over who deserved the money from the sale of textiles woven by a woman but given to a man. Women frequently complained to me about having to weave a new belt for a husband to wear at an upcoming festival because he had sold the latest one she had woven for him—"and then kept the money, too!"

Protest Tactics

Both nearby Puno and other Peruvian cities and towns regularly experience protests by women participating in popular associations and organizations. Assemblies, marches, strikes, and road blockades, some of which become violent clashes between popular and government or paramilitary forces, are a common part of life in Peru, and this was exacerbated during Peru's undeclared civil war, though not on Taquile. Thus many or most

Taquilean women are aware, personally or through the radio, of many protest tactics. The 1989 Taquilean women's one-day strike against a non-island boat agency I describe below represented a qualitative change in tactics employed by Taquileans against outsiders. It is not so unusual, however, in the history of women's activism in South America, where a legacy of direct protest by women remains a part of popular culture.

In Peru, the reference point is Micaela Bastidas, married to and a co-strategist of the indigenous revolutionary Túpac Amaru. Together they led the eighteenth-century "Great Rebellion" against the Spanish empire (she is said to have directed the uprising against Cuzco); like him, Bastidas was executed for rebellion. In Bolivia during the same years, Bartolina Sisa, married to and a co-strategist of Túpac Katari, remains a popular figure of indigenous female rebellion. There are many others, not all indigenous, including the mestizas "Heroínas de la Coronilla," who detained the advance of royal troops into southern Bolivia by defending the city of Cochabamba in 1812, using sticks, stones, and a few weapons, in Bolivia's fight for independence from Spain (Mesa, Gisbert, and Mesa 1997:298).[2]

Overall, Taquilean women and men responded in distinctive gendered ways to the battle for control of transportation, with men acting through government agencies and NGOs, and (even if only once) women acting directly. Women's and men's different responses can be understood as deriving from historical experiences of gendered relations with the Peruvian nation-state, as well as the experience of tourism.

In April 1989, a group of indigenous women on Taquile Island, Peru, spontaneously started a strike (*huelga*) to block a particularly abusive tour agency's boats from docking on their island's hand-built stone jetty, high on Andean Lake Titicaca. For years, Taquileans had been trying to reassert their right to control tourism on their island, and control of transportation was central to this effort, but community efforts to monopolize transportation and regulate tour boats were unsuccessful.

April is autumn in the Andes and the rainy season had recently ended. Taquile's many stone terraces would be emerald green with the crops almost ready for harvest. At midday, when the boats arrived from mainland Puno, the Andean sky was brilliant blue, the vast lake shimmering, the tropical sun burning. The Taquileans saw the tourists, in their travel-worn clothing and high-tech mountaineering gear, approach in the boats, after the three-and-a-half-hour-long voyage across the lake.

The boat captains attempted to maneuver their boats along Taquile's steep and rocky coast to its three stone docks, but on that day Taquilean women kept the motorboats full of tourists, boat crews, and guides from landing by pushing the boats away with long wooden poles that are used to maneuver boats in and out of the island's docks. Some months after the event I was told that the "women's strike" had "shamed" Taquilean men into joining to try to physically block docking and entry onto the island; as women pushed the boats away, groups of men raced from steep hilltop to hilltop and lobbed stones with handwoven slings at the non-Taquilean boats below. The tour agency's motorboats finally left, to make their way across the lake to the mainland city of Puno.

None of the women held community office or were involved in any Peruvian political organization; this single battle, with its demonstration of female courage, was followed by a short-term victory when a regional office of the Peruvian government granted Taquileans a monopoly on transportation for a few years. This monopoly was impossible to enforce, however, and it was successfully contested by non-Taquileans under President Fujimori's neoliberal government during the 1990s. A direct protest against boat owners was never repeated.

The indigenous men of Taquile, accustomed to negotiating with regional and national agencies, hoped to receive assistance from the Peruvian nation. They found, however, that in the neoliberal environment of former president Fujimori's 1990s government, indigenous peasant communities enjoyed no special rights in the scramble for economic survival. When confronted with non-Taquileans illegally docking on the island, men's responses were largely in the passive mode expected of them, rather than directly confrontational. (Taquileans generally avoid direct physical conflict, and the island is characterized by an unusually low level of violence.) This allowed the tourist guides successfully to get around paying docking fees by saying that their bosses hadn't given them enough money or with delaying tactics. It is important to note that in such interactions the racially subordinate position of Taquileans is implicit but largely determines the modes of the interactions.

When I visited Taquile in 2002, interactions with public agencies were still carried out exclusively by men, with male non-islanders interacting with male Taquileans. Taquilean men continue to monopolize all offices on committees and in associations. Women were, however, increasingly active in the work of committees in terms of the tasks they perform, including serving turns in the cooperative store, collecting information from boat passengers, and occasionally attending to tourists in Taquile's intermittently functioning tour agency in Puno. This change reflects both increased assertiveness as well as improvements in women's education and literacy. In 2002, men as well as women were anticipating the election of women to committees and community offices. Men are respected after they serve as rotative authorities, especially Taquile's governor or *teniente* and head mayor or *alcalde mayor*. My compadre Francisco Huatta told me women also are recognized and respected for their community service, as the wives of male authorities, adding that, "maybe next year there will be a female governor?" Women I asked about this, such as Alejandrina Huatta (his daughter), said "and why not?" which I took to mean they agreed. To date, however, there has been no female governor.

Tourism and Indigenous Identity

Opportunities from tourism led to travel abroad by several dozen community members, either individually or in groups. Personal contacts with individuals continued to be important resources, though there were important differences between the experiences of women and men. Groups that traveled to international folklore and/or museum festivals were mostly composed of men, though they included at least one woman. This was usually at the insistence of the international groups who negotiated with male representatives of Taquile's various "folklore" associations to plan trips abroad, including two trips to Washington, D.C., for the Smithsonian Institution's 1991 and 1994 Festivals of American Folklife. Various factors, including word of mouth, Internet advertising, publications in popular and scholarly periodicals, and advertising by Peruvian agencies such as the Ministry of Industry and Tourism (MITINCI), about either the spectacular beauty of the island and its beautifully dressed inhabitants or the Taquilean "model" for community control of tourist enterprises, led to Taquile becoming not only a highly visited tourist site but also a model for "indigenous control of tourism."

Despite steady increases in tourism to Taquile, as I have noted there are clear indications that problems are developing there. The 2000 report by a consultant for a U.S. Agency for International Development–funded project to develop tourism in the Puno corridor (Gartner and Morton 2000), which I cite above, recommends that tourism be directed toward the little-visited Island of Amantani and other permanent islands on the Peruvian side of Lake Titicaca. Gartner states that the tourist experience on the "picturesque" island of Taquile has become diluted for tourists seeking an "authentic cultural experience." Gartner and his assistant, who did not stay overnight, write that this is due to the extremely high numbers of tourists going to Taquile, whose brief stay provided little more than a glimpse of "inhabitants wearing colorful clothing" (ibid.).

This report confirms Taquile's importance as a tourism site in southern Peru, but also the loss of its brief and shining moment as a "world model for indigenous control of tourism." The report's recommendation to encourage tourism to other islands is based on what the authors describe as the poor quality of the "tourist experience" on Taquile. Taquileans blame this on their loss of control: "They [the private non-Taquilean tour agencies] control everything, we can't do anything: their boats come whenever they please; some guides are rude and tell untruths and call us 'dirty indians'; and the tourists are only here for a half hour, an hour" (ibid.). Local tour agencies say it is because Taquile is "modernizing," building cement houses rather than thatched huts. What kind of indians are Taquileans supposed to be, on whose terms?

Tourism to Andean communities has multiple effects on how Andeans imagine, embody, perform, and negotiate being "indian," as tourists seek authenticity in the homes, acts, and bodies of indians. Race, in particular indigeneity, is both foregrounded and erased in tourism. Representations of indianness are key to the attractiveness of the island of Taquile as a tourist site, and indeed of tourism to Peru and South America. Tourists travel to see indians. Peruvian government tourist brochures about the islands in Lake Titicaca code race through expressions such as "descendants of the Incas" and, in Spanish, "millennial peoples." Government documents code indians as peasants, referring to Taquile as a Comunidad Campesina Reconocida. Consultants' reports express disappointment in Taquile's ability to continue offering an "authentic cultural experience," which appears to be something that only indians can provide tourists (but are no longer doing).

The voluminous and rich literature on race and ethnicity in the Andes has examined multiple aspects of the social construction of the status of indian, as evaluated etically in terms of class and cultural beliefs and practices and, to a lesser degree, emically in terms of notion of personhood and self (Canessa 1998). While indian status is highlighted in a racially homogeneous community such as Taquile when residents travel outside home, research such as that by Canessa (ibid.) and Mary Weismantel (2001), and the contributors to this volume shows that conflicts over social roles are fought in the most intimate spaces of peoples' homes and hearths.

Social status may be examined at any given moment as constitutive or at least imbricated in virtually any given action or belief, but race and ethnicity are not always foregrounded and considered consciously every minute of every day, for most people. Taquileans at home sometimes think about what they do in terms of their indianness, but sometimes they do not. Except for the poorest Taquileans, people usually wear good Taquilean clothing when going to community events, such as the weekly assembly, but commonly wear worn clothing, which may include items of factory-made western dress, when working around the house, where they are thinking more about practicality than whether a tourist might spot them in western dress. Given the prevailing racism in Peru, the opposite occurs when outside the community—virtually every gesture and action is interpreted and framed in terms of social identity, of being indian, or mestizo, or white. Tourism has changed the in-community/out-community consciousness of race by potentially foregrounding race on a minute-by-minute basis, and by adding additional imaginings of indianness in addition to those of local people, regional mestizos, and national "whites."

Many tourists seek exotic locales, and exotic indians, acting in exotic indian ways. Beautiful little Taquile, set in Lake Titicaca, can seem almost too much to the ironic tourist. A colleague told me after a visit in 2001 to Taquile that they are "almost too perfect"—an exotic island in an exotic lake, people wearing gorgeous costumes (which turned out to be good daily dress). Yet, in general, when tourists tour, they expect the people they visit to be frozen into timeless subjects. The nature of Taquile's earlier "face-to-face" model of tourism, wherein visitors traveled on Taquilean-run boats, and stayed in Taquilean homes, both intensified and ameliorated this desire.

Community-controlled tourism created a space for many or most Taquileans to practice an agency that they are losing and that is rarely possible outside the island, given poverty and discrimination. Taquileans who operate boats, cook and serve meals, sell textiles, register tourists, and invite endless visitors to become godparents, project agency to tourists in a way that does not occur to passive tourists brought by possibly racist tour agencies. More important, and relevant to this volume, is that Taquileans experience this agency themselves. The loss of Taquile's monopoly of transportation to and from their island has profound implications for tourists' imaginings of indianness and, at least as important, for the imaginings of Taquileans. Taquileans told me repeatedly that they want to regain their former monopoly of transportation, both to earn income and to be able to control the comings and goings of tourists. They are frustrated that internal debates, on topics such as whether they should limit the total number of tourists, or not have travel on particular days of the week or dates in the year, are meaningless when they have no control over the arrival and departure of private, non-Taquilean tour boats. Ironically, Taquile continues to serve as a model for the control of tourism in their community to other indigenous communities, including Charazani and Coroma in Bolivia, at the same time that they continue to seek alliances with NGOs that might help them regain their former monopoly on transportation.

It is easy to enumerate the very real problems and disadvantages of tourism, including unequal distribution of benefits, unwanted garbage, disorderly behavior, intrusions into daily life, trampling of fields, and so on. Yet tourism, insofar as it has been controlled by Taquileans, also has provided many benefits, both economic and psychological, and in a poor region of a poor country, that clearly are worth fighting for. Following the growth of tourism, population in the community increased from around 900 to around 1,700, primarily due to reduced mortality, improved health, and return migration from Taquileans hoping to make a living at home once again, reversing the more common pattern of rural exodus. As significant is the fact that the height and weight of many teenagers has increased, suggesting improved diet or at least increased calories.

Somewhat surprisingly, the transport sector proved to be very important in terms of benefits to the Taquilean community as a whole (Zorn 1997). The modest amount charged tourists was sufficient to subsidize travel by islanders to and from the mainland, which was resoundingly perceived as a significant benefit. Taquileans learned new skills in the course of developing a transport sector: managing businesses, operating and repairing motors, and even building large motor boats, using hand tools (Healy and Zorn 1982–83, Zorn 2004).

But one very important benefit is an intangible but frequently stated pride in the value of local "costumbres" (customs), which stands for local practices; this perhaps should have been expected by outsiders like me, given the disdain or worse with which the outside world generally regarded people like Taquileans, who are considered lowly indian peasants. The other side of this coin is, however, a requirement for Taquileans to look—and act—like the brochures that increasingly advertise them, leading to a "freezing" of practices to meet tourist expectations.

The "diluted" Taquilean experience creates problems for the department of Puno, which sorely needs income, and relies on tourism, however poorly executed, as a primary source of it. The dissatisfaction of tourists visiting Taquile could result in decreased tourism to Puno, since it is clear that the spectacular islands in the lake next to Puno are responsible for much of the draw to Puno.

As a result of the loss of their former monopoly over transportation, Taquileans no longer receive the economic benefits they did before, and also are no longer able to regulate tourism to the extent that they were hitherto able. Furthermore, Taquileans told me that they feel that they have lost control of their lives: "We can't say anything; they [the outside tour agencies] command." In the words of the report on tourism in the Puno corridor, Taquileans have been reduced to being the "inhabitants wearing colorful clothing." The interesting problem here is that what tourists come to see is indians, and it is the combination of overly high volume, and lack of regulation by Taquileans, that is diminishing the "quality" of the Taquilean "product."

At present a few young Taquilean men are trying to compete for tourists by going to the Internet, but there are numerous problems, ranging from Taquile's lack of electricity to the island being "off the grid" for Internet service. Another strategy may be to have a few young Taquileans—almost certain to be men—who can train as guides; this is problematic due to limited literacy, expense, and scarce educational opportunities, but may be possible, in cooperation with interested individuals in Peru and Bolivia.

The more general problem of the regulation of behavior of non-Taquileans on the island is a part of the relationship between Taquile and the Peruvian nation. In the contemporary neoliberal climate, Taquileans can enjoy no special protection, which I believe they and other communities coping with mass tourism require in order to realize economic benefits. Communities such as these need, if not state assistance, at least the absence of state resistance to their efforts to control other components of tourism, including the frequency of tours, where tours go, and what guides say (or don't say) about the inhabitants and their homes.

Discussion

At the beginning of the twenty-first century, at the same time that Taquileans in general, and women in particular, were participating more actively in community, regional, and national affairs, a series of constraints served to limit increased participation. The primary factors were tourism (though not necessarily in ways that might have been expected) and economics.

Considered by many policy makers the most traditional, and therefore "backward," group in the Andes, women, through their cloth, emerge as dynamic mediators between their community and the outside. As weavers, women are the key creators of powerful symbolic representations of ideology that locates men's and women's places in the cosmos. This is particularly important since many Andean women literally lose their public "voices" after marriage (in many Bolivian indigenous ethnic groups, only unmarried females sing in public). Through cloth, Andean women also play an active role in the negotiation of "tradition" and "modernity" within their societies, a role often ascribed to men in general, and to male authorities in particular. Berlo (1991), focusing primarily on Maya women of Chiapas, Mexico, and highland Guatemala, makes a similar point, arguing that native women in the Americas, through the medium of textiles, are "agents of transformation." Furthermore, women weave the Andean cloth that has been most heavily commercialized in the ethnic arts market, which means that the commercialization of ethnic cloth is likely to have a special effect on women and gender relations.

In 2002, I could see that Taquilean women were attending school in greater numbers than ever before, and had increased their direct participation in tourism by taking on tasks in community organizations, and by opening small shops and restaurants. This coincided with scattered talk about whether Taquileans soon would elect female authorities.

Tourism and the sale of textiles made it possible for Taquileans to earn cash primarily at home, which was rare indeed in the impoverished altiplano. While income from tourism increased social stratification, it also allowed most Taquileans to improve their lives (Zorn 2004) in many ways. Women earned money from the sale of textiles and this impacted gender roles. While mass tourism means that more visitors than ever before come to Taquile, islanders no longer control the transport sector, and the numerous day tourists spend less time—and money—on the island than did earlier visitors. There is no doubt that tourism still brings in money, but the "leakage" of profits away from the community (which commonly occurs with tourism) has increased greatly, and Taquileans are competing for a dwindling share of income. The trend toward increased visitors and reduced profit per visitor seems likely to continue, and this will bring decreasing opportunities for Taquilean women to earn money from selling textiles and from businesses associated with tourism.

A rather less obvious effect of tourism, in both its community-controlled and mass forms, is the more general effect that tourism has had on Taquilean identity, including gender norms and relations. An important benefit of Taquile's fame as a tourist destination has been the development of an intangible but frequently stated pride in the value of local costumbres; this is not insignificant, given the disdain or worse with which the outside world generally regarded people like Taquileans, who are considered lowly indian peasants. Tourism has helped Taquileans become proud of their indigenous identity, and the attention lavished on Taquile and Taquileans, and money from tourism, has brought grudging respect from non-islanders in the region and even the nation. The other aspect of appreciation for indigenous identity is, however, a requirement for Taquileans to look—and act—like the brochures that increasingly advertise them.

More broadly, continuing severe economic problems in the region and nation have constrained women's, as well as men's, opportunities. Taquilean men and, increasingly, women were ready to become more active in their region and nation, but their opportunities to do so have become fewer as Peru continues to experience tremendous poverty and social inequality.

Conclusions

Tourism, gender, indigeneity, and the nation are all woven together in the case of Taquile, a beautiful remote island in Lake Titicaca near Puno. Taquile's tourism is based on a perception of authentic indigeneity for the adventurous tourist seeking contact with native peoples (ethnotourism). This perception of Taquileans as ur-Andean is held not only by foreigners, but also by metropolitan Peruvians as well, and Taquile is used as the authentic Andean backdrop for presidential public relations events, claiming legitimacy by association with an authentic indigenous reality.

Taquileans' widely recognized status as ur-indian gave them a stronger voice in direct appeals to the national government. Taquileans have a broader and more successful strategy of engagement with international NGOs than their mainland peasant cousins, which over the years has brought benefits to the community.

This leads us to a paradox: Taquile's traditionalism is what allows it to modernize. The wealth accumulated through tourism and sales of handicrafts ironically has meant Taquileans can now afford to build cement houses with tin roofs and buy machine-spun, commercially dyed yarns for their textiles, operate modern motorboats for transport, educate their children to speak Spanish, and attempt to enter Internet-based marketing, all of which undermines the perceived authenticity of their indigeneity.

The wealth provided by tourism-related activities has also affected traditional relationships between the genders, providing increased access to cash for women. With tourism, as a result of their increased economic importance, Taquilean women have in recent years begun to be more active in the public domain, working more with external organizations, a previously male domain. Taquileans are also choosing to educate their female children more, further affecting gender relations and sources of power and legitimacy for women. But Taquilean women and men have responded differently to the threat to business presented by the breakdown of the Taquilean transport monopoly. Men's response has been, on the one hand, to appeal to the traditional patron-client relationships with external organizations for their intervention, and on the other to go "straight to the top" and appeal to the national government directly. The men's strategy is much more grounded in traditional Andean notions of power relations, ritual kinship, or compadrazgo, and so on. Women's strategy, on the other hand, has been one of less reliance on intermediaries, and more one of direct public action, blocking the rival boats from landing and "shaming" their men into more direct public action to assert their prior rights. Despite the fact that both men and women see women as being more "traditional," women's strategy in this instance is actually less traditional. Ironically, this nontraditional approach may in fact prove more successful under neoliberal regimes than the men's more traditional one.

Although the net effect of tourism might be seen to be undermining the traditional indigenous cultural forms in Taquile, it has paradoxically served to make indigenous identity more salient to the Taquileans themselves. Tourism has made indigenous identity prominent not only in the outside world (where all their actions are judged as indian, other) but at home as well. The constant gaze of the tourist has made Taquileans aware of their indigeneity in an unusual way, and in fact Taquileans express pride that their costumbres are so noteworthy and important. Although tourism has changed Taquilean lifeways forever, and had deep implications for gender relations, it has also given Taquileans a very strong sense of their own proud identity as indigenous.

Taquile and its struggle to control tourism highlights many of the problems facing indigenous communities today. With a long history of dispossession, marginalization, and racism, international tourism has the positive benefit of raising the status of indigenous culture, "costumbres" in the eyes of the Peruvian nation, as well as indigenous people themselves. At the same time, indigenous communities such as Taquile face the paradox that if tourism gives them more control over their lands and lives, makes them less marginal within the nation and more able to resist racism by raising the status of an indigenous identity, it also appears to undermine the very uniqueness that attracts tourism in the first place.

Acknowledgments

I would like to thank the people of Taquile Island, especially my compadres Natividad Machaca and Francisco "Pancho" Huatta, and their families; Juan Quispe and his family; and the many Taquilean authorities, for their hospitality and assistance for nearly three decades. I gratefully acknowledge the support of many institutions that have funded my research and writing on Taquile, including the Brooklyn Museum, and the National Endowment for the Humanities (Fellowship FB-35257-98), and before that the Inter-American Foundation and the Institute for International Education. I thank the American Ethnological Society and the Society for Latin American Anthropology of the American Anthropological Association for their support of the 2001 double session that preceded this volume. The session's excellent panelists, and the enthusiastic audience at both sessions, provided many thought-provoking ideas for which I am grateful. I thank Andrew Canessa for his insightful comments, fine editorial suggestions, and patience; I am particularly grateful to him for taking on the task of editing this volume on his own. I also wish to thank the two anonymous reviewers for their careful comments on an earlier draft, and friends and colleagues for their comments on earlier ideas and drafts. I hope they will forgive me for not naming them individually here. Any errors are, of course, my responsibility.

Notes

1. I thank Kevin Healy for sharing this email with me, along with decades of collaboration concerning Taquile. All translations from Quechua and Spanish are mine unless otherwise noted.

2. I thank one of the anonymous reviewers for pointing this out.

Bibliography

Albó, Xavier. 1999. "Andean People in the Twentieth Century." In *The Cambridge History of the Native Peoples of the Americas*, vol. 3: *South America*, part 2, ed.

Frank Salomon and Stuart B. Schwartz, 765–871. Cambridge: Cambridge University Press.

Avalos de Matos, Rosalía. 1951a. "Changements culturels dans les îles du Lac Titicaca." Travaux de l'Institut Français d'Études Andines 3:40–50.

———. 1951b. "L'organisation sociale dans l'île de Taquile." *Travaux de l'Institut Français d'Études Andines* 3:74–87.

Berlo, Janet C. 1991. "Beyond Bricolage: Women and Aesthetic Strategies in Latin American Textiles." In *Textile Traditions of Mesoamerica and the Andes: An Anthology*, ed. Margot B. Schevill, Janet C. Berlo, and Edward B. Dwyer, 437–79. New York: Garland Publishing.

Blondet, Cecilia. 1990. "Establishing an Identity: Women Settlers in a Poor Lima Neighbourhood." In *Women and Social Change in Latin America*, ed. Elizabeth Jelin, 12–46. London: UNRISD/Zed Books.

Canessa, Andrew. 1998. "Procreation, Personhood, and Ethnic Difference in Highland Bolivia." *Ethnos* 63, no. 2:227–47.

Colloredo-Mansfeld, Rudi. 1999. *The Native Leisure Class: Consumption and Cultural Creativity in the Andes*. Chicago: University of Chicago Press.

Contorno, Elena, and Lucia Tamayo Flores. 2000. Informe de viaje a las islas Taquile y Amantaní. Email, May 16, 2000.

Dore, Elizabeth, ed. 1997. *Gender Politics in Latin America: Debates in Theory and Practice*. New York: Monthly Review Press.

Dore, Elizabeth, and Maxine Molyneux, eds. 2000. *Hidden Histories of Gender and the State in Latin America*. Durham, N.C.: Duke University Press.

Flores Huatta, Alejandro, and Paula Quispe Cruz. 1994. "Preserving Our Culture." In *All Roads Are Good: Native Voices on Life and Culture*, ed. Terence Winch, 167–75. New York, Washington, D.C.: National Museum of the American Indian, Smithsonian Institution.

Gartner, William C., and Molly Morton. 2000. "Estrategia de Desarrollo de Turismo para el Corredor Económico del PRA: Analisis de la Oferta" (May 2000). Electronic document, *http://www.chemonicspe.com/boletin2/Publicaciones/Estudio_Oferta_Turistica_Puno.pdf*, accessed November 19, 2001.

Gill, Leslie. 1990. "Like a Veil to Cover Them: Women and the Pentecostal Movement in La Paz, Bolivia." *American Ethnologist* 17, no. 4:708–21.

Healy, Kevin, and Elayne Zorn. 1982–1983. "Lake Titicaca's Campesino-Controlled Tourism." *Grassroots Development, Journal of the Inter-American Foundation* 6, no. 2/7, no. 1:3–10.

———. 1994. "Taquile's Homespun Tourism." In Cultural Expression and Grassroots Development: Cases from Latin America and the Caribbean, ed. Charles Kleymeyer, 135–48. Boulder, Colo.: Lynne Rienner Publications.

Jelin, Elizabeth, ed. 1990. *Women and Social Change in Latin America*, trans. J. A. Ammit and M. Thomson. London: UNRISD/Zed Books.

Luykx, Aurolyn. 2000. *The Citizen Factory: Schooling and Cultural Production in Bolivia*. Albany: State University of New York Press.

Mar, José Matos. 1951a. "La propriedad en la isla de Taquile (Lago Titicaca)." *Revista del Museo Nacional* 26 (1951): 211–71.

———. 1951b. "La propriété dans l'Ile Taquile." *Travaux de l'Institut Français d'Études Andines* 3:51–73.

———. 1960. "El trabajo en una comunidad andina." In *Etnología e Arqueología: Instituto de Etnología y Arqueología* 1, 9–23. Lima: Universidad Nacional Mayor de San Marcos.

———. 1964. "La propriedad en la isla de Taquile (Lago Titicaca)." In *Estudios sobre la cultural actual del Perú*, 66–124. Lima: Universidad Nacional Mayor de San Marcos.

———. 1986. *Taquile en Lima: Siete familias cuentan*. Lima: Instituto de Estudios Peruanos.

Meisch, Lynn. 2002. *Andean Entrepreneurs: Otavalo Merchants and Musicians in the Global Arena*. Austin: University of Texas Press.

de Mesa, José, Teresa Gisbert, and Carlos D. Mesa. 1997. *Historia de Bolivia*. La Paz: Ed. Gisbert.

Patterson, Amy S. 2000. "Women in Global Politics: Progress or Stagnation?" *USA Today* magazine, September. Electronic document, http://www.findarticles.com/p/articles/mi_m1272/ai_65230199, accessed August 4, 2004.

Stephen, Lynn. 1997. *Women and Social Movements in Latin America: Power from Below*. Austin: University of Texas Press.

Weismantel, Mary. 1988. *Food, Gender, and Poverty in the Ecuadorian Andes*. Philadelphia: University of Pennsylvania Press.

———. 2001. *Cholas and Pishtacos: Stories of Race and Sex in the Andes*. Chicago: University of Chicago Press.

Zorn, Elayne. n.d. "Taquileños on the Mall/Washingtonians (and others) in Taquile: The Smithsonian Folklife Festival, International Tourism, and the 'Last Inkas.'" Paper presented at the 94th Annual Meeting of the American Anthropological Association, Washington, D.C. 1995.

———. 1997. *Marketing Diversity: Global Transformations in Cloth and Identity in Highland Peru and Bolivia*. Ph.D. diss., Dept. of Anthropology, Cornell University, Ithaca, N.Y.

———. 2004. *Weaving a Future: Tourism, Cloth, and Culture on an Andean Island*. Iowa City: University of Iowa Press.

Afterword
Andean Identities:
Multiplicities, Socialities, Materialities
Mary Weismantel

This summer in Lima, two different Peruvians gave me some insight into what Andean identity looks like from the perspective of that coastal city. The first was a taxi driver who described himself angrily as "the last Limeño": a lonely survivor in a city full of immigrants from the highlands. "They drive like they're still driving llamas up in the mountains," he complained, and pretended to roll down his window and shout at the car ahead of him. "Hey, it's a car, not an alpaca!" A young sales clerk, the daughter of those same immigrants, spoke defensively of her trips up to visit the highland community where her parents were born. "It's nice there, beautiful," she said. "It's not like people say, you know, like there's nothing modern. People are the same there as here; they know how to tell time and everything like that."

The authors of the chapters in this book move deftly between these two contrasting sensibilities. They know what the sales clerk knows: that the Andean region is indian but it is hardly timeless. Yet they are also aware that in the eyes of people like my taxi driver, there is an inherent incompatibility between the indigenous body and modernity. For the "natives" of the Andean nations, this dual awareness—which Krista Van Vleet (chap. 4) compares to DuBois' notion of double consciousness—is built into everyday existence, which demands both that they negotiate the complexities of life in the twenty-first century and navigate the deep and troubled waters of a racism that denies their capacity to do so. The six essays presented here explore this duality within six very different ethnographic and historical contexts; taken together, they provide a rich and finely nuanced view of contemporary Andean life.

They also reveal how far contemporary anthropological understandings of identity have come. What we see here, rather than an essence rooted within the individual consciousness, is something constantly produced and reproduced through exchange. Andrew Canessa opens the book by quoting Michael Taussig, who says that identity takes its form not at the central core with its fantasied "satisfying solidity" (Canessa, introduction, citing Taussig 1993:151) but on the borders of the body and the self, through the "mutually implicating dyad of alterity and identity" (Canessa 2000). The essays that follow document this process of identity formation taking place in and through social intercourse.

These Andean essays thus privilege social interaction as the site of identity production. The interactions may be informal and discursive: conversations actual or imagined, such as the taxi driver shouting about alpacas (but not so loudly that another driver might shout back), the sales clerk phrasing her statements in response to an invisible chorus of dismissive commentary about the highlands, or worried parents listening to their daughter talk about her teacher. Or they may be more formal performances: a concert or a ritual dance, official statements written by government employees, or the classroom presentations of a teacher charged with making backward indians into modern citizens. In each case, whether dancing together or talking to one another, the people in these essays create identity through processes that are inherently social and interactive.

This process is symbolic, but also material: it takes place when bodies interact, and objects are made, bought, sold, and consumed. Identities are simultaneously formed out of ideas and beliefs, and constituted through physical media: voices and gestures, clothing and money. The physicality of these processes highlights their production within space and time—two especially significant dimensions that illuminate the multiplicity of social realities within which contemporary Andean actors move. The spaces involved include the actual physical locations where people meet and interact, but also metaphorical places: the symbolically charged landscapes of the Andes, with their strong racial and sexual connotations. The temporal dimension is equally complex: as the Lima shopgirl insisted, the highlands are a place where people know how to tell time—but in these essays, we see them telling several different kinds of time. At school and at work, indigenous people are as mindful as any others of what E. P. Thomson famously characterized as capitalist time, but Marcia Stephenson's essay, for example, deals with Aymara people who also reenact precapitalist temporal and spatial structures through the ritual of the chuqila.

Both dimensions are brought together by bodies in movement through space and time, whether at work, in ritual, or at play. Hands, feet, and

eyes move in distinctive temporal and spatial patterns when herding a llama or driving a car, putting on a poncho or a new pair of shoes, weaving
an ancient textile pattern or learning a new kind of sex. Music, especially,
moves the body to particular rhythms, each signifying a race, a region,
and a moment in history: in song or in dance, people find themselves
transported to the warm lowlands or the cold highlands, into indian bodies or metropolitan spaces. The identities encountered here, then, are not
primarily singular, individual, and symbolic; they are also *multiple, social,*
and *material.*

Multiplicities

Like other forms of social identity in the twentieth and twenty-first centuries, indigenous Andean identity takes shape as mobile actors shift between performances within an ever-changing social landscape. The double consciousness noted above and the many intersections between race
and gender, and between metropolitan and marginal arenas, are among
the forces that create "communities of practice" (Eckert and McConnell-
Ginet 1995 quoted in Van Vleet, chap. 4): multiple social spaces within
and between which individuals move during the course of their days and
lives. These movements can be unpredictable—as when a young woman
chooses to buy polleras for a fiesta, rather than an airplane ticket to Europe—and so too are the alignments between race, sex, class, and nation
within each context. One of the contributions these chapters make to
Andean studies is to amplify—and confound—the conjunctions of race
and sex noted by previous scholars such as that encapsulated in Marisol
de la Cadena's memorable phrase, "women are more indian." Canessa
explores the corollary of this premise: indian men are more feminized.
Van Vleet, in contrast, finds that when young rural women make money
in the city, people in their home communities may make a quite different association: between youthful femininity and commodities, urbanity,
and prosperity. Her essay shows that the association between modernity
and tradition can be convoluted as well: it is by stockpiling polleras that
these young women showcase their urban success.

Michelle Bigenho interrogates two other widely accepted associations
between gender and race in the Americas: the privileging of the indigenous female body as the unique source of cultural authenticity, and of
the sexual-racial dyad of white male and non-white female as the central
emblem of colonial relations. She documents a different, unexplored

national imaginary, in which white women mined the cultural production of indigenous men in order to create a new Bolivian musical identity. Canessa, in a novel and welcome exploration of the sexual experiences of indigenous men with non-indigenous women, similarly finds new national identities taking shape in these sexual unions as well. But when these men return home, de la Cadena's original formulation still holds: these newly cosmopolitan husbands find their own wives too indian. The point, then, is not to disprove particular symbolic relationships noted by other scholars, but rather to underscore the dynamic, volatile nature of these connections, which constantly create their own antitheses even as they are continually reinforced and reproduced over time.

It is also important not to overstate the possibilities for mobility: while the move within sociological thinking from rigid notions of identity to an emphasis on fluidity was a welcome advance, we must not forget that race, sex, and class can still be iron cages from which escape is difficult and comes with a heavy cost. Within specific spaces there are opportunities for individual expression, such as shedding one's jeans and platform shoes for a pollera, and for the kind of collective resistance that THOA finds in the chuqila; by the same token, however, opportunities that are confined to circumscribed spaces are not available to everyone. The movement of actors between these spaces is continually constrained. The singers Bigenho interviewed were careful to describe the limits within which they kept themselves in order to preserve feminine decorum, avoiding any hint of indulgence in the masculine pleasures of the night. It is difficult to believe that they never envied their male colleagues their greater freedoms, or wished to indulge in the forms of social and sensual intercourse—at a minimum, of drinking together, smoking together, laughing together in the liminal spaces of nightclubs and bars—that their own performances were intended to facilitate. The barriers of class and race are brought to light in the telling examples provided by Canessa, where an educated urban professional may find it advantageous to list Aymara or Quechua language skills on a job application, and "cool" to chew coca in a jazz bar. In the places where rural people seek work or pleasure, the same practices still stigmatize them as uneducated and backward. Indeed, the same middle-class urbanite who may enjoy exploring his inner "indian" in socially selective venues, may nevertheless recoil in disgust from a "real" indian encountered in a less protected setting.

These convoluted realities suggest the need to think more about the relationship between the ideologies of identity that are so critical to the nation-state as imagined community, and the lived experiences of those on the margins of the nation, who have so often served as the sources for metropolitan imaginaries. This duality, we are beginning to realize, is neither simple nor unidirectional. When what has been produced—in this case, a national ideology—is exchanged, it undergoes unexpected transformations as it moves between communities of practice. As a result, the political valences may veer sharply or even reverse themselves: images of indians advanced by metropolitan elites in aid of progressive ideologies may instead reinforce existing inequalities, while racist imagery can be redeployed on the periphery for antiracist ends.

Even such seemingly simplistic and derogatory assertions as "indians are dirty," or "like mules," prove to be multivocal. The trope of the dirty indian can become part of the antimodern discourse of romantic primitivism, in which dirtiness becomes closeness to the earth (Orlove 1998), and I have heard indigenous speakers turn the clichéd symbolic association of indians and mules into a politically charged statement about the indigenous capacity for steadfast resistance and unshakeable endurance (Weismantel 1988). Furthermore, as Brooke Larson demonstrates in her analysis of Bolivian educational policy statements, while state rhetorics about the need to bring modernity to their nonwhite citizens may seem numbingly repetitive over decades, a close reading reveals meaningful differences between the modernizing policies of leftist governments desirous of lifting the oppressive weight of poverty, and more conservative efforts that focused on gendering indigenous women on a white model, while encouraging the indian citizen to remain within his appropriately "limited sphere" and creating bourgeois nuclear families everywhere.

Furthermore, the relationship between metropolitan ideologies and peripheral lives is one of reciprocal influence, not merely a one-way street in which outsiders mistake and fantasize about a putatively real social experience that they do not know directly. Although scholars now eschew any notion of an authentic native, our critiques of the indigenista fabrications of nationalist intellectuals can reproduce the fantasy that a "real," untheorized indigenous identity still exists, just outside our vision. But indigenous, rural, and popular class identities do not simply arise unmediated out of everyday practice; they also take form in response to metropolitan fantasies—whether the fantasies are racist, nationalist, or both. One striking example that hints at the unwritten cultural and intellectual histories of the Andes is the long-standing image of the Aymara as stoic. On the one hand, this stereotype is a vicious lie that renders its victims less than human, as in Canessa's example of the caricatural grimacing Aymara portrayed by an urban Bolivian. In the latter's statement that "they don't feel pain like we do," we can see something of how this trope has been used to excuse the most brutal and degrading of living and working conditions.

But this image, like other racial imaginaries, may work very differently within the "unimagined" communities of Aymara people themselves. For while there is a vast political and historical chasm between the dramatic descriptions of Aymara women in Frontaura's 1932 publication (quoted in Larson, chap. 1) as "made of steel . . . her will power stronger than any other race on earth," and THOA's late-twentieth-century insistence on the immutable Aymara resistance to centuries of colonial oppression, there are nevertheless continuities between the two as well. Indigenous intellects have been consumers of metropolitan myths about the nation—and about themselves. Reworked and reimagined, nationalist images of stoic indians, noble indians, dirty indians, and mulish indians are part of indigenous cultural heritage, and they shape and influence the work of indigenous writers, artists, and activists. The history of indigenous intellectual life in the Andes has yet to be written, but it will be a history of dynamic interaction between the steadfast resistance to outside pressures to assimilate emphasized by THOA, and a creative responsiveness to Bolivian and Peruvian intellectual trends such as Marxism, Maoism, Catholic and Protestant theologies, nationalisms of all stripes, and even neoliberalism.

In sum, the production of ideas about the nation and its citizens was never as fully controlled or limited as political elites might have hoped. White metropolitan men may have seen themselves as the authors of the new nation, created through poems and polemics that were the unique outpourings of a visionary soul. But as their ideas entered into social life, they too began to move between communities of practice in unanticipated ways, changing forms and multiplying meanings as they went.

Socialities

These essays document the formation of identities as an inherently social, dialogic, interactive process. They thus provide a means to amplify Judith Butler's notion of performativity, which has been enormously influential in Andean studies as elsewhere in anthropology. Butler's model of difference is far more flexible and nuanced than earlier notions of ethnicity, enabling us to readily understand the young indigenous woman who dons a pollera and embroidered blouse one minute, and jeans and platform shoes the next. It incorporates the individual agency of the actor, who delivers or subverts the performance expected of her, and also the enormous weight of the discursive regimes within which she makes these choices. However, Butler's theory in the abstract can seem oddly absent of social intercourse: identity formation takes place on the part of a single, performing individual who creates herself in the face of an enormous but rather disembodied and anonymous world of discourses and regimes. Missing or not fully theorized is the interactive and invasive presence of mothers, neighbors, co-workers and compadres through whom we actually experience and respond to ideological notions of our society and the nation.

The concept of mimesis, developed by Taussig and other authors, is inherently binary rather than ego-centered. It allows us to see not only the individual actor surrounded by an intangible but powerful social field, as in Butler, but an interaction between two actors, real or imaginary: self and alter, differentiated through race or sex. Here the boundaries of the self are presented as permeable, but not in such a way that one identity will merge or collapse into one another: these are exchanges in which the two parties remain intact and separate, albeit not unaltered. Few if any of the stories told in this volume are of permanent crossing; instead, dancers enact the role of hunters, indigenous men experiment with novel sex acts and novel sex partners, white women borrow the voices of musical instruments in order to sound like indians without sounding like indian women. In the process, each constructs an alter inside him- or herself—the wild hunter, the cosmopolitan Bolivian citizen, the truly indigenous Bolivian—but without completely ceasing to be what s/he was before—agriculturalist, indigenous miner, urban mestiza.

Although not all these chapters focus on mimesis, they often allow us to catch glimpses of the processes by which indian and white, metropolitan and rural, feminine and masculine are defined against—and created through—one another. Larson documents the weirdly fantastic yet specifically detailed Aymara women imagined by bourgeois female professional educators. In describing these women of "stone" and "steel," stupefied by coca until they are unable to have sex, enduring cold climates and colder mothers, or traveling unchaperoned in the company of men and animals, these authors created a negative image against which to compare other Bolivian femininities, not only their own but also the warmer Quechua woman, and of course the improved Bolivian woman of the future, perfected through education.

These fearsome images in turn can help us comprehend the difficulties faced by Bigenho's musicians, who gradually converted the imaginary highland indian into something more readily internalized, a figure of desire. To do so required a convoluted series of gender transformations, in which mestiza women are the vehicles of a purely masculine indigenous cultural form. The form in which indigeneity would become palatable to all Bolivians, then, was brought some distance from the actual bodies of indian women: first through the masculinity of the style, and then through the whitened femininity of the performer. In the end, previously racially contaminated cultural forms were fully integrated, not only into the national imaginary, but into the individual fantasy life of every Bolivian. Today, the growing numbers of immigrants who have left the Andes for the United States, Italy, or Spain continue to teach their children to know and love their distant Andean homelands by inculcating in them an intimate and embodied familiarity with these musical forms.

We often associate mimesis with performances such as these, as race is enacted through the minstrels' song and dance, sex through the transvestite's costumed theatricality. Canessa takes us into less charted territory, in which the boundaries of self and other are crossed and recrossed through actual physical exchange between bodies. The phenomenon of men having sex with women of many races, and thus achieving a new sense of Bolivian citizenship, is not literally a case of mimicry of a perceived alter; but mimesis is surely involved when the memory of a temporary physical intimacy with a stranger's body initiates a permanent transformation in one's sense of self. This newly cosmopolitan masculinity then in turn prompts the rejection of a previous intimacy, when men beat wives who have remained too indian (see also Ellis 1996; Weismantel 2001). Here, mimesis does not involve performing the desired other, but rather inflicting pain and harm upon the despised alter, who too closely resembles what is feared and rejected in the self. The intimate moments within white Peruvian families described by Robert Ellis, when fathers strike sons whom they call "faggots" and "women," and Canessa's tales of Aymara husbands who hit wives while calling them "dirty indians," are echoed in institutional contexts such as the military, where violence awaits those who speak Aymara, and punishment may entail not only being called a woman, but being forced to dress and act as a female caricature.

These examples illustrate the symbolic violence that lies within less physical acts of mimesis, such as the frequent verbal allusions to brutal or vulgar behavior as expressions of "the indian within." The two seem frightening close: the verbal use of racial, sexual, and gender slurs to accompany actual blows, and the way in which the painful perception of racial or sexual inadequacy gives rise to the desire to inflict physical pain. And yet, in the Andean context as in many other American contexts, a sense of closeness to one's racial and sexual alters gives rise to strong sensations of pleasure and desire as well. Bigenho is quite right to point to the visceral emotions associated with feeling authentically indigenous for mestizo Latin Americans, and to the sense of being truly Bolivian that arises from the mimetic performances of indigenous alterity. Elayne Zorn's case study touches upon another example of romantic primitivism: the desire of foreign tourists to witness the existence of a cultural reality alternative to their own, and imagined as the alter of modernity itself. The ironies of these desires and their effects remain: brutal racism and racial fantasy, homophobia and transvestic performance, misogynist violence and the idealization of femininity all co-occur within contexts across the Americas. Indeed, in the case of tourism, the desire to perceive the fantasied other inevitably seems to lead to the distortion or even the destruction of the object of desire itself.

Mimesis, then, gives us a model to envision identities taking form at the borders of the self; the examples provided here demonstrate that this process is not only one of fantasy and imagination, but something that takes place within actual social and even physical exchanges between husbands and wives, sex workers and their clients, teachers and pupils, officers and men, tourists and tour guides. If ideas about race and the nation find expression in the lofty sentiments penned by Larson's educators, who sought to uplift and purify a degraded and decadent race, they come to ground in the daily exchanges where abstractions became embodied in hats and hair, insults and blows.

Materialities

The singer Bigenho interviewed was not Aymara, and in fact belonged to the landowning class that lost power and economic privilege during the agrarian reforms of the Bolivian revolution. Nonetheless, she finds profound pleasure and significance in the physical act of speaking Aymara, and asks to be buried wearing the indigenous clothing in which she performs, "with her hat on top of the coffin." Zorn tells us that on the island of Taquile, conflicts over tourism flare because tour guides don't like seeing indian houses made of nontraditional materials, and residents can't control which boats land at their docks—although they have tried, using rocks and boat hooks. Van Vleet gives us a puzzling sequence of conversations about other conversations—what a teacher might have said to a student, and what that student's father might have said to the teacher—with a concrete outcome: a very happy child in expensive new shoes. Canessa talks to men who experience modernity through a shaved pudendum, a dirty movie, and a new sexual vocabulary—but don't feel that any of this can be brought home to their wives. Larson is struck by the mundane (if impractical) means through which rural educators set out to create a new nation: instructions on place settings for houses without tables, and tips on flattering a slim figure addressed to women whose preferred dressing style produces shapes more closely resembling a mountain.

Identity, then, is made visible and tangible through material means: a hat or a rock, feet dancing or in shoes, a razor or a fork. By documenting the deployment of these material vehicles in specific contexts, these essays provide a concrete demonstration of how Andean identities work—and so expand our understanding of identity once more. Thus although the theme of this book is the relationship between the nation and racial and gendered identities—a topic that has been the focus of much recent scholarship, to which these Andean cases are a welcome addition—this collection, because it focuses so intently on the concrete manifestations of subaltern identity, also heightens our awareness of the materiality of oppression and inequality, and thus of privilege and pleasure. Detailed and finely grained portrayals such as these could become building blocks for forms of analysis that combine the postcolonial themes of race, gender, and nation with a renewed attention to structural inequality and political economy—the absorbing preoccupations of an earlier generation of Latin Americanists, made newly salient by the economic crises of the 1990s and the depredations wrought by neoliberal state policies. The benefits of such an analysis would be twofold. First, it would enable us to think hard about the extent to which issues of class and the distribution of wealth remain submerged within subaltern political discourses and movements overtly concerned with ethnicity, race, gender, and sexuality—just as we now discern the latter questions suppressed within the earlier, class-based movements of the twentieth century, as for example in Guatemala, where Maya identity has supplanted Marxist ideology as the driving force behind oppositional political movements. Secondly, we could reengage those older scholarly works about Latin America, with their many rich insights—not by abandoning more recent theoretical and substantive interests, but by moving toward a synthetic approach. Zorn's ethnography of the conflicts over control of the tourist trade, for example, is redolent of the ironies of life as an iconic indian continually on display for the delectation of tourists; but these ironies seem less compelling to Taquile's inhabitants than the bread-and-butter issues of the right to make a living, to gain adequate access to the political process, and to protect the physical environment in which one lives. The interplay of touristic fantasy and lived reality, political economy and the politics of identity, is precisely what make this case study so fascinating.

A focus on material life can be productive for scholars who do not wish to engage historical materialism or political economy as well; it can also enrich postmodernist anthropology taken on its own terms. Butler, like Foucault, has struggled with the notion of materiality, as she confessed in the introduction to her second book, *Bodies that Matter* (1993). And yet, as we see in the examples presented here, her own notion of iteration comes to life when understood as a material process through which an imagined identity becomes concretized over time through physical engagement with things. Van Vleet introduces us to a young woman who undergoes several transformations, made visible through clothing: the rural indigenous child thrilled to own a pair of shoes; the "imilla" with her long, loose hair; the successful chola with her carefully amassed wardrobe of polleras. These are the visible, tangible aspects of the body and the world out of which identity is fashioned and displayed—and Van Vleet introduces them not only as vehicles for symbolic expression, but also as physical objects and habits to which the body reacts differently depending on whether they are familiar or new. New shoes make the feet dance, but the pollera is initially approached hesitantly, its femininity off-putting—only to be gradually discovered as the source of pleasure and pride. Landscapes, too, may exist as eternal symbols in the imagination—the high world of the hunter and the wild vicuña, embodied in the dancers of the chuqila—but real landscapes can suffer from gradual degradation, as in Taquile, until changed beyond recognition by the repeated assaults of too many tourist feet.

Perhaps the most striking statement about the materiality of identity production is made by Stephenson, who details the movements of a dance that outsiders like John Cohen and insiders like the THOA intellectuals have alike found significant enough to video—even when the dancers are unable or unwilling to provide an exegesis for their acts. For Cohen, the lack of a verbal interpretation is troubling, and lessens the significance of the dance and the culture alike. But THOA, with its emphasis upon the simple fact of endurance, seems to imply that the embodied knowledge of space and time enacted through the gestures of a dance is itself a form of cultural capital, like the repeated words of a myth or the verbal exegesis of a symbol. Carefully cultivated and taught, these bodily movements and rhythms position the dancers within the Andean environment in specific and meaningful ways, even when accompanying texts are absent or, as in the words of the song provided by Stephenson, occluded. In fact, the cultural knowledge contained within song and dance may be more meaningful because it is enacted through the body: a physical and experiential reshaping of time and space that offers concrete (albeit silent) resistance to the enormous, continual, crushing pressure to assimilate and to forget.

However, in focusing only on Stephenson's essay, we run the risk of repeating an old mistake: that of consigning indigenes to an unthinking sphere of everyday practices and practical reason, while associating elites only with ideologies disassociated from reality. In actuality, the dialectic between lived reality and ideology is to be found in both places. At times, the essays in this volume capture something of the complex and interesting relationships, acknowledged and unacknowledged, between utopian dreams and small daily practices as these intersect in both the metropolis and the peripheries of the nation. Bigenho's singers speak of the pragmatic details of their lives as performers, as well as of their larger aspiration to change Bolivian musical culture; and Zorn documents the tensions on Taquile, where tour operators from outside sell authentic indians to an eager public—while indigenous entrepreneurs struggle to retain a share of this market—*in themselves*. Here, the contradictions of elite discourse come to roost with a vengeance, as residents simultaneously find themselves celebrated as the "hyperreal indians" of international discourse and denigrated as no longer authentic enough to attract tourists, while being subjected to older forms of racial and economic disadvantage that have allowed local non-indians to take over the lucrative tourist trade.

In sum, by keeping tightly focused on bodily practices, whether quotidian or ritual, these authors are able to situate their analyses in the theoretical terrain of postcolonial and queer studies, making reference to hybridity, multiplicity, performance, and mimesis, while grounding these notions in specific bodies, acts, and landscapes. This collection thus signals a certain maturation of the literature on identity, in which the postmodern body—that rather phantasmic creation of contemporary theory—takes on a more muscular and unmistakably physical presence, possessed not only of a phallus (or its absence), but also of feet that dance, hands that weave, skin that gets bruised, and even teeth that get brushed (or not). Best of all, this is a rigorously social body, formed not only through its interactions with disembodied ideologies and regimes of power, but more immediately through daily intercourse with sisters, fathers, spouses, anthropologists, bosses, and whores.

Bibliography

Butler, Judith. 1993. *Bodies that Matter: On the Discursive Limits of Sex*. New York: Routledge.

Canessa, Andrew. 2000. "Fear and Loathing on the Kharisiri Trail: Alterity and Identity in the Andes." *Journal of the Royal Anthropological Institute (incorporating Man)* 6, no. 4:705–20

Eckert, Penelope, and Sally McConnell-Ginet. 1995. "Constructing Meaning, Constructing Selves: Snapshots of Language, Gender, and Class from Belten High." In *Gender Articulated: Language and the Socially Constructed Self*, ed. Kira Hall and Mary Bucholtz, 469–507. New York: Routledge.

Ellis, Robert. 1996. "The Inscription of Masculinity and Whiteness in the Autobiography of Mario Vargas Llosa." *Bulletin of Latin American Research* 17(2): 223–36.

Orlove, Benjamin. 1998. "Down to Earth: Race and Substance in the Andes." *Bulletin of Latin American Research* 17(2): 207–22.

Weismantel, Mary. 1988. *Food, Gender, and Poverty in the Ecuadorian Andes*. Philadelphia: University of Pennsylvania Press. Reprinted 1998 by Westview Press.

———. 2001. *Cholas and Pishtacos: Stories of Race and Sex in the Andes*. Chicago: Chicago University Press.

CONTRIBUTORS

Michelle Bigenho, assistant professor of anthropology at Hampshire College, is author of *Sounding Indigenous: Authenticity in Bolivian Music Performance* (Palgrave, 2002). In her field research on music performance in Peru and Bolivian she has drawn on her skills as a performing musician. She is currently working on a manuscript that examines the globalization of "Andean" music through an ethnography of Bolivian music in Japan.

Andrew Canessa received his Ph.D. in social anthropology from the London School of Economics in 1994 and is director of the Centre for Latin American Studies at the University of Essex. He has conducted regular fieldwork in the Aymara-speaking village of Pocobaya since 1989, working on diverse themes such as procreation, identity, gender, religion, and schooling. Recent publications include *Pocobaya: Género e identidad en una aldea andina* (Mamahuaco Press, 2005) and "Reproducing Racism: Schooling and Race in Highland Bolivia" (*Journal of Race and Education,* 2004). He is working on a monograph, *"We Will Be People No More": Ethnicity, Identity, and Change in Highland Bolivia.*

Brooke Larson is professor of history at Stony Brook University. Her books include *Cochabamba, 1550–1900: Colonialism and Agrarian Transformation in Bolivia* (2d ed., Duke, 1998); *Ethnicity, Markets, and Migration in the Andes* (with O. Harris and E. Tandeter; Duke, 1995); and most recently, *Trials of Nation Making: Liberalism, Race, and Ethnicity in the Andes, 1810–1910* (Cambridge, 2004). Her current book project explores the politics of land, schools, and identity on the Aymara altiplano.

Marcia Stephenson is associate professor of Spanish and women's studies at Purdue University. Her research and publications focus on issues related to gender, race, and ethnicity in Bolivia. She is working on a book project studying colonialism and the international trade in Andean camelids.

Krista Van Vleet is assistant professor of anthropology in the Department of Sociology and Anthropology at Bowdoin College. Her research focuses on gender and kinship, emotion, and narrative among Quechua speakers in Bolivia. Recent publications include "The Intimacies of Power" (2001), which examines violence between mothers- and daughters-in-law and "Partial Theories" (2003), a discussion of envy and gossip in a rural Andean community. She is working on a book called *Relative Intimacies: Performing Kinship and Narrating Lives in the Bolivian Andes.*

Mary Weismantel is professor of anthropology and director of Latin American and Caribbean studies at Northwestern University. She is the author of two books on the Andes, *Food, Gender, and Poverty in the Ecuadorian Andes* and *Cholas and Pishtacos: Tales of Race and Sex in the Andes,* as well as numerous articles.

Elayne Zorn received her Ph.D. in anthropology from Cornell University and is associate professor of anthropology in the Department of Sociology and Anthropology, University of Central Florida. A cultural anthropologist, she has carried out twenty-five years of fieldwork with Quechua-speaking people in highland Peru and Bolivia on topics including material culture (cloth), tourism, and tourist arts. Her most recent publication is *Weaving a Future: Tourism, Cloth, and Culture on an Andean Island* (University of Iowa Press, 2004).

INDEX

21, 50; production, 167; and race, 111; and tourism, 171, 174. *See also* costume; pollera

Cochabamba: dress, 73; elites, 70, hinterland, 67; migration to, 109, 118; and music, 63; and Quechua, 74; water privatization, 18

Cohen, J., 87, 99, 102n. 3, 191, 192

Comaroff, J., and J. Comaroff, 53, 56

compadrazgo, 161, 163, 170, 172, 177, 187

CONAIE, 4

Corrigan, P., and D. Sayer, 36

costume, 73, 74, 92, 116, 172, 188. *See also* clothing; pollera

creoles, 26; elites, 36–39, 90; and republics, 11–13; women and singing, 60–77

Cuzco: *indigenistas*, 14, 55, 62; race, 33; rebellion, 168; tourism, 157, 161

dance: adolescents, 20, 114, authenticity, 91; Carnival, 109, 116–18; *chuqila*, 20, 87–88; *cueca*, 70; folklore, 111, identity, 23, 88, 94, 115, 124, 192; memory, 90, 92; and the nation, 20, 23, 88, 92–93, 97, 111, 124; race, 91, 94, 111, 183, 188; *tango*, 71; tourist brochures, 165; *vals*, 71

Desjarlais, R., 108

Desmond, J., 89, 91, 93

Donoso Torres, V., 47–49

Douglas, M., 92

Duviols, P., 96

earth: earth goddess, 18; and race, 132; relation to, 16, 88, 132, 185; ritual significance of, 96

Eckert, P., and S. McConnell-Ginet, 119

elites, 22, 38, 43, 87, 124, 132, 134, 192; Bengali, 22; creole, 12, 13, 33, 35, 36, 39, 62, 90; landed, 68, 76, 86, 93; and the nation, 6, 55, 61, 133; performers, 119; political, 3, 11, 21, 22, 54, 55, 186; Puno, 162; regional, 45, 62, 70; social, 3, 11, 19, 22; urban, 11, 12, 17, 33, 44, 70, 83, 87, 185

eugenics, 15, 33, 34, 36, 52

EZLN, 4

family, 34, 36, 46, 48, 51, 56, 108, 147, 164, 167; Aymara family, 35, 41, 42; Bolivian family, 42, 48; indian family, 42, 43, 52, 141, 148; music, 63, 71; and the nation, 34, 120, 122; peasant family, 45, 46, 48

Findlay, E., 34

folklore, 4, 69–71, 73, 88; dances, 90, 111; and dress, 151; events, 156, 157, 170; and indigeneity, 71, 73, 75, 92, 111; nightclubs, 64; and Rigoberto Paredes, 90–91; singers, 61–63;

food: and identity, 16, 22, 134; and public policy, 48, 52; ritual food, 116; sharing, 22, 120

Foster, S., 93, 94

Foucault, M., 6, 53, 107, 191

Frontaura, M., 41, 42, 48

Fujimori, A., 157, 164, 169

Geographic Society of La Paz, 90, 91

Gill, L., 77n. 1, 137

godparents. *See* compadrazgo

Gow, D., and J. Rappaport, 5

guanaco, 89, 96

Guillén Pinto, A., 40

hacienda, 17, 36, 42, 45, 67, 86, 132, 141; indians, 14; land reform, 15, 70; unrest, 43, 68

Harris, O., 85, 94, 95, 103n. 8

highlands, 53, 54, 130, 131, 181, 182, 183; music, 69; resistance, 43, 54

homosexuality: and the army, 136; female, 140; male, 151, 188

household, 15, 34, 114, 118, 119, 131, 147; and gender division of labor, 142, 149, 151n. 11; indian, 46; peasant, 45, 46, 51, 141

Huari, 96, 97, 103n. 7

identity, 4–9; gender and identity, 23, 101, 158; indian identity, 4, 7, 14, 15, 20, 21, 24, 132–33, 158, 176–78, 185; national identity, 8, 13, 16, 19, 22, 41, 82, 107; racial identity, 10, 22, 149. *See also* indian identity.

Illimani, 66, 77n. 2; Radio Illimani, 64, 68, 69

Wari. *See* Huari
weaving, 19, 22, 157, 159, 165, 175,
    183, 193; and gender, 23, 61, 142,
    167; and historical memory, 84

youth, 108, 114–16, 120, 121, 125n. 3,
    125n. 4, 126n. 9, 183; indigenous,
    44; and nations, 22, 124. *See also*
    adolescents; sipas

CPSIA information can be obtained at www.ICGtesting.com
Printed in the USA
LVOW070303260911

247838LV00004B/4/P